Annie's Favorite Afghans™

Editorial Director
Andy Ashley
Production Director
Ange Van Arman

EDITORIAL
Senior Editor
Jennifer McClain
Associate Editor
Donna Scott
Editorial Staff
Shirley Brown, Alva Lea Edwards, Liz Field, Donna Jones,
Nina Marsh, Diane Simpson, Ann White

PHOTOGRAPHY
Scott Campbell, Tammy Coquat-Payne, Rusty Lingle

BOOK DESIGN & PRODUCTION
Danny Martin

PRODUCTION
Minette Collins Smith, Joanne Gonzalez

PRODUCT PRESENTATION
Design Coordinator
Sandy Kennebeck
Inhouse Designer
Mickie Akins
Design Copy
Linda Moll Smith

Sincerest thanks to all the designers and other professionals whose
dedication has made this book possible.
Special thanks to David Norris and Kaye Stafford
of Quebecor Printing Book Group, Kingsport, Tennessee.

Library of Congress Cataloging-in-Publication Data
ISBN: 0-9655269-0-9
First Printing: 1996
Library of Congress Catalog Card Number: 96-79702
Published and Distributed by
Annie's Attic, LLC, Big Sandy, Texas 75755
Printed in the United States of America.

Cover: *Antique Afghan*, pattern instructions begin on page 88.

Dear Friends,

Whether it's a favorite dessert, a favorite song or a favorite vacation spot, a favorite is a familiar something to which we return again and again for a reward we know awaits us.

So it is with those of us who crochet.

Much of the joy of sitting down with a set of hooks and a skein of yarn to stitch an afghan comes from its comforting reliability. But it is this very familiarity with the pleasure of working with our hands that transports us from the realm of the mundane to the heights of joyous creativity.

It is the constancy of crochet that engages our hearts.

So, after almost 20 years of publishing crochet patterns, it's only natural that we gather together some of our favorites in this book.

Or, to be more accurate, these are your favorites, a compendium of beloved patterns that you've kept requesting over the years.

What makes these 50 afghans, arranged by theme and motif in chapters that attempt to categorize their long-lived charms, so special?

Look through Annie's Favorite Afghans and you'll find collectible heirlooms, convenient "take-it-and-make-it" motifs, charmers for children, cozy quilts and floral fantasies, as well as reliable granny squares, repeating ripples, gifts for celebration, afghans just for him and favorite stitches galore. But, in the midst of this variety, we've taken care to provide you with proven designs. Each of these popular patterns has met the test of time.

From humble to grand, this touchstone collection spans the designs of our own lives which are but memories hooked together a little at a time. Like the afghans we crochet, the everyday moments we share with family and friends are remembered in skeins and stitches, which, when fully assembled, enfold us with warmth and blanket us with comfort.

In discovering your own favorites, may you cherish every day with a little bit of crochet.

Happy Crocheting,

Annie

Contents

Floral Fantasies

The heady delights of flowers fresh from the garden are yours year-round with this hand-selected bouquet of patterns. Here, gardening glories are entwined on our afghan-stitched Floral Trellis. Or crochet exuberant poppies, refined roses, sprightly bluebonnets. Take your pick—each is an ever-blooming forget-me-not!

by Michele Maks

Floral Trellis

FINISHED SIZE: About 42" × 45½".

MATERIALS:
- ❑ Worsted yarn:
    - 75 oz. cream
    - 8 oz. dk. pink
    - 3 oz. each green, dk. aqua, turquoise, dk. blue, med. blue, lt. blue, dk. purple, med. purple, lavender and lt. pink
    - 1 oz. each orange, maroon, lt. aqua, yellow and white
- ❑ Tapestry needle
- ❑ F crochet hook and G afghan hook or size needed to obtain gauges

GAUGES: F hook, 9 sc = 2"; 9 sc rows = 2".
G afghan hook, 9 vertical bars = 2"; 4 afghan st rows = 1".

AFGHAN

Row 1: With afghan hook and cream, ch 184, work row 1 of afghan stitch *(see Stitch Guide).*

Rows 2–173: Work row 2 of afghan stitch *(see Stitch Guide).* At end of last row, fasten off.

Rnd 174: Using F hook and working around outer edge in ends of rows and in sts, join dk. pink with sc in first st, sc in each st and in each row around with 3 sc in each end of first and last rows, join with sl st in first sc, turn.

Rnds 175–178: Ch 1, sc in each st around with 3 sc in each center corner st, join as before. At end of last rnd, fasten off.

Using cross-stitch *(see Stitch Guide),* work design according to graph. ❧

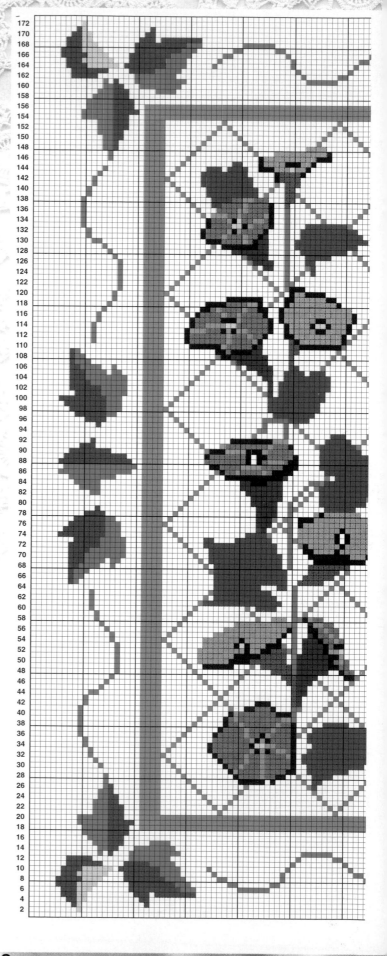

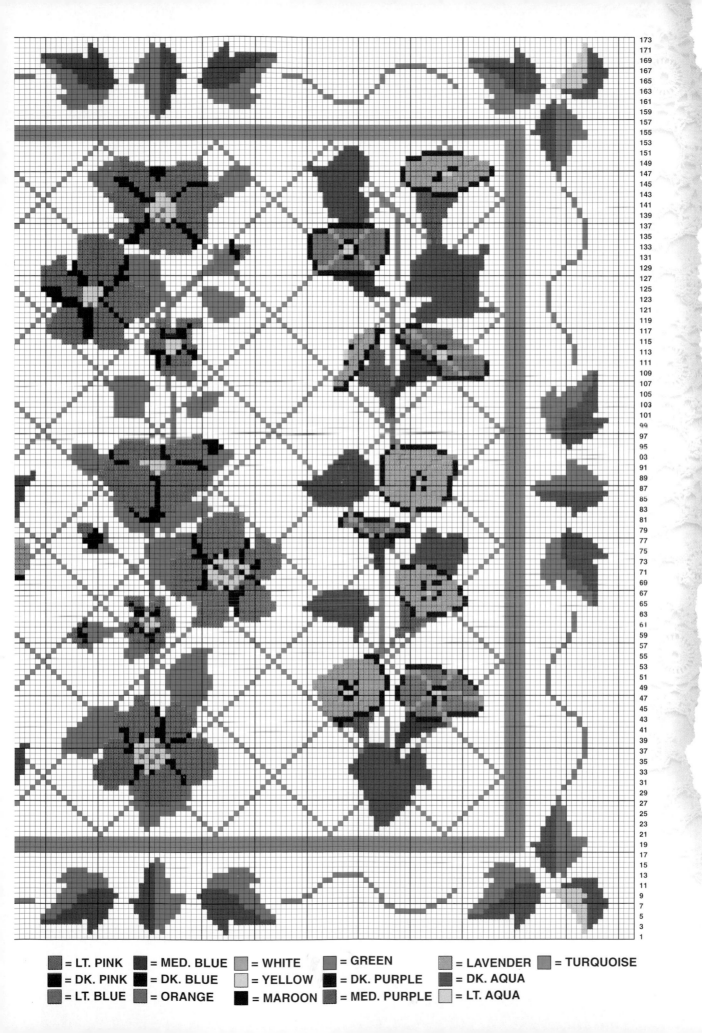

173
171
169
167
165
163
161
159
157
155
153
151
149
147
145
143
141
139
137
135
133
131
129
127
125
123
121
119
117
115
113
111
109
107
105
103
101
99
97
95
03
91
89
87
85
83
81
79
77
75
73
71
69
67
65
63
61
59
57
55
53
51
49
47
45
43
41
39
37
35
33
31
29
27
25
23
21
19
17
15
13
11
9
7
5
3
1

	= LT. PINK		= MED. BLUE		= WHITE		= GREEN		= LAVENDER		= TURQUOISE
	= DK. PINK		= DK. BLUE		= YELLOW		= DK. PURPLE		= DK. AQUA		
	= LT. BLUE		= ORANGE		= MAROON		= MED. PURPLE		= LT. AQUA		

by Liz Field

Bluebonnet Afghan

FINISHED SIZE: About 45" × 58".

MATERIALS:
- ❑ Worsted yarn:
     40 oz. off-white
     8 oz. lt. blue
     8 oz. dk. blue
- ❑ F hook or size needed to obtain gauge

GAUGE: 5 dc = 1"; 2 dc rows = 1". Flower Motif is 5½"; Center Motif is 2".

SPECIAL STITCHES:

For **sc popcorn (sc pc)**, 3 sc in first st, drop lp from hook, insert hook in first st of group, pull dropped lp through.

For **dc popcorn (dc pc)**, 4 dc in ch sp or st, drop lp from hook, insert hook in first st of group, pull dropped lp through.

FLOWER MOTIF (make 80)

Rnd 1: With off-white, ch 4, sl st in first ch to form ring, ch 1, 8 sc in ring, join with sl st in first sc. *(8 sc made)*

Rnd 2: Ch 1, **sc pc** *(see Special Stitches)*, (ch 1, sc pc) in each st around, ch 1, join with sl st in top of first pc. Fasten off. *(8 pc)*

NOTE: *Ch 3 is not used or counted as a st in popcorn rnds.*

Rnd 3: Join lt. blue with (sl st, ch 3, **dc pc**—*see Special Stitches*) in any ch-1 sp on rnd 2, ch 1, (dc pc in next ch-1 sp, ch 1) around, join. Fasten off.

Rnd 4: Join dk. blue with (sl st, ch 3, dc pc) in any ch-1 sp on rnd 3, ch 2, dc pc in top of next pc, (ch 2, dc pc in next ch-1 sp, ch 2, dc pc in top of next pc, ch 2) around, join. Fasten off. *(16 pc)*

Rnd 5: Join off-white with (sl st, ch 3, dc, ch 1, 2 dc) in any ch-2 sp on rnd 4, 2 dc in next ch-2 sp, *(2 dc, ch 1, 2 dc) in next ch-2 sp, 2 dc in next ch-2 sp; repeat from * around, join with sl st in top of ch 3. *(48 dc)*

Rnd 6: Sl st in next st, (sl st, ch 3, dc, ch 1, 2 dc) in next ch-1 sp, skip next 2 sts, (2 dc in next sp between sts, skip next 2 sts) 2 times, *(2 dc, ch 1, 2 dc) in next ch-1 sp, skip next 2 sts, (2 dc in next sp between sts, skip next 2 sts) 2 times; repeat from * around, join. *(64 dc)*

Rnd 7: Sl st in next st, (sl st, ch 3, dc, ch 1, 2 dc) in next ch-1 sp, skip next 2 sts, (2 dc in next sp between sts, skip next 2 sts) 3 times, *(2 dc, ch 1, 2 dc) in next ch-1 sp, skip next 2 sts, (2 dc in next sp between sts, skip next 2 sts) 3 times; repeat from * around, join. Fasten off. *(80 dc)*

CENTER SQUARE (make 63)

Rnd 1: With off-white, ch 5, sl st in first ch to form ring, ch 1, 8 sc in ring, join with sl st in first sc. *(8 sc made)*

Rnd 2: Ch 1, 2 sc in each st around, join. *(16)*

Rnd 3: (Ch 3, dc, ch 1, 2 dc) in first st, ch 1, skip next st, dc in next st, ch 1, skip next st, *(2 dc, ch 1, 2 dc) in next st, ch 1, skip next st, dc in next st, ch 1, skip next st; repeat from * around, join with sl st in top of ch 3.

Rnd 4: Ch 1, sc in each st and in each ch around with (sc, ch 1, sc) in each corner ch-1 sp, join. Fasten off.

ASSEMBLY

Arrange Motifs and Squares *(see illustration)* having 8 Motifs across by 10 Motifs down; matching ch-1 sps at corners, sew together, stitching through **back lps** *(see Stitch Guide)* of sts only.

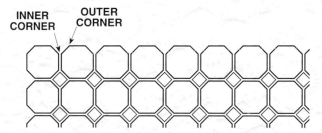

INNER CORNER   OUTER CORNER

EDGING

Rnd 1: Join lt. blue with (sc, ch 1, sc) in any outer corner ch-1 sp, sc in each st around with 2 sc in each outer corner and skip 2 sts at each inner corner, join with sl st in first sc. Fasten off.

Rnd 2: Join dk. blue with sc in first st, sc in each st around, join. Fasten off. ❧

by Betty Dernulc

Perky Poppies

FINISHED SIZE: About 53" × 67", including Fringe.

MATERIALS:
❑ Worsted yarn:
   44 oz. white
   13 oz. burnt orange
   4 oz. green
   4 oz. brown
❑ H hook or size needed to obtain gauge

GAUGE: 4 dc = 1"; 3 dc rows = 2".

SPECIAL STITCH:
For **treble crochet cluster (tr cl)**, yo 2 times, insert hook in st, yo, pull lp through, (yo, pull through 2 lps on hook) 2 times, *yo 2 times, insert hook in same st, yo, pull lp through, (yo, pull through 2 lps on hook) 2 times; repeat from *, yo, pull through all lps on hook.

FIRST STRIP
First Square
Rnd 1: With brown, ch 6, sl st in first ch to form ring, ch 5, (dc in ring, ch 2) 7 times, join with sl st in third ch of ch 5. Fasten off. *(8 ch-2 sps made)*

Rnd 2: Join burnt orange with sc in any ch-2 sp, (4 dc, sc) in same ch sp *(petal made)*, (sc, 4 dc, sc) in each ch-2 sp around, join with sl st in first sc. *(8 petals)*

Rnd 3: Working behind petals, (ch 4, sc in first sc of next petal on rnd 2) 8 times, do not join.

Rnd 4: (Sc, 6 dc, sc) in each ch-4 sp around, join. Fasten off.

Rnd 5: For edging on petals, join white with sc in first sc on rnd 2, *(ch 3, sc in next st) 5 times, sc in first sc of next petal; repeat from * 6 more times, (ch 3, sc in next st) 5 times. *(48 sc)*

Rnd 6: Sc in first sc on rnd 4, *(ch 3, sc in next st) 7 times, sc in first sc on next petal; repeat from * 6 more times, (ch 3, sc in next st) 7 times, join. Fasten off. *(64 sc)*

Rnd 7: Join green with sc in first sc on rnd 6, *ch 5, skip next 7 sc, (**tr cl**—see Special Stitch—ch 2, tr cl, ch 2, tr cl) in next sc, ch 5, skip next 7 sc, sc in next sc; repeat from * 2 more times, ch 5, skip next 7 sc, (tr cl, ch 2, tr cl, ch 2, tr cl) in next sc, ch 5, skip next 7 sc, join. Fasten off.

Rnd 8: Join white with sl st in next ch-5 sp, ch 3, 5 dc in same ch sp, *3 dc in next ch-2 sp, (dc, ch 2, dc) in center cluster for corner, 3 dc in next ch-2 sp, 6 dc in next 2 ch-5 sps; repeat from * 2 more times, 3 dc in next ch-2 sp, (dc, ch 2, dc) in center cluster, 3 dc in next ch-2 sp, 6 dc in ch-5 sp, join with sl st in top of ch 3. *(80 dc)*

Rnd 9: Ch 4, dc in next st, (ch 1, skip next st, dc in next st) 4 times, *ch 1, (dc, ch 2, dc) in corner, ch 1, dc in next st, (ch 1, skip next st, dc in next st) 9 times, ch 1, dc in next st; repeat from * 2 more times, ch 1, (dc, ch 2, dc) in corner; ch 1, dc in next st, (ch 1, skip next st, dc in next st) 4 times, ch 1, skip next st, join with sl st in third ch of ch 4. *(52 dc)*

Rnds 10–12: Ch 4, (dc, ch 1) in each dc around with (dc, ch 2, dc, ch 1) in each corner, join. *(60, 68, 76 dc)*

Rnd 13: Ch 3, dc in each ch sp and st around with (dc, ch 2, dc) in each corner, join with sl st in top of ch 3. Fasten off. *(156 dc)*

Rnd 14: For **ruffle**, join burnt orange with sl st in any top corner on rnd 11, ch 3, 2 dc in same sp, *turn square quarter turn to right, **dc fp** *(dc front post, see Stitch Guide)* around post of next dc on rnd 11; turn square back to left, 3 dc in ch-1 sp on rnd 10; turn square to left, 3 dc fp around post of next dc on rnd 11; turn to right, 3 dc in next ch-1 sp of rnd 11; repeat from * around, ending with 3 dc fp around post of last dc on rnd 11; join. Fasten off.

Rnd 15: Join white with sc in any st on rnd 13, (ch 3, skip next st, sc in next st) around with (ch 3, sc) 2 times in each corner, join. Fasten off.

Second Square
Rnds 1–15: Repeat rnds 1–15 of First Square.
Row 16: Join white with sc in any corner of this square; for **corner joining**, ch 1, sc in corner ch-3 sp on previous square, ch 1, sc in same corner on this square; (ch 1, sc in next ch-3 sp on previous

continued on page 17

by Sandra Smith

Bed of Roses

FINISHED SIZE: Afghan is about 34" × 48". Pillow is 12" square.

MATERIALS:
❑ Worsted yarn:
    24 oz. off-white
    18 oz. red
    18 oz. green
❑ Two 14" squares off-white fabric
❑ Polyester fiberfill
❑ Sewing needle and off-white thread
❑ G hook or size needed to obtain gauge

GAUGE: 4 sc = 1"; 4 sc rows = 1". Each Block is 7½" square.

SPECIAL STITCH:

For **split sc (ssc**—*see illustration),* insert hook between vertical strands of next sc, complete as sc.

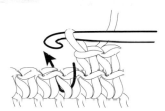

BLOCK (make 24)

Flower Base

NOTES: *Do not join rnds unless otherwise stated. Mark first st of each rnd.*

Work Base in **back lps** *(see Stitch Guide) only.*

Rnd 1: With red, ch 2, 8 sc in second ch from hook. *(8 sc made)*

Rnd 2: 2 sc in each st around. *(16)*

Rnd 3: (2 sc in next st, sc in next st) around. *(24)*

Rnd 4: (2 sc in next st, sc in next 2 sts) around. *(32)*

Rnd 5: (2 sc in next st, sc in next 3 sts) around, join with sl st in first st. Fasten off. *(40)*

Leaves

Row 1: Working this row in **back lps,** join green with sc in first st on rnd 5, sc in next 4 sts, turn. *(5 sc made)*

Rows 2–3: Ch 1, sc in each st across, turn.

Row 4: Ch 1, skip first st, sc in next 2 sts, skip next st, sc in last st, turn. *(3)*

Row 5: Ch 1, skip first st, sc in next 2 sts, turn. *(2)*

Row 6: Ch 1, skip first st, sc in next st. Fasten off.

Row 7: Working around edge of leaf, join green with sl st in same st as first st on row 1 of leaf, sc in end of each row across to row 6, sc in side of st on row 6, (sc, ch 1, sc) in top of same st, sc in opposite side of same st, sc in end of each row across to row 1, sl st in same st as last st on row 1 of leaf. Fasten off. *(14 sc)*

(For next leaf, skip next 5 sts on rnd 5 of Base; repeat rows 1–7) 3 times.

Background

Rnd 1: Working this rnd in **back lps,** join off-white with sc in ch at tip of any leaf, ch 2, sc in same ch, *[sc in next 2 sts, skip next st, hdc in next st, dc in next 2 sts, tr in next st, dtr in next st of rnd 5 on Base, dtr in next 4 sts, tr in first st on next leaf, dc in next 2 sts, hdc in next st, skip next st, sc in next 2 sts], (sc, ch 2, sc) in next ch; repeat from * 2 more times; repeat between [ ], join with sl st in first sc. *(76 sts made)*

Rnd 2: Sl st in first ch sp, ch 1, *(sc, ch 2, sc) in next ch sp, sc in each st across to next corner ch sp; repeat from * around, join. *(84 sc)*

Rnd 3: (Sl st, ch 3, 2 dc, ch 2, 3 dc) in first ch sp, *[ch 2, skip next 3 sts, (dc in next st, ch 2, skip next 2 sts) 6 times], (3 dc, ch 2, 3 dc) in next ch-2 sp; repeat from * 2 more times; repeat between [ ], join with sl st in top of ch 3.

Rnd 4: Ch 1, sc in first st, *[sc in next 2 sts, (2 sc, ch 1, 2 sc) in next ch sp, sc in next 3 sts, (2 sc in next ch sp, sc in next st) 6 times, 2 sc in next ch sp], sc in next st; repeat from * 2 more times; repeat between [ ], join. Fasten off. *(120)*

Petals

NOTE: *Work all petals in* **front lps** *of Flower Base.*

For **first Petal,** join red with sl st in first st on row 1, hdc in same st, dc in next 9 sts, (hdc, sl st) in next st.

continued on page 16

continued on page 16

continued from page 15

For **second, third and fourth Petals,** *(sl st, hdc) in next st, 2 dc in next 3 sts, (hdc, sl st) in next st; repeat from * 2 more times.

For **fifth and sixth Petals,** *(sl st, hdc) in next st, 2 dc in next 4 sts, (hdc, sl st) in next st; repeat from * one time.

For **seventh, eighth and ninth Petals,** *(sl st, hdc) in next st, 2 dc in next 6 sts, (hdc, sl st) in next st; repeat from * 2 more times.

For **tenth, eleventh and twelfth Petals,** *(sl st, hdc) in next st, 2 dc in next 7 sts, (hdc, sl st) in next st; repeat from * 2 more times. At end of last Petal, join with sl st in next st. Fasten off.

For assembly, matching sts and working in **back lps,** sl st blocks together with four across and six down.

Border

Rnd 1: With right side facing you and working this rnd in **back lps,** join off-white with (sc, ch 2, sc) in any corner ch-1 sp, sc in each st and joining seam around with (sc, ch 2, sc) in each corner ch-1 sp, join with sl st in first sc. Fasten off. *(624 sc made)*

Rnd 2: Working across long edge first, join green with (sc, ch 2, sc) in either corner ch-2 sp, sc in each st around with (sc, ch 2, sc) in each corner ch-2 sp, join. *(632 sc)*

Rnd 3: (Sl st, ch 1, sc, ch 2, sc) in corner ch-2 sp, *(ch 2, skip next 2 sts, **ssc**—*see Special Stitch*) 62 times, ch 2, skip next st, (sc, ch 2, sc) in corner ch-2 sp, ch 2, skip next 2 sts, (ssc in next st, ch 2, skip next 2 sts) 41 times*, (sc, ch 2, sc) in corner ch-2 sp; repeat between first and second *, join. *(214 dc)*

Rnd 4: Ch 1, ssc in first st, (sc, ch 2, sc) in corner ch-2 sp, (ssc in next st, 2 sc in next ch-2 sp) around with (sc, ch 2, sc) in each corner ch-2 sp, join. *(640 sc)*

Rnd 5: Sl st in next st, (sl st, ch 1, sc, ch 2, sc) in next corner ch-2 sp, *[ch 1, skip next st, (ssc in next st, ch 2, skip next 2 sts) across to last 2 sts before corner ch-2 sp, ssc in next st, ch 1, skip next st*, (sc, ch 2, sc) in corner ch-2 sp]; repeat between [ ] 2 times; repeat between first and second *, join. *(888 sc)*

Rnds 6–8: Repeat rnds 4 and 5 alternately. At end of rnd 8, fasten off.

PILLOW SIDE (make 2)

Block

Work same as Afghan Block. At end of rnd 4 on background, **do not fasten off.**

Border

Rnd 1: Ch 1, sc in next st, [ch 2, skip next 2 sts, sc in next st], *ch 2, skip next st, (sc, ch 1, sc) in next corner sp, ch 2, skip next st*; (repeat between [ ] across to last st before corner sp; repeat between first and second *) 3 times; repeat between [ ] 7 times, ch 2, join. *(48 sc made)*

Rnd 2: Ch 1, sc in each st and 2 sc in each ch-2 sp around with (sc, ch 1, sc) in each corner sp, join. *(144 sc)*

Rnd 3: Ch 1, *sc in next st, (ch 2, skip next 2 sts, sc in next st) across to last st before corner sp, ch 2, skip next st, (sc, ch 1, sc) in next corner sp, ch 2, skip next st; repeat from * 3 more times, (sc in next st, ch 2, skip next 2 sts) across, join. *(56 sc)*

Rnd 4: Repeat rnd 2. Fasten off. *(168 sc)*

Rnd 5: Join green with sl st in first st; repeat rnd 3. *(64 sc)*

Rnd 6: Ch 1, ssc in each sc and 2 sc in each ch-2 sp around with (sc, ch 1, sc) in each corner sp, join. *(192 sc)*

Rnd 7: Ch 1, *ssc in next st, (ch 2, skip next 2 sts, ssc in next st) across to last st before corner ch sp, ch 2, skip next st, (sc, ch 1, sc) in next corner sp, ch 2, skip next st; repeat from * 3 more times, (ssc in next st, ch 2, skip next 2 sts) across, join. *(72 sc)*

Rnds 8–9: Repeat rnds 6–7. At end of rnd 9, fasten off. *(216 sc, 80 sc)*

ASSEMBLY

For **pillow,** allowing ½" seams, sew fabric squares wrong sides together, leaving 3" opening; turn, stuff, sew opening closed.

Hold Pillow Sides wrong sides together; working through both thicknesses, join green with sc in any corner ch sp, (sc, ch 1, 2 sc) in same ch sp, (ssc in next st, 2 sc in next ch-2 sp) around with (2 sc, ch 1, 2 sc) in each corner ch sp; insert **pillow** before closing, join. Fasten off. ❧

continued from page 13

square, ch 1, skip next dc on this square, sc in next dc) across ending with corner joining. Fasten off.

Third Square
Rnd 1–Row 16: Repeat rnd 1–row 16 of Second Square.
Rnd 17: Working around outer edge of entire strip, join white with sc in any ch-3 sp, ch 3, (sc, ch 3) in each ch-3 sp around with (sc, ch 3, sc, ch 3) in each corner. Fasten off.

SECOND STRIP
First & Second Squares
Repeat First and Second Squares of First Strip.

Third Square
Rnd 1–Row 16: Repeat rnd 1–row 16 of Second Square of First Strip. At end of row 16, fasten off.
Rnd 17: Join white with sc in corner on this Strip, ch 1, sc in upper right-hand corner of First Square on First Strip, (ch 1, skip next dc on this Strip, sc in next dc, ch 1, sc in next ch sp on previous Strip) across; working in ch-3 sps around remaining sides of this Strip, (sc, ch 3) in each ch sp around with (sc, ch 3, sc, ch 3) in each corner. Fasten off.

For Third and Fourth Strips, repeat Second Strip.

EDGING
Rnd 1: Join white with sc in any corner, ch 3, sc in same ch sp, ch 3, (sc, ch 3) in each ch sp around with (sc, ch 3, sc, ch 3) in each corner, join with sl st in first sc.
Rnd 2: (Sl st, ch 4, 3 dc) in corner, (skip next ch-3 sp, sc in next ch-3 sp, ch 4, 3 dc in same ch sp) around, join with sl st in first ch of ch 4. Fasten off.

FRINGE
For each ch-4 sp, cut 8 strands each 22" long. Fold in half, insert hook from back of ch-4 sp, pull folded end through, pull ends through fold and tighten. Repeat around entire edge. To knot Fringe, combine 8 strands from one group and 8 strands from next group, tie overhand knot (*see Stitch Guide*) 1½" down; repeat around entire outer edge 2 times. ❧

by Dot Drake

Yellow Rose of Texas

FINISHED SIZE: About 44" × 66".

MATERIALS:
- ❑ Worsted yarn:
  - 9 oz. each dk. yellow, lt. yellow and green
  - 18 oz. each off-white and gold
- ❑ G hook or size needed to obtain gauge

GAUGE: 4 sc = 1"; 4 sc rows = 1".

SPECIAL STITCHES:

For **beginning cluster (beg cl)**, ch 3, (yo, insert hook in same st, yo, pull through, yo, pull through 2 lps on hook) 2 times, yo, pull through all 3 lps on hook.

For **cluster (cl)**, yo, insert hook in next st, yo, pull through, yo, pull through 2 lps on hook, (yo, insert hook in same st, yo, pull through, yo, pull through 2 lps on hook) 2 times, yo, pull through all 4 lps on hook.

LARGE MOTIF (make 24)

Rnd 1: With lt. yellow, ch 8, sl st in first ch to form ring, ch 1, (2 sc, 2 dc) 5 times in ring, join with sl st in first sc. *(20 sts made)*

Rnd 2: Working this rnd over starting ch behind rnd 1, ch 1, sc in sp between first 2 sc, ch 3, (sc in sp between next 2 sc, ch 3) 4 times, join. *(5 ch sps)*

Rnd 3: (Sl st, ch 1, sc, 3 dc, sc) in first ch sp of rnd 2, (sc, 3 dc, sc) in each ch sp around, join. *(10 sc, 15 dc)*

Rnd 4: Working this rnd behind rnd 3, ch 1, sc around post *(see Stitch Guide)* of first sc on rnd 2, ch 4, (sc around post of next sc on rnd 2, ch 4) 4 times, join.

Rnd 5: (Sl st, ch 1, sc, 5 dc, sc) in first ch sp of rnd 4, (sc, 5 dc, sc) in each ch sp around, join. Fasten off. *(10 sc, 25 dc)*

Rnd 6: Working this rnd behind rnd 5, join dk. yellow with sc around post of first sc on rnd 4, ch 5, (sc around post of next sc on rnd 4, ch 5) 4 times, join.

Rnd 7: (Sl st, ch 1, sc, dc, 5 tr, dc, sc) in first ch sp of rnd 6, (sc, dc, 5 tr, dc, sc) in each ch sp around, join. *(10 sc, 10 dc, 25 tr)*

Rnd 8: Working this rnd behind rnd 7, ch 1, sc around post of first sc on rnd 6, ch 6, (sc around post of next sc on rnd 6, ch 6) 4 times, join.

Rnd 9: (Sl st, ch 1, sc, dc, 4 tr, ch 1, 4 tr, dc, sc) in first ch sp of rnd 8, (sc, dc, 4 tr, ch 1, 4 tr, dc, sc) in each ch sp around, join. Fasten off. *(10 sc, 10 dc, 40 tr)*

Rnd 10: Working this rnd in **back lps** *(see Stitch Guide)*, join lt. yellow with sl st in first st of rnd 9, sl st in each st around, join with sl st in first sl st. Fasten off.

Rnd 11: Working this rnd behind rnd 10, join green with sc in any ch-1 sp of rnd 9, ch 11, (sc in next ch-1 sp, ch 11) 4 times, join with sl st in first sc. *(5 sc)*

Rnd 12: Beg cl *(see Special Stitches)*, ch 3, skip next 2 ch, sc in next ch, ch 3, skip next 2 ch, (**cl**—see *Special Stitches*, ch 3, skip next 2 ch, sc in next ch, ch 3, skip next 2 ch) around, join with sl st in top of ch 3. *(10 cl)*

Rnd 13: (Beg cl, ch 3, cl) in first st, ch 3, dc next 2 ch-3 sps tog skipping sc, ch 3, *(cl, ch 3, cl) in top of next cl, ch 3, dc next 2 ch-3 sps tog skipping sc, ch 3; repeat from * around, join. Fasten off. *(20 cl)*

Rnd 14: Join off-white with sl st in any ch-3 sp, ch 1, 4 sc in each ch-3 sp around, join with sl st in first sc. *(120 sc)*

Rnd 15: Working this rnd in **back lps**, ch 1, sc in each st around, join.

Rnd 16: Working this rnd in **back lps**, ch 4, skip next st, (dc in next st, ch 1, skip next st) around, join with sl st in third ch of ch 4. *(60 dc)*

Rnd 17: Working this rnd in **back lps**, ch 1, sc in each st and ch around, join with sl st in first sc. Fasten off. *(120 sc)*

SMALL MOTIF (make 15)

Rnd 1: With lt. yellow, ch 5, sl st in first ch to form ring, (beg cl, ch 3) in ring, (cl, ch 3) 5 times in ring, join with sl st in top of ch 3. Fasten off. *(6 cl made)*

Rnd 2: Join dk. yellow with (sl st, beg cl, ch 3, cl) in any ch-3 sp, ch 3, (cl, ch 3, cl, ch 3) in each ch sp around, join. Fasten off. *(12 cl)*

continued on page 20

continued from page 19

Rnd 3: Join off-white with sl st in any ch-3 sp, ch 1, 4 sc in each ch-3 sp around, join with sl st in first sc. *(48 sc)*

Rnd 4: Working this rnd in **back lps,** ch 1, sc in each st around. Fasten off.

LARGE MOTIF ASSEMBLY

First Panel

For **First Motif,** join gold with sc in any st of rnd 17 on one Motif, ch 3, skip next st, (sc in next st, ch 3, skip next st) around, join with sl st in first sc. Fasten off. *(60 sc made)*

For **Second Motif,** join gold with sc in any st of rnd 17 on Second Motif; with wrong sides together, ch 1, sc in ch sp between 38th and 39th sc of gold rnd on First Motif, ch 1, skip next st on Second Motif, sc in next st, (ch 1, sc in next ch sp of First Motif, ch 1, skip next st on Second Motif, sc in next st) 7 times, ch 3, skip next st, (sc in next st, ch 3, skip next st) around, join. Fasten off. *(68 sc)*

Repeat Second Motif instructions, joining Third Motif to Second Motif, Fourth to Third, Fifth to Fourth and Sixth to Fifth.

Second Panel

For **First Motif,** working in ch sp between 23rd and 24th sc of First Motif on last panel, repeat Second Motif.

For **Second Motif,** join gold with sc in any st of rnd 17 on Second Motif; with wrong sides together, ch 1, sc in ch sp between 53rd and 54th sc of First Motif, *ch 1, skip next st on Second Motif, sc in next st, (ch 1, sc in next ch sp of First Motif, ch 1, skip next st on Second Motif, sc in next st) 7 times*, ch 3, skip next st, (sc in next st, ch 3, skip

next st) 36 times, sc in next st, ch 1, sc in ch sp between 23rd and 24th sc of next Motif on last panel; repeat between first and second *, ch 3, skip next st, (sc in next st, ch 3, skip next st) 6 times, join. Fasten off.

Repeat Second Motif instructions, joining Third Motif to Second Motif, Fourth to Third, Fifth to Fourth and Sixth to Fifth.

For **Third and Fourth Panels,** repeat Second Panel two more times.

SMALL MOTIF ASSEMBLY

Holding one Small Motif in center of four Large Motifs, join gold with sc in any st on rnd 4 of Small Motif, skip one ch sp on Large Motif, *(ch 1, sc in next ch sp of Large Motif, ch 1, skip next st of Small Motif, sc in next st) 5 times, ch 3, skip next st of Small Motif, sc in next st, skip one ch sp on next two Large Motifs; repeat from * 3 more times, ending with ch 3, join with sl st in first sc. Fasten off.

Repeat with remaining Motifs.

BORDER

Rnd 1: Join gold with sc in any ch sp on outer edge of any Large Motif, ch 3, (sc in next ch sp, ch 3) around, join with sl st in first sc.

Rnd 2: Sl st across to center of first ch sp, ch 6, dc in same ch sp, (dc, ch 3, dc) in each ch sp around, join with sl st in third ch of ch 6. Fasten off.

FRINGE

For each Fringe, cut 3 strands each 12" long. Fold strands in half, insert hook in one ch sp of rnd 2 on Border, pull fold through, pull ends through fold and tighten. ❧

IN PRAISE OF FLOWERS

Carnations in a buttonhole, lavender in the drawer,
Honeysuckle on the fence, wisteria o'er a door.
In windowbox, garden plot or trellis a'curl,
Their wondrous comeliness, they gaudily unfurl.

They enrich our celebrations in table bouquets,
and untamed, enliven our paths and highways.

They flame a front post and border a yard,
and are praised in poetry by the Bard.
Is a rose just a rose? Hardly so.
It's a symbol of all the blessings we know.

In the short space of bees, in sun or shade,
Flowers bespeak all our Dear Lord has made.

Verbenas, petunias, hydrangeas and sage,
Sending wishes with flowers is all the rage.
No wonder crocheters cultivate their transient graces
And capture blooming beauties in clusters and laces.

The best gift of all? One that will e'er bloom—
Budding joy stitched in afghans, one per room.

Linda Moll Smith

Crochet Quilts

Warm-hearted as a grandmother's hug, cozy as a cat curled by the fire, these old-fashioned quilts create a new heritage of comfort. Here, Double Wedding Ring unites sweetheart roses with lacy panels. Cherish timeless designs: our flower basket motif, bow tie, crazy bow tie and Amish-styled diamond lapghan—all updated in fabulous crochet.

by Dereck Lockwood

Double Wedding Ring

FINISHED SIZE: About 45" × 60" without Fringe.

MATERIALS:
- ❏ Worsted yarn:
    - 14 oz. white
    - 3½ oz. each lt. pink, burgundy, med. green and dk. green
    - 7 oz. each med. pink, dk. pink, pale green and lt. green
- ❏ Bobby pins for markers
- ❏ Tapestry needle
- ❏ G hook or size needed to obtain gauge

GAUGE: 4 sc = 1"; 4 sc rows = 1".

EYE MOTIF (make 31)

Row 1: For **First Side**, with burgundy, ch 6, sc in second ch from hook, sc in next 4 ch, turn. *(5 sc made)*

NOTE: *Ch 1 at beginning of row is not used or counted as a st.*

Rows 2–3: Ch 1, sc in each st across, turn.

Row 4: Ch 1, sc in first 3 sts, 2 hdc in next st, hdc in last st, turn. *(6 sts)*

Row 5: Ch 1, hdc in first 3 sts, sc in last 3 sts, turn. Fasten off.

Row 6: Join lt. pink with sl st in first st, ch 1, hdc in same st as sl st, hdc in next 2 sts, sc in last 3 sts, turn.

Rows 7–10: Ch 1, sc in each sc and hdc in each hdc across, turn. At end of row 10, fasten off.

Row 11: Join dk. pink with sl st in first st, ch 1, sc in each sc and hdc in each hdc across, turn.

Rows 12–15: Ch 1, sc in each sc and hdc in each hdc across, turn. At end of row 15, fasten off.

Row 16: Join med. pink with sl st in first st, ch 1, sc in each sc and hdc in each hdc across, turn.

Rows 17–20: Ch 1, sc in each sc and hdc in each hdc across, turn. At end of row 20, fasten off.

Row 21: Join lt. green with sl st in first st, ch 1, sc in each sc and hdc in each hdc across, turn. Mark first st of row 21.

Rows 22–25: Ch 1, sc in each sc and hdc in each hdc across, turn. At end of row 25, fasten off.

Row 26: Join med. green with sl st in first st, ch 1, sc in each sc and hdc in each hdc across, turn.

Rows 27–30: Ch 1, sc in each sc and hdc in each hdc across, turn. At end of row 30, fasten off.

Row 31: Join pale green with sl st in first st, ch 1, sc in each sc and hdc in each hdc across, turn.

Rows 32–35: Ch 1, sc in each sc and hdc in each hdc across, turn. At end of row 35, leaving an 8" end for sewing, fasten off.

Row 36: For **Second Side,** with dk. green, ch 6, sc in second ch from hook, sc in next 4 ch, turn. *(5 sc made)*

Rows 37–38: Ch 1, sc in each st across, turn.

Row 39: Ch 1, sc in first 3 sts, 2 hdc in next st, hdc in last st, turn. *(6 sts)*

Row 40: Ch 1, hdc in first 3 sts, sc in last 3 sts, turn. Fasten off.

Rows 41–70: Work same as rows 6–35 of First Side.

NOTE: *Front of row 1 and row 36 is right side of work.*

With right side of both pieces facing you, sew sts of row 35 to ends of rows 36–40; sew sts of row 70 to ends of rows 1–5 *(see Eye Motif illustration).*

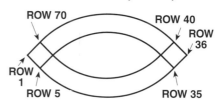

Row 71: For **Center,** working in ends of rows on inside edges of assembled pieces, with right side facing you, join white with sc in end of row 34, sc in each row across to row 6, sc row 6 and 70 together, sc in each row across to row 41, sc row 41 and row 35 together, join with sl st in first sc. *(58 sc)*

Row 72: Ch 4, skip first 3 sts, sc in next st, ch 5, skip next 2 sts, sc in next st, ch 6, skip next 2 sts, sc in next st, ch 7, skip next 2 sts, sc in next st, ch 8, skip next 2 sts, sc in next st, ch 7, skip next 2 sts, sc in next st, ch 6, skip next 2 sts, sc in next st, ch 5, skip next 2 sts, sc in next st, ch 4, skip next 2 sts, sc in next st, turn.

Row 73: To close opening, ch 2, sl st in last ch-4 sp on row 72, ch 2, skip next 3 unworked sts on rnd 71, sc in next st; *work steps A–G to complete the row:*

A: Ch 2, sl st in next ch-5 sp on row 72, ch 2, skip next 2 sts on rnd 71, sc in next st;

B: Ch 3, sl st in next ch-6 sp on row 72, ch 3, skip next 2 sts on rnd 71, sc in next st;

C: Ch 3, sl st in next ch-7 sp on row 72, ch 3, skip next 2 sts on rnd 71, sc in next st;

D: Ch 4, sl st in next ch-8 sp on row 72, ch 4, skip next 2 sts on rnd 71, sc in next st;

E: Ch 3, sl st in next ch-7 sp on row 72, ch 3, skip next 2 sts on rnd 71, sc in next st;

F: Ch 3, sl st in next ch-6 sp on row 72, ch 3, skip next 2 sts on rnd 71, sc in next st;

G: Ch 2, sl st in next ch-5 sp on row 72, ch 2, skip next 2 sts on rnd 71, sc in next st, ch 2, sl st in next ch-4 sp on row 72, ch 2, skip next 3 sts on rnd 71, sl st in last sc on rnd 71. Fasten off.

RING ASSEMBLY

1: For **First Ring,** sew unworked ends of rows 36–40 on one Eye Motif to opposite side of row 1 on next Motif; repeat until four Eye Motifs are joined to form a Ring *(see Ring illustration).*

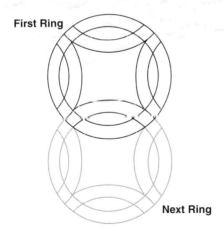

First Ring

Next Ring

2: For **Next Ring,** sew three more Eye Motifs together and sew to previous Ring in same manner, always sewing unworked ends of rows 36–40 to opposite side of row 1 to maintain color pattern.

3: Repeat Next ring until all Eye Motifs are joined according to assembly illustration.

LACE FILL-IN

Rnd 1: Working in ends of rows around edges of diamond-shaped area at center of any Ring, join

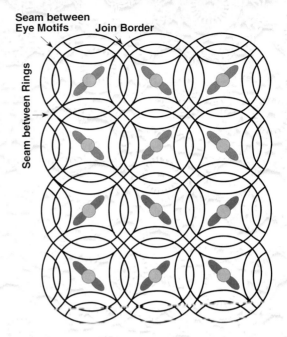

Seam between Eye Motifs   Join Border

Seam between Rings

white with sl st in end of row 21 on any Eye Motif, ch 1, *sc in marked row 21, sc in next row, (2 sc in next row, sc in next 4 rows) 2 times, 2 sc in next row, sc in next row, sc next row *(row 35)* and row 36 on next Eye Motif together, sc in next row, (2 sc in next row, sc in next 4 rows) 2 times, 2 sc in next row, sc in next 2 rows; repeat from * 3 more times, join with sl st in first sc. *(140 sc made)*

Rnd 2: Ch 4 *(counts as dc and ch 1)*, skip next st, dc in next st, (ch 1, skip next st, dc in next st) 3 times; *work steps A—I to complete the rnd:*

A: For **corner decrease,** yo 2 times, skip next st, insert hook in next st, yo, pull through st, (yo, pull through 2 lps on hook) 2 times leaving 2 lps on hook;

B: Yo 3 times, skip next st, insert hook in next st, yo, pull through st, (yo, pull through 2 lps on hook) 3 times leaving 3 lps on hook;

C: Yo 4 times, skip next st, insert hook in next st, yo, pull through st, skip next 5 sts, insert hook in next st, yo, pull through st, yo, pull through 3 lps on hook, (yo, pull through 2 lps on hook) 3 times leaving 4 lps on hook;

D: Yo 3 times, skip next st, insert hook in next st, yo, pull through st, (yo, pull through 2 lps on hook) 3 times leaving 5 lps on hook;

E: Yo 2 times, skip next st, insert hook in next st, yo, pull through st, (yo, pull through 2 lps on hook) 2 times leaving 6 lps on hook, yo, pull through all 6 lps on hook *(corner decrease complete);*

F: Skip next st, dc in next st, (ch 1, skip next st,

continued on page 26

continued from page 25

dc in next st) 9 times;

G: Repeat A–F 2 more times;

H: Repeat A–E;

I: Skip next st, dc in next st, (ch 1, skip next st, dc in next st) 4 times, ch 1, skip next last st, join with sl st in third ch of ch 4. *(10 dc on each side, 4 corner decreases)*

NOTE: *For remainder of Lace Fill-in, skip each ch-1 sp unless otherwise stated.*

Rnd 3: Ch 5 *(counts as tr and ch 1)*, tr in next st, ch 1; *work steps A–I to complete rnd;*

A: For **corner decrease**, yo 2 times, insert hook in next st, yo, pull through st, (yo, pull through 2 lps on hook) 2 times, leaving 2 lps on hook;

B: Yo 3 times, insert hook in next st, yo, pull through st, (yo, pull through 2 lps on hook) 3 times leaving 3 lps on hook;

C: Yo 4 times, skip next st, insert hook in next corner decrease st, yo, pull through st, (yo, pull through 2 lps on hook) 4 times leaving 4 lps on hook;

D: Yo 3 times, skip next st, insert hook in next st, yo, pull through st, (yo, pull through 2 lps on hook) 3 times leaving 5 lps on hook;

E: Yo 2 times, insert hook in next st, yo, pull through st, (yo, pull through 2 lps on hook) 2 times leaving 6 lps on hook, yo, pull through all 6 lps on hook *(corner decrease completed)*;

F: Ch 1, (tr in next st, ch 1) 4 times;

G: Repeat A–F 2 more times;

H: Repeat A–E;

I: Ch 1, (tr in next st, ch 1) 2 times, join with sl st in fourth ch of ch 5, *(4 tr on each side, 4 corner decrease)*

Rnd 4: Ch 5; *work steps A–F to complete the rnd:*

A: For **corner decrease**, yo 2 times, insert hook in next st, yo, pull through st, (yo, pull through 2 lps on hook) 2 times leaving 2 lps on hook;

B: Yo 3 times, insert hook in next corner decrease st, yo, pull through st, (yo, pull through 2 lps on hook) 3 times leaving 3 lps on hook;

C: Yo 2 times, insert hook in next st, yo, pull through st, (yo, pull though 2 lps on hook) 2 times leaving 4 lps on hook, yo, pull through all 4 lps on hook;

D: Ch 1, (tr in next st, ch 1) 2 times;

E: Repeat A–D 2 more times;

F: Repeat A–C, ch 1, tr in next st, ch 1, join. *(8 tr, 4 corner decreases)*

Rnd 5: Ch 4; *work steps A–F to complete rnd:*

A: Yo 3 times, insert hook in next corner decrease st, yo, pull through st, (yo, pull through 2 lps on hook) 3 times leaving 2 lps on hook;

B: Yo 2 times, insert hook in next st, yo, pull through st, (yo, pull through 2 lps on hook) 2 times leaving 3 lps on hook; yo, pull through all 3 lps on hook;

C: Yo 2 times, insert hook in next st, yo, pull through st, (yo, pull through 2 lps on hook) 2 times leaving 2 lps on hook;

D: Yo 3 times, skip next st, insert hook in next corner decrease st, yo, pull through st, (yo, pull through 2 lps on hook) 3 times leaving 3 lps on hook;

E: Yo 2 times, insert hook in next st, yo, pull through st, (yo, pull through 2 lps on hook) 2 times leaving 4 lps on hook, yo, pull through all 4 lps on hook;

F: Repeat C–E 2 more times, join with sl st in top of ch 4. Fasten off.

BORDER

NOTE: *In rnd 1, you will be working in ends of rows, in sts and in ch on opposite side of row 36; sts, ch and rows are all referred to as rows.*

Rnd 1: Working around entire Afghan, with white, place lp on hook, insert hook in last row on Eye Motif at the right *(see arrow on assembly illustration)*, yo, pull through row, yo, insert hook in first row on next Eye Motif to the left, yo, pull through row, yo, pull through all 3 lps on hook *(joining sc 2 tog made)*, *[sc in next row, 2 sc in next row, sc in next 2 rows, (sc in next 2 rows, 2 sc in next row, sc in next 2 rows) across to last 5 rows before next seam between Rings (this will take you past the seam between Eye Motifs on corner Ring—see assembly illustration), sc in next 2 rows, 2 sc in next row, sc in next row], sc last row on this Eye Motif and first row on next

Eye Motif together; repeat from * around entire Afghan to last Eye Motif; repeat between [ ], join with sl st in first sc. *(94 sc on each corner ring, 46 sc on each Eye Motif, 10 sc 2 tog at seams)*

Rnd 2: For **beginning decrease (beg dec)**, ch 4, skip next st, tr in next st; *work steps A–H to complete the rnd:*

A: Working around corner Ring, (ch 1, skip next st, tr in next st) 4 times, skip next st; for **V st,** ch 1, (tr, ch 1, tr) in next st; *(ch 1, skip next st, tr in next st) 5 times, skip next st, V st in next st; repeat from * 5 more times, (ch 1, skip next st, tr in next st) 3 times;

B: Working across seam, for **3-st dec,** ch 1, skip next st, *yo 2 times, insert hook in next st, yo, pull through st, (yo, pull through 2 lps on hook) 2 times*, skip next 2 sts; repeat between first and second *, skip next st; repeat between first and second *, yo, pull through all 4 lps on hook *(3-st dec complete);*

C: Working across Eye Motif, (ch 1, skip next st, tr in next st) 4 times, *skip next st, V st in next st, (ch 1, skip next st, tr in next st) 5 times; repeat from *, skip next st, V st in next st, (ch 1, skip next st, tr in next st) 3 times;

D: Repeat B, C, B;

E: Repeat A, B, C, B;

F: Repeat A–D;

G: Repeat A–C;

H: Skip next 2 sts; for **end dec,** ch 1, yo 2 times, insert hook in next st, yo, pull through st, (yo, pull through 2 lps on hook) 2 times, skip first ch 4, insert hook in next tr, yo, pull through all lps on hook. *(Beg and end decs count as one 3 st dec—250 tr, 46 V sts, 10 3-st decs)*

NOTES: *For remainder of Border, skip each ch-1 sp unless otherwise stated.*

For **treble decrease (tr dec),** *yo 2 times, insert hook in next st, yo, pull through st, (yo, pull through 2 lps on hook) 2 times; repeat from * 2 more times, yo, pull through all lps on hook.*

Rnd 3: Ch 4, tr in next st, *(ch 1, tr) in each st—*including both tr of V sts—*and in ch sp of each V st across to last tr before next 3-st dec; work tr dec (see Notes);* repeat from * 8 more times, (ch 1, tr) in each st—*including both tr of V sts—*and in ch sp of each V st across to last tr, end dec. *(368 tr, 10 tr decs)*

Rnd 4: Ch 4, tr in next st, *(ch 1, tr) in each st and V st in each st worked into ch sp of V st on rnd 2 across to last tr before next tr dec; work tr dec; repeat from * 8 more times, (ch 1, tr) in each st and V st in each st worked into ch sp of V st on rnd 2 across to last st, end dec. Fasten off. *(302 tr, 46 V sts, 10 tr decs)*

Rnd 5: Count back to second V st from end of rnd 4 *(this is the center V st above Eye Motif on short edge of Afghan),* join med. pink with sl st in ch sp of this V st, ch 4, dc in next tr of V st, (ch 1, dc in next st) 3 times, (ch 1, tr in next st) 7 times, work tr dec; *work steps A–F to complete rnd:*

A: Working around corner, (ch 1, tr in next st) 7 times, (ch 1, dc in next st) 9 times, (ch 1, tr in next st) 9 times, (ch 1, dtr in next st) 5 times, dtr in next ch sp of V st *(this is corner st),* (ch 1, dtr in next st) 5 times, (ch 1, tr in next st) 8 times, (ch 1, dc in next st) 9 times, (ch 1, tr in next st) 7 times, work tr dec;

B: Working across edge above Eye Motif, *(ch 1, tr in next st) 7 times, (ch 1, dc in next st) 5 times, ch 1, dc in ch sp of V st, (ch 1, dc in next st) 4 times, (ch 1, tr in next st) 7 times, work tr dec;

C: Repeat B;

D: Repeat A and B;

E: Repeat A–C;

F: Repeat A, (ch 1, tr in next st) 7 times, (ch 1, dc in next st) 5 times, ch 1, join with sl st in third ch of ch 4. Fasten off. *(384 sts, 10 tr decs)*

Rnd 6: Join dk. pink with sl st in first st, ch 4, dc in next st, (ch 1, dc in next st) 6 times, (ch 1, tr in next st) 3 times, (ch 1, dtr in next st) 3 times; *work steps A–F to complete rnd:*

A: Working around corner, (ch 1, tr in next st) 3 times, (ch 1, dc in next st) 16 times, (ch 1, tr in next st) 3 times, (ch 1, dtr in next st) 7 times, (ch 1, dtr, ch 1, dtr) in next st, mark last ch sp made for corner, (ch 1, dtr in next st) 7 times, (ch 1, tr in next st) 3 times, (ch 1, dc in next st) 15 times, (ch 1, tr in next st) 3 times, (ch 1, dtr in next st) 3 times;

B: Working across edge above Eye Motif, *(ch 1, tr in next st) 3 times, (ch 1, dc in next st) 16 times, (ch 1, tr in next st) 3 times, (ch 1, dtr in next st) 3 times;

C: Repeat B;

D: Repeat A and B;

E: Repeat A–C;

F: Repeat A, (ch 1, tr in next st) 3 times, (ch 1, dc in next st) 8 times, ch 1, join. Fasten off. *(398 sts, 4 corner ch sps)*

Rnd 7: Join pale green with sl st in first st, ch 4, dc in next st, *(ch 1, dc in next st) across to last 8 sts before next marked corner ch sp, (ch 1, tr in next st) 3 times, (ch 1, dtr in next st) 5 times, (ch 1, dtr, ch 1, dtr, mark last st made for corner, ch 1, dtr) in marked corner ch sp, (ch 1, dtr in next

continued on page 37

by Dorothy Kunkel

Flower Basket

FINISHED SIZE: Afghan is about 54" × 70"; Pillow is 20" × 18".

MATERIALS:
- ❑ Worsted yarn:
  - 51 oz. beige
  - 39 oz. brown
  - 9 oz. green
  - 3½ oz. yellow
  - 3 oz. each lt. orange, dk. orange, lt. blue, dk. blue, purple, lavender, burgundy and pink
- ❑ Polyester fiberfill
- ❑ Tapestry needle
- ❑ F hook or size needed to obtain gauge

GAUGE: Each Motif is 1½" across.

AFGHAN
Motif
Ch 5, sl st in first ch to form ring, ch 3, 2 dc in ring, ch 2, (3 dc in ring, ch 2) 5 times, join with sl st in top of ch 3. Fasten off. *(18 dc made)*

Assembly
Make 18 dk. orange, 30 each of lt. orange, dk. blue, lt. blue, purple, lavender, burgundy and pink; 38 yellow; 176 green; 394 brown and 706 beige Motifs.

With wrong sides of Motifs facing you and stitching through **front lps** *(see Stitch Guide)*, sew Motifs together according to diagram using matching colors.

Edging
Working around entire outer edge, join brown with sc in ch-2 sp of top left corner Motif, 2 sc in same sp, sc in each st, 3 sc in each outer ch-2 sp and skipping each of next 2 ch-2 sps at joining seam of Motifs around, join with sl st in first sc. Fasten off.

PILLOW
Motif
Following instructions for Afghan Motif, make 96

beige, 76 brown, 16 green, 8 yellow and 6 each of all other colors.

Assembly
Sew Motifs together same as for Afghan according to diagram. Hold wrong sides together, matching sts; working through both thicknesses, repeat edging of Afghan, stuffing before closing. ❧

by Marie Leo

Crazy Bow Tie

FINISHED SIZE: About 35" × 46".

MATERIALS:
- ❑ Worsted yarn:
    - 9 oz. yellow
    - 6 oz. green
    - 4 oz. lt. blue
    - 4 oz. pale peach
- ❑ Tapestry needle
- ❑ I hook or size needed to obtain gauge

GAUGE: 1 shell = 1"; 4 shell rows = 3"; 1 Square = 5½" square.

NOTE: Pattern is worked diagonally from bottom right-hand corner to top left-hand corner.

SQUARE (make 48)

Row 1: With green; for **increase diagonal shell (inc), ch 6, dc in fourth ch from hook, dc in next 2 ch;** turn. Fasten off. *(1 shell, 1 ch-3 sp)*

Row 2: Join lt. blue with sl st in first st, inc; for **diagonal shell (shell), (sl st, ch 3, 3 dc)** in ch-3 sp on row 1; turn. Fasten off. *(2 shells, 2 ch-3 sps)*

Row 3: Join pale peach with sl st in first st, inc, shell in each ch-3 sp across, turn. Fasten off. *(3 shells, 3 ch-3 sps)*

Row 4: Join green with sl st in first st, inc, shell in each ch-3 sp across, turn. Fasten off. *(4 shells, 4 ch-3 sps)*

Row 5: Join lt. blue with sl st in first st, inc, shell in each ch-3 sp across, turn. Fasten off. *(5 shells, 5 ch-3 sps)*

Row 6: Join pale peach with sl st in first st, inc, shell in each ch-3 sp across, turn. Fasten off. *(6 shells, 6 ch-3 sps)*

Row 7: Join green with sl st in first st, inc, shell in each ch-3 sp across, turn. Fasten off. *(7 shells, 7 ch-3 sps)*

Row 8: Join yellow with (sl st, ch 3, 3 dc) in first ch-3 sp, shell in each ch-3 sp across to last ch sp, sl st in last sp, turn. *(6 shells, 6 ch-3 sps)*

Rows 9–13: Ch 1, sl st in next 3 sts, shell in each ch-3 sp across to last ch sp, sl st in last sp, turn. At end of last row, fasten off. *(1 shell)*

ASSEMBLY

Sew Squares together according to illustration.

EDGING

Rnd 1: Working in sps between sts at end of shell rows and in ends of rows around outer edge, join green with sc in any row, sc in same row, 2 sc in each row around with 3 sc in each corner, join with sl st in first sc. Fasten off.

Rnd 2: Join lt. blue with sc in first st, sc in each st around with 3 sc in center st of each corner, join. Fasten off.

Rnd 3: Join pale peach with sc in first st, sc in each st around with 3 sc in center st of each corner, join. Fasten off.

Rnd 4: Join green with sc in first st, sc in each st around with 3 sc in center st of each corner, join. Fasten off.

Rnd 5: Join yellow with sc in first st, sc in each st around with 3 sc in center st of each corner, join. Fasten off. ❦

by Marie Leo

Diamond Lapghan

FINISHED SIZE: About 35" × 46".

MATERIALS:
- ❏ Worsted yarn:
    - 10 oz. lt. purple
    - 10 oz. dk. purple
- ❏ Tapestry needle
- ❏ I hook or size needed to obtain gauge

GAUGE: 1 shell = 1"; 4 shell rows = 3"; 1 Square = 5½" square.

NOTE: Pattern is worked diagonally from bottom right-hand corner to top left-hand corner.

SQUARE (make 48)
Row 1: With lt. purple; for **increase diagonal shell (inc), ch 6, dc in fourth ch from hook, dc in next 2 ch**; turn. *(1 shell, 1 ch-3 sp)*

Row 2: Inc; for **diagonal shell, (shell), (sl st, ch 3, 3 dc)** in ch-3 sp on row 1; turn. *(2 shells, 2 ch-3 sps)*

Rows 3–7: Inc, shell in each ch-3 sp across, turn. At end of last row, fasten off. *(7 shells, 7 ch-3 sps)*

Row 8: Join dk. purple with sl st in first ch-3 sp, ch 3, 3 dc in same sp, shell in each ch-3 sp across to last ch sp, sl st in last sp, turn. *(6 shells, 6 ch-3 sps)*

Rows 9–13: Ch 1, sl st in first 3 sts, shell in each ch-3 sp across to last ch sp, sl st in last sp, turn. At end of last row, fasten off. *(1 shell)*

ASSEMBLY
Sew Squares together according to illustration.

EDGING
Rnd 1: Working in sps between sts at ends of shell rows and in ends of rows around outer edge, join dk. purple with sc in any row, sc in same row, 2 sc in each row around with 3 sc in each corner, join with sl st in first sc.

Rnd 2: Ch 2, hdc in each st around with 3 hdc in center st of each corner, join with sl st in top of ch 2, turn.

Rnd 3: Ch 1, sc in first 2 sts, ch 3, sl st in third ch from hook, (sc in next 2 sts, ch 3, sl st in third ch from hook) around, join with sl st in first sc. Fasten off. ❧

LP=Lt. Purple   DP=Dk. Purple

by Lorain Axup

Bow Tie Afghan

FINISHED SIZE: Afghan is about 69" × 85"; Pillow is 20" square.

MATERIALS:
- ❑ Worsted yarn:
    - 2½ oz. of desired color (CC) for each Block
    - 60 oz. main color (MC)
    - 8 oz. green
- ❑ Polyester fiberfill
- ❑ Tapestry needle
- ❑ H hook or size needed to obtain gauge

GAUGE: 7 sts = 2"; 7 rows = 2". Block is 16" square.

NOTES:
To change colors (see Stitch Guide), drop first color; with second color, pull through last 2 lps of st. Drop first color, pick up when needed. When increasing one color and decreasing other color in each row, carry dropped yarn behind one st after color change so it will be in correct position for next color change.
Do not fasten off unless otherwise stated.

AFGHAN
Motif (make 4 of each desired color)
Row 1: With MC, ch 14, drop MC, pull up lp with first desired color (CC), ch 15, sc in second ch from hook, sc in next 13 ch, sc in next ch changing to MC, sc in next 14 ch, turn. *(28 sc made)*

Row 2: Ch 1, sc in first 14 sts changing to CC in last st made, sc in last 14 sts, turn.

Row 3: Ch 1, sc in first 14 sts changing to MC in last st made, sc in last 14 sts, turn.

Rows 4–11: Repeat rows 2 and 3 alternately.

Row 12: Ch 1, sc in first 13 sts changing to CC in last st made, sc in last 15 sts, turn.

Row 13: Ch 1, sc in first 16 sts changing to MC in last st made, sc in last 12 sts, turn.

Row 14: Ch 1, sc in first 11 sts changing to CC in last st made, sc in last 17 sts, turn.

Row 15: Ch 1, sc in first 18 sts changing to MC in last st made, sc in last 10 sts, turn.

Row 16: Ch 1, sc in first 9 sts changing to CC in last st made, fasten off MC, sc in last 19 sts, turn. Fasten off CC.

Row 17: Join MC with sc in first st, sc in next 9 sts changing to CC in last st made, sc in last 19 sts, turn.

Row 18: Ch 1, sc in first 18 sts changing to MC in last st made, sc in last 10 sts, turn.

Row 19: Ch 1, sc in first 11 sts changing to CC in last st made, sc in last 17 sts, turn.

Row 20: Ch 1, sc in first 16 sts changing to MC in last st made, sc in last 12 sts, turn.

Row 21: Ch 1, sc in first 13 sts changing to CC in last st made, sc in last 15 sts, turn.

Row 22: Ch 1, sc in first 14 sts changing to MC in last st made, sc in last 14 sts, turn.

Row 23: Ch 1, sc in first 14 sts changing to CC in last st made, sc in last 14 sts, turn.

Rows 24–32: Repeat rows 22 and 23 alternately ending with row 22. Fasten off MC and CC.

Block (make 20)
Matching colors, sew four matching Motifs together as shown in illustration.

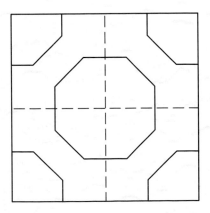

continued on page 36

Bow Tie Afghan

continued from page 35

Assembly
Matching colors, sew Blocks together, four wide and five long.

Edging
Rnd 1: Join green with sc in any st, sc in each st and end of each row around with 3 sc in each corner st, join with sl st in first sc.

Rnds 2–4: Ch 1, sc in each st around with 3 sc in each corner st, join. At end of rnd 4, fasten off.

Rnd 5: Join MC with sc in any st, sc in each st around with 3 sc in each corner st, join.

Rnds 6–8: Ch 1, sc in each st around with 3 sc in each corner st, join.

Rnd 9: Ch 1, reverse sc *(see Stitch Guide)* in each st around, join. Fasten off.

PILLOW
For Pillow, make 8 Motifs. Sew four together as shown in illustration for each Pillow Side.

Edging
Rnds 1–8: Repeat rnds 1–8 of Afghan Edging. At end of rnd 8, fasten off.

Assembly
Rnd 1: Hold both pieces wrong sides together; working through both thicknesses, join MC with sc in any st, sc in each st around with 3 sc in each corner st, stuffing before closing, join with sl st in first sc.

Rnd 2: Ch 1, reverse sc in each st around, join. Fasten off. ❧

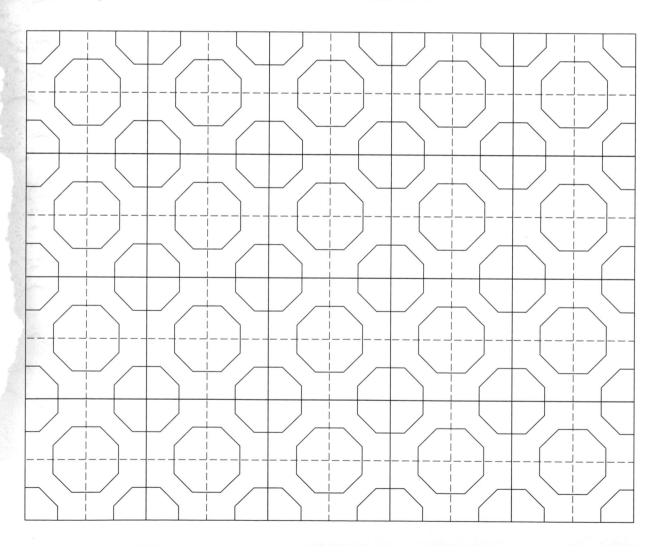

Double Wedding Ring

continued from page 27

st) 5 times, (ch 1, tr in next st) 3 times; repeat from * 3 more times, (ch 1, dc in next st) across, ch 1, join. Fasten off. *(410 sts)*

Rnd 8: Join med. green with sl st in first st, ch 3, *dc in each st and in each ch sp across to 7 ch sps before next marked corner st, (tr in next ch sp, tr in next st) 3 times, (dtr in next ch sp, dtr in next st) 3 times, 2 dtr in next ch sp, (dtr, ch 2, dtr) in next corner st, 2 dtr in next ch sp, (dtr in next st, dtr in next ch sp) 3 times, (tr in next st, tr in next ch sp) 3 times; repeat from * 3 more times, dc in each st and in each ch sp across, join with sl st in top of ch 3. Fasten off. *(406 sts, 4 corner ch sps)*

Rnd 9: Join dk. green with sc in first st, sc in each st around with 3 sc in each corner ch sp, join with sl st in first sc. Fasten off.

KNOTTED FRINGE

1: Alternating one Green Fringe and one Pink Fringe, work Fringe in every other stitch across each short edge as follows:

For **Green Fringe,** cut one strand each of pale green, lt. green and med. green each 12" long. Holding all strands together, fold in half, pull fold through stitch, pull all six ends through fold, pull tight.

For **Pink Fringe,** with one strand each of lt. pink, med. pink and dk. pink work same as Green Fringe.

2: Separating each Fringe with one strand of each color on each side, tie with overhand knots *(see Stitch Guide),* then separate each Fringe and tie six strands of green together and tie six strands of pink together *(see illustration at right).*

ROSE (make 12)

Base: With white, ch 52. Fasten off.

Center Petal: Join lt. pink with sc in first ch, (hdc, dc) in next ch, (tr, dc) in next ch, (hdc, sc) in next ch changing to med. pink in last st made *(see Stitch Guide); work nine more Petals as follows:*

Next 3 Petals: *(Hdc, dc) in next ch, 2 tr in next ch, (tr, dc) in next ch, (hdc, sc) in next ch; repeat from * 2 more times changing to dk. pink in last st made;

Last 6 Petals: *(Hdc, dc) in next ch, 2 tr in next

ch, 2 dtr in next ch, (dtr, tr) in next ch, (tr, dc) in next ch, (hdc, sc) in next ch; repeat from * 5 more times. Fasten off.

Beginning at Center Petal, roll the white Base in a circle and sew together forming a Rose.

Sew Base of one Rose to center of each Lace Fill-In.

LEAF (make 24)

With dk. green, beginning at stem end, ch 12, sc in second ch from hook, sc in next 2 ch, hdc in next ch, dc in next ch, 2 tr in each of next 4 ch, dc in next ch, (hdc, sc changing to pale green, hdc) in end ch; continuing on opposite side of ch, dc in next ch, 2 tr in each of next 4 ch, dc in next ch, hdc in next ch, sc in last 3 ch. Fasten off.

Sew stem ends to two Leaves under edge of Rose at center of each Lace Fill-In *(see assembly illustration).* ❦

KNOTTED FRINGE

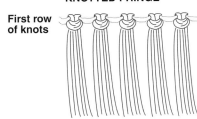

First row of knots

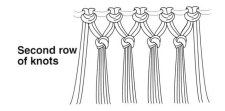

Second row of knots

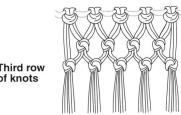

Third row of knots

More Motifs

"Take it and make it," is the recurring motif of these afghans-to-go. Our Floral Baby Shawl is a pattern of portability to make in bits and pieces. Joining our array of notable totables are swirling spirals, puffed clusters, dazzling starbursts and repeating roses—gifted travelers all.

by Dorothy Hamilton

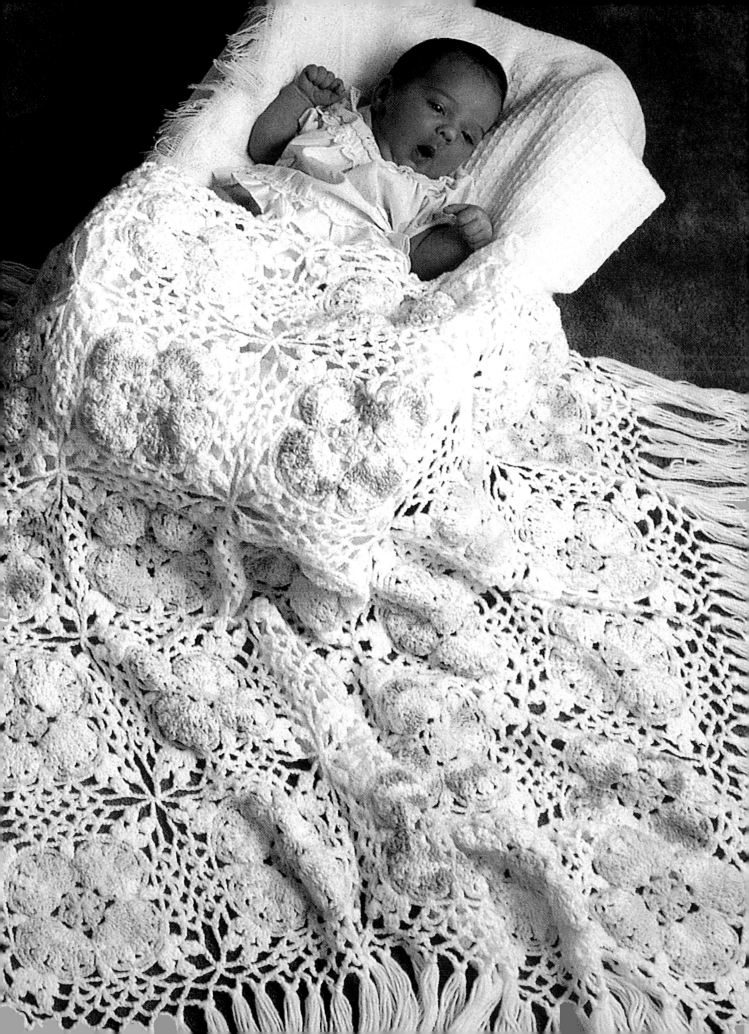

Floral Baby Shawl

FINISHED SIZE: About 36" × 36" without Fringe.

MATERIALS:
- ❑ Sport yarn:
  - 8 oz. white
  - 2 oz. green
- ❑ 2 oz. each 5 flower colors in baby yarn
- ❑ 14" square pillow form
- ❑ D hook or size needed to obtain gauge

GAUGE: 1 Motif = 7" square.

SPECIAL STITCHES:

For **3-dc cluster (3 dc-cl)**, (yo, insert hook in st, yo, pull through, yo, pull through 2 lps) 3 times, yo, pull through all lps on hook.

For **2-dc cluster (2 dc-cl)**, (yo, insert hook in same st, yo, pull through, yo, pull through 2 lps) 2 times, yo, pull through all 3 lps on hook.

NOTE: After first Motif is made, all following Motifs are joined to each other while working last rnd.

FIRST STRIP

First Motif

Rnd 1: With green, ch 6, sl st in first ch to form ring, ch 3, 2 dc in ring, (ch 3, 3 dc in ring) 3 times, ch 3, join with sl st in top of ch 3. *(12 dc made)*

Rnd 2: Working this rnd in **back lps** *(see Stitch Guide)*, ch 5, (skip next st, sc in next st, ch 5, skip next ch-3 sp, sc in next st, ch 4) 3 times, skip next st, sc in next st, ch 5, join with sl st in first ch of beginning ch 5. Fasten off. *(8 ch sps)*

Rnd 3: Join flower color with (sl st, ch 3, 8 dc) in any ch-4 sp, (ch 1, sc in next ch-5 sp, ch 1, 9 dc in next ch-4 sp) 3 times, ch 1, sc in next ch-5 sp, ch 1, join with sl st in top of ch 3. *(40)*

Rnd 4: Ch 2, hdc in next 2 sts, 2 dc in next 3 sts, hdc in next 3 sts, ch 2, sc in next st, ch 2, (hdc in next 3 sts, 2 dc in next 3 sts, hdc in next 3 sts, ch 2, sc in next st, ch 2) 3 times, join with sl st in top of ch 2. *(52 sts)*

Rnd 5: Ch 3, 2-dc cl *(see Special Stitches)*, (ch 3, skip next st, 3-dc cl—*see Special Stitches*—in next st) 5 times, skip next st, *ch 2, skip next ch-2 sp, sc in next st, ch 2, skip next ch-2 sp, 3-dc cl in next st, ch 3, (skip next st, 3-dc cl in next st, ch 3) 4 times, skip next st, 3-dc cl in next st, skip next st; repeat from * 2 more times, ch 2, skip next ch-2 sp, sc in next st, ch 2, skip next ch-2 sp, join with sl st in top of first cl. Fasten off. *(24 cl, 4 sc)*

Rnd 6: Working this rnd in **back lps**, join green with sl st in first cl, ch 1, *(ch 4, sc in next cl) 5 times, ch 2; for **long dc (ldc)**, yo, insert hook in next ch-5 sp of rnd 2, pull up long lp, complete as dc; ch 2, sc in next cl; repeat from * 3 more times ending with sl st in first ch 1. Fasten off. *(28)*

Rnd 7: Join white with sl st in first ldc of last rnd, ch 3, 2 dc in same st, *ch 4, skip next sc, (sc in next sc, ch 4) 4 times, skip next sc, 3-dc cl in next ldc; repeat from * 2 more times, ch 4, skip next sc, (sc in next sc, ch 4) 4 times, join with sl st in top of first cl. *(4 cl, 16 sc)*

Rnd 8: Ch 7, dc in same st; for **V stitch (V st)**, **(dc, ch 4, dc)** in next st; *ch 4, skip next ch-4 sp, (3-dc cl, ch 4, 3-dc cl, ch 4, 3-dc cl) in next ch-4 sp *(corner made)*; ch 4, V st in next st, V st in next cl, V st in next st; repeat from * 2 more times, ch 4, skip next ch-4 sp, (3-dc cl, ch 4, 3-dc cl, ch 4, 3-dc cl) in next ch-4 sp, ch 4, V st in next st, join with sl st in third ch of beginning ch 7. *(12 cl, 12 V sts)*

Rnd 9; Ch 7, dc in same st, skip next dc, V st in next 2 dc, *ch 4, skip next ch-4 sp, 3-dc cl in next ch-4 sp, ch 7, 3-dc cl, in next ch-4 sp, ch 4, (V st in next dc, skip next dc) 2 times, V st in next 2 dc; repeat from * 2 more times, ch 4, skip next ch-4 sp, 3-dc cl in next ch-4 sp, ch 7, 3-dc cl in next ch-4 sp, ch 4, V st in next dc, join with sl st in third ch of ch 7. Fasten off.

Next Motif

Rnds 1–8: Repeat rnds 1–8 of First Motif. At end of rnd 8, fasten off.

Rnd 9: Join white with sl st in ch-4 sp between first 2 cl of first corner on rnd 8, ch 3, 2-dc cl in same sp, ch 3; to join Motifs, sl st in fourth ch of last ch-7 sp on rnd 9 of last Motif; ch 3, 3-dc cl in next ch-4 sp on rnd 8, ch 4, (*dc in next dc, ch 2, sl st in next V st on rnd 9 of last Motif, ch 2, dc in same st at last dc*, skip next dc on rnd 8) 2 times; repeat between * 2 more times, ch 3, 3-dc cl in next ch-4 sp, ch 3, sl st in fourth ch of next ch-7 sp on rnd 9 of last Motif; now working in rnd 8, ch 3, (3-dc cl in next ch-4 sp, ch 4, V st in next dc, skip next dc, V st in next dc, skip next dc, V st in next 2 dc, ch 4, skip next ch-4 sp, 3-dc cl in next ch-4 sp, ch 7) 2 times, 3-dc cl in next ch-4 sp, ch 4, (V st in next dc, skip next dc) 2 times, V st in next 2 sts, ch 4, join with sl st in top of first cl. Fasten off.

Repeat for next 3 Motifs.

SECOND STRIP
First Motif

Rnds 1–8: Repeat rnds 1–8 of First Motif on First Strip.

Rnd 9: Working on right side of First Motif of last Strip, repeat rnd 9 of Second Motif of First Strip.

Next Motif

Rnds 1–8: Repeat rnds 1–8 of First Motif on First Strip. Fasten off.

Rnd 9: Join white with sl st in ch-4 sp between first 2 cl of first corner on rnd 8, ch 3, 2-dc cl in same sp, [ch 3, sl st in fourth ch of third ch-7 sp of last completed Motif on this Strip, ch 3, 3-dc cl in next ch-4 sp on rnd 8, ch 4, (*dc in next dc, ch 2, sl st in next V st of rnd 9 on last Motif, ch 2, dc in same dc of rnd 8*, skip next dc) 2 times; repeat between * 2 more times, ch 4, skip next ch-4 sp, 3-dc cl in next ch-4 sp]; to join right side of Next Motif of last Strip, repeat between [ ], ch 3, sl st in fourth ch of ch-7 sp, ch 3, 3-dc cl in next ch-4 sp, ch 4, (V st in next dc, skip next dc) 2 times, V st in next 2 dc, ch 4, skip next ch-4 sp, 3-dc cl in next ch-4 sp, ch 7, 3-dc cl in next ch-4 sp, ch 4, (V st in next dc, skip next dc) 2 times, V st in next 2 dc, ch 4, join with sl st in top of first cl. Fasten off.

Repeat for next 3 Motifs on Second Strip with first joining of each Motif in only ch-7 sp of rnd 9 on previous Motif.

NEXT STRIPS

Repeat Second Strip 3 more times.

TRIM

Rnd 1: Join white with sl st in any ch sp, (ch 7, sc in next ch sp) around, do not join.

Rnd 2: (Ch 7, sc in next ch sp) around, join with sl st in first ch of first ch 7. Fasten off.

For **Fringe,** cut 6 strands each 12" long; with wrong side of Afghan facing you, working in ch sps around outer edge, fold strands in half, pull fold through ch sp; pull ends through fold. Repeat in each ch sp around.

PILLOW

For each **Pillow Side,** work first two Motifs of First and Second Strips. Work Trim around edges of each side.

With wrong sides together, matching ch-7 sps, Join white with sc in any 2 ch sps held together, ch 3, (sc in next 2 ch sps, ch 3) around, inserting pillow form before closing, join. Fasten off. Work Fringe around edge of Pillow. ❧

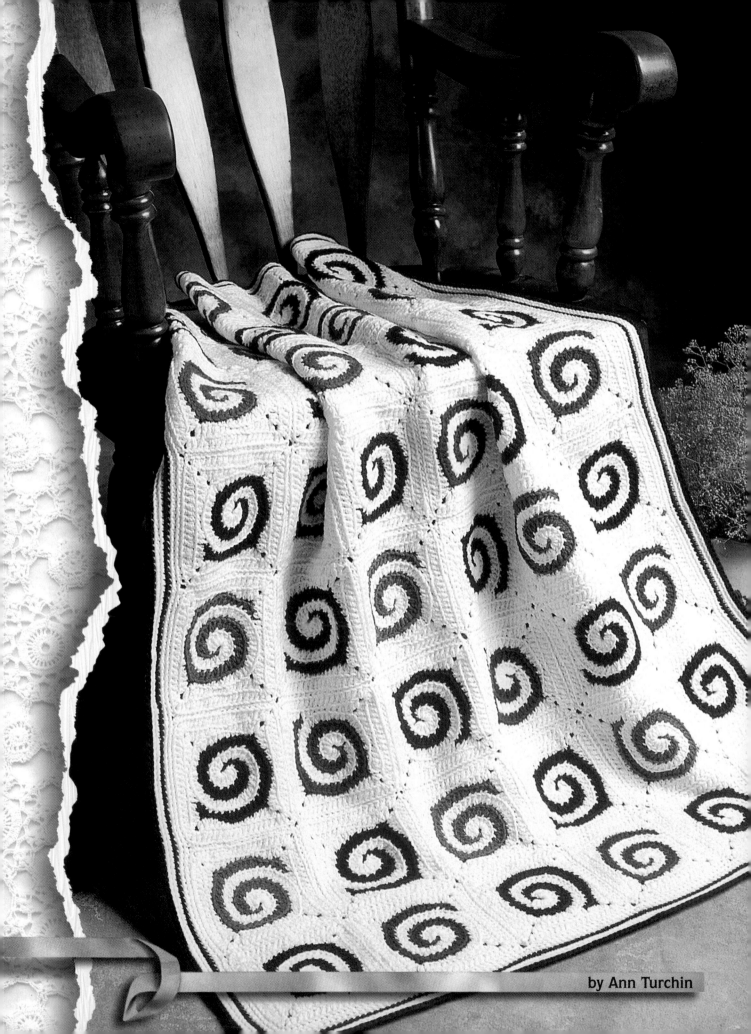

by Ann Turchin

Swirls & Squares

FINISHED SIZE: About 32" × 42".

MATERIALS:
- ❑ Worsted yarn:
  - 26 oz. white (MC)
  - 3½ oz. pink (CC)
  - 3½ oz. purple (CC)
  - 3½ oz. turquoise (CC)
  - 3½ oz. rust (CC)
- ❑ Tapestry needle
- ❑ G hook or size needed to obtain gauge

GAUGE: 4 dc = 1"; 2 dc rows = 1".

NOTES:

Work in continuous rnds, do not join or turn unless otherwise stated.

Work in **back lps** (see Stitch Guide) unless otherwise stated.

BASIC SQUARE (make 12 of each CC)

Rnd 1: With MC, ch 4, sl st in first ch to form ring, ch 3, 10 dc in ring, loosen lp and drop from hook. *(11 dc made)*

Rnd 2: Join desired CC with sl st in ring, ch 1, sc in first 2 ch on ch 3, 2 dc in next ch, 2 dc in each st around, drop lp. *(22 dc, 2 sc)*

Rnd 3: With dropped lps of rnd 1, 2 dc in first 3 sts, dc in next st, (2 dc in next st, dc in next st) around, drop lp. *(37 dc)*

Rnd 4: With dropped lp of rnd 2, (dc in next st, 2 dc in next st) 5 times, (dc in next 2 sts, 2 dc in next st) 3 times, hdc in next 2 sts, 2 hdc in next st, hdc in next st, sc in next st, sl st in next st leaving remaining sts on rnd 3 unworked, **fasten off CC**; with dropped lp of rnd 3, working in sts on rnd 4, dc in next st, 2 hdc in next st, hdc in next st, sc in next st, 2 sc in next st, sc in next st, sl st in next st. *(21 MC sts, 27 CC sts)*

Rnd 5: Ch 3, dc in same st as sl st, *[dc in next st, hdc in next 2 sts, sc in next 4 sts, hdc in next 2 sts, dc in next st, 2 dc in next st], ch 2, 2 dc in next st; repeat from * 2 more times; repeat between [ ], ch 2, join with sl st in top of ch 3. *(56 sts)*

Rnd 6: Ch 3, dc in next 13 sts, *(2 dc, ch 3, 2 dc) in next ch-2 sp, dc in next 14 sts; repeat from * 2 more times; repeat between ( ) in next ch-2 sp, join. *(72 dc)*

BLOCK (make 12)

For each Block, using one Square of each CC, matching edges on Squares, sew dc together in **back lps** according to photograph; sew center ch of each ch 3 together at center of Block.

Sew Blocks together in same manner.

EDGING

Rnd 1: Join MC with sc in first ch of any outside corner ch-3 sp, 3 sc in next ch, sc in next ch, sc in next 18 sts, (sc in next ch, ch 1, sc in third ch on next square, sc in next 18 sts) across to corner, *sc in next ch, 3 sc in next ch, sc in next ch, sc in next 18 sts; repeat between ( ) across to corner; repeat from * 2 more times, join with sl st in first sc.

Rnd 2: Ch 1, sc in each st around with 3 sc in center st of each corner, join. Fasten off.

Rnd 3: Join pink with sc in first st, sc in each st around with 3 sc in center st of each corner, join. Fasten off.

Rnd 4: Join MC with sc in first st, sc in each st around with 3 sc in center st of each corner, join. **Do not fasten off.**

Rnd 5: Ch 1, sc in each st around with 3 sc in center st of each corner, join. Fasten off.

Rnd 6: Join purple with sc in first st, sc in each st around with 3 sc in center st of each corner, join. Fasten off. ❦

by Joanne Whitwell

Starburst Afghan

FINISHED SIZE: About 50" × 64".

MATERIALS:
- ❑ Worsted yarn:
    - 29½ oz. burgundy
    - 25 oz. black
    - 15 oz. raspberry
    - 10½ oz. dk. pink
    - 8½ oz. lt. pink
- ❑ I hook or size needed to obtain gauge

GAUGE: Motif is 4¾" square.

AFGHAN

Work First Motif; work 1-Side Joined Motif for total of 14 Motifs or to desired length of Afghan.

*Work 1-Side Joined Motif onto right-hand side of First Motif on last strip of Motifs; work 2-Side Joined Motif to length of Afghan; repeat from * for total of 11 strips or to desired width of Afghan.

FIRST MOTIF

Rnd 1: With lt. pink, ch 4, 2 dc in fourth ch from hook, ch 3, (3 dc, ch 3) in same ch 3 times, join with sl st in top of ch 3. Fasten off. *(12 dc made)*

Rnd 2: Join burgundy with sc in any ch-3 sp, ch 3, sc in same ch-3 sp, *[ch 1, skip next st, sc in next st, ch 1, skip next st], (sc, ch 3, sc) in next ch-3 sp; repeat from * 2 more times; repeat between [ ], join with sl st in first sc. Fasten off.

Rnd 3: For **first corner,** join dk. pink with sc in any ch-3 sp on rnd 2, ch 1; holding yarn on front of work, dc in ch-3 sp on rnd 1, ch 1, sc in same ch-3 sp on rnd 2; ch 1, *[**front post (fp**—*see Stitch Guide)* around dc on rnd 1, sc in next sc on rnd 2, skip next dc on rnd 1, fp around next dc on rnd 1, ch 1]; for **next corner,** sc in next ch-3 sp on rnd 2, ch 1, dc in ch-3 sp on rnd 1, ch 1, sc in same ch-3 sp on rnd 2; ch 1; repeat from * 2 more times; repeat between [ ], join. Fasten off.

Rnd 4: For **beginning ch corner (beg ch corner), join burgundy with sc in first ch-1 sp of any corner, ch 3, sc in next ch-1 sp;** ch 1, *[sc in next ch-1 sp, ch 1, skip next st, sc in next st, ch 1, skip next st, sc in next ch-1 sp, ch 1]; for **ch corner, sc in next ch-1 sp, ch 3, sc in next ch-1 sp;** ch 1; repeat from * 2 more times; repeat between [ ], join. Fasten off.

Rnd 5: For **beg fp corner, join raspberry with sc in any ch-3 sp, ch 1, fp around dc on row before last, ch 1, sc in same ch-3 sp;** ch 1; *[skip next st, fp around next sc on row before last, (sc in next st, fp around next fp on row before last) 2 times, sc in next st, fp around next sc on row before last, ch 1]; for **fp corner, sc in next ch-3 sp, ch 1, fp around next dc on row before last, ch 1, sc in same ch-3 sp;** ch 1; repeat from * 2 more times; repeat between [ ], join. Fasten off.

Rnd 6: With black, beg ch corner, ch 1, *[skip next st, sc in next ch-1 sp, ch 1, (skip next st, sc in next st, ch 1) 3 times, skip next st, sc in next ch-1 sp, ch 1], ch corner, ch 1; repeat from * 2 more times; repeat between [ ], join. Fasten off.

Rnd 7: With burgundy, beg fp corner, ch 1, *[fp around next sc on row before last, sc in next st, (fp around next fp on row before last, sc in next st) 4 times, fp around next sc on row before last, ch 1], fp corner, ch 1; repeat from * 2 more times; repeat between [ ], join. Fasten off.

Rnd 8: Join black with sc in first ch-1 sp of any corner, ch 1, *[fp around next fp, ch 1, sc in next ch-1 sp, ch 1, skip next st, (sc in next st, ch 1, skip next st) 5 times, sc in next ch-1 sp, ch 1], sc in next ch-1 sp, ch 1; repeat from * 2 more times; repeat between [ ], join. Fasten off.

1-SIDE MOTIF

Rnds 1–7: Repeat rnds 1–7 of First Motif.

Rnd 8: Join black with sc in first ch-1 sp of any corner, ch 1, *fp around next fp, [ch 1, sc in next ch-1 sp, ch 1, sc in next ch-1 sp, ch 1, skip next st, (sc in next st, ch 1, skip next st) 5 times, sc in next ch-1 sp, ch 1], sc in next ch-1 sp, ch 1, fp around next fp*, sl st in next matching ch-1 sp on next corresponding Motif, ch 1, sc in next ch-1 sp on this Motif, (sl st in next ch-1 sp on same corresponding Motif, ch 1, skip next st, sc in next st on this

continued on page 47

by Karen Saul

Winter Roses

FINISHED SIZE: About 47½" square.

MATERIALS:
- ❏ Worsted yarn:
    - 20 oz. red
    - 18 oz. white
    - 8 oz. green
- ❏ Tapestry needle
- ❏ K hook or size needed to obtain gauge

GAUGE: 3 dc = 1"; 1 Granny Square = 6½" square.

GRANNY SQUARE (make 49)

Rnd 1: With green, ch 4, sl st in first ch to form ring, ch 2, 2 dc in ring, (ch 2, 3 dc in ring) 3 times, ch 2, join with sl st in top of ch 2.

Rnd 2: Sl st in next 2 dc, sl st in next ch-2 sp; for **beg corner, (ch 2, 2 dc, ch 2, 3 dc)** in same sp; * for **corner, (3 dc, ch 2, 3 dc)** in next ch-2 sp; repeat from * 2 more times, join. Fasten off.

Rnd 3: Join white with sl st in any corner ch sp, work beg corner in same ch sp as sl st, *skip next 3 dc, 3 dc between corners, work corner in ch sp of next corner; repeat from * 2 more times, skip next 3 dc, 3 dc between corners, join.

Rnd 4: Sl st to ch sp of first corner, work beg corner, *(skip next 3 dc, 3 dc in next sp) 2 times, corner in next corner; repeat from * 2 more times, skip next 3 dc, 3 dc in next sp, join. Fasten off.

Rnd 5: Join red with sc in any corner ch sp, 4 sc in same ch sp, sc in each st across to corner, (5 sc in corner ch sp, sc in each st to corner ch sp) around, join with sl st in first sc. Fasten off.

Rose (make 49)

With red, ch 14, sc in second ch from hook, hdc in next ch, dc in next 9 ch, hdc in next ch, sc in last ch. Leaving 9" end, fasten off.

Using tapestry needle, thread end of yarn through first ch, starting at one end, roll piece to other end, weave yarn through bottom of stitches, being careful to catch all stitches and pulling firmly to form Rose. Sew Rose to center of Granny Square.

Assembly

With tapestry needle and red yarn, sew Granny Squares together in **back lps** *(see Stitch Guide)*, making seven rows of seven Squares. Sew rows together.

Edging

Rnd 1: Join red with sc in first st of any corner, sc in same st, 2 sc in next 2 sts, sc in each st across to next corner, (2 sc in first 3 corner sts, sc in each st across to next corner) 3 times, join with sl st in first sc. Fasten off.

Rnd 2: Join white with sc in any st, (ch 3, sc in third ch from hook, skip next st, sc in next st) around, join. Fasten off. ❧

continued from page 45

Motif) 5 times, (sl st in next ch-1 sp on same corresponding Motif, ch 1, sc in next ch-1 sp on this Motif) 2 times, ch 1; repeat between first *; repeat between [ ], join. Fasten off.

2-SIDE MOTIF

Rnds 1–7: Repeat rnds 1–7 of First Motif.

Rnd 8: With black, join with sc in first ch-1 sp of any corner, ch 1, [fp around next fp, (ch 1, sc in next ch-1 sp) 2 times, ch 1, skip next st, (sc in next st, ch 1, skip next st) 5 times, sc in next ch-1 sp, ch 1, sc in next ch-1 sp, ch 1], *fp around next fp, sl st in next matching ch-1 sp on next corresponding Motif, ch 1, sc in next ch-1 sp on this Motif, (sl st in next ch-1 sp on same corresponding Motif, ch 1, skip next st, sc in next st on this Motif) 5 times, (sl st in next ch-1 sp on same corresponding Motif, ch 1, sc in next ch-1 sp on this Motif) 2 times, ch 1; repeat from *; repeat between [ ], join. Fasten off.

EDGING

Rnd 1: Working around outer edge, join black with sc in any st, sc in each st and in each joining with 3 sc in each corner fp, join with sl st in first sc.

Rnd 2: Ch 1, **reverse sc** *(see Stitch Guide)* in each st around, join. Fasten off. ❧

by Joanne Whitwell

Heartland Home

FINISHED SIZE: About 51" × 61".

MATERIALS:
- ❑ 67 oz. off-white worsted yarn
- ❑ J hook or size needed to obtain gauge

GAUGE: Motif is 2½" square.

AFGHAN

Work First Motif; work 1-Side Joined Motif for total of 24 Motifs or to desired length.

*Work 1-Side Joined Motif onto right-hand side of First Motif on last strip of Motifs; work 2-Side Joined Motif to length of afghan; repeat from * for total of 20 strips or to desired width of Afghan.

FIRST MOTIF

Rnd 1: Ch 4, sl st in first ch to form ring; for **beginning popcorn (beg pc), ch 3, 4 dc in ring, drop lp from hook, insert hook in top of ch 3, pull dropped lp through ch 3;** ch 3; *for **popcorn (pc), 5 dc ring, drop lp from hook, insert hook in top of first dc of group, pull dropped lp through st;** ch 3; repeat from * 2 more times, join with sl st in top of ch 3. *(4 pc made)*

Rnd 2: Ch 2, dc in first ch-3 sp, ch 2; for **picot corner, *dc in same sp, ch 3, sl st in third ch from hook, dc in same sp;** ch 2, dc same sp and next ch-3 sp tog, ch 2, repeat from * 2 more times; picot corner, ch 2, join with sl st in top of first ch 2. Fasten off.

1-SIDE JOINED MOTIF

Rnd 1: Ch 4, sl st in first ch to form ring, beg pc, ch 3, (pc, ch 3) 3 times, join with sl st in top of first ch 3. *(4 pc made)*

Rnd 2: Ch 2, dc in first ch-3 sp, ch 2, picot corner, ch 1, join with sl st in first ch-2 sp after any picot corner on last Motif made, ch 1, dc same sp and next ch-3 sp on this Motif tog, ch 1, sl st in next ch-2 sp on last Motifs made, ch 1, (picot corner, ch 2, dc same sp and next ch-3 sp tog, ch 2) 2 times, picot corner, ch 2, join with sl st in top of first ch 2. Fasten off.

2-SIDE JOINED MOTIF

Rnd 1: Ch 4, sl st in first ch to form ring, beg pc, ch 3, (pc, ch 3) 3 times, join with sl st in top of first ch 3. *(4 pc made)*

Rnd 2: Ch 2, dc in first ch-3 sp, ch 2, picot corner, ch 1, sl st in corresponding ch-2 sp on last Motif made, ch 1, dc same sp and next ch-3 sp on this Motif tog, ch 1, sl st in next ch-2 sp on last Motif, ch 1, picot corner, ch 1, sl st in corresponding ch-2 sp on next joined Motif, ch 1, dc same sp and next ch-3 sp on this Motif tog, ch 1, sl st in next ch-2 sp on Joined Motif, ch 1, picot corner, ch 2, dc same sp and next ch-3 sp on this Motif tog, ch 2, picot corner, ch 2, join with sl st in top of first ch 2. Fasten off.

BORDER

Rnd 1: Join with sc in any ch-2 sp after outside picot corner, ch 2, sc in next ch-2 sp, ch 2, *[sc next 2 picots tog, ch 2, (sc in next ch-2 sp, ch 2) 2 times]; repeat between [ ] across to next outside picot corner, sc in next picot, ch 2, (sc in next ch-2 sp, ch 2) 2 times; repeat from * 2 more times; repeat between [ ] across to last outside picot corner, sc in last picot, ch 2, join with sl st in first sc.

Rnd 2: Beg pc, ch 2, *(pc in next st, ch 2) across to sc in picot corner, (pc, ch 3, pc) in next sc, ch 2; repeat from * around, join with sl st in top of ch 3. Fasten off. ❦

Children's Charmer

Winsome as a boyish dimple, enchanting as a girlish curl, these afghans capture the universal cuteness of the younger set. Carnival Clown is a colorful play on childhood merriment. Hook up with classic Overall Sam and Sunbonnet Sue, stitch a snuggly bear blanket or build ABCs in blocks—it's fun being a kid again!

by Lorraine White

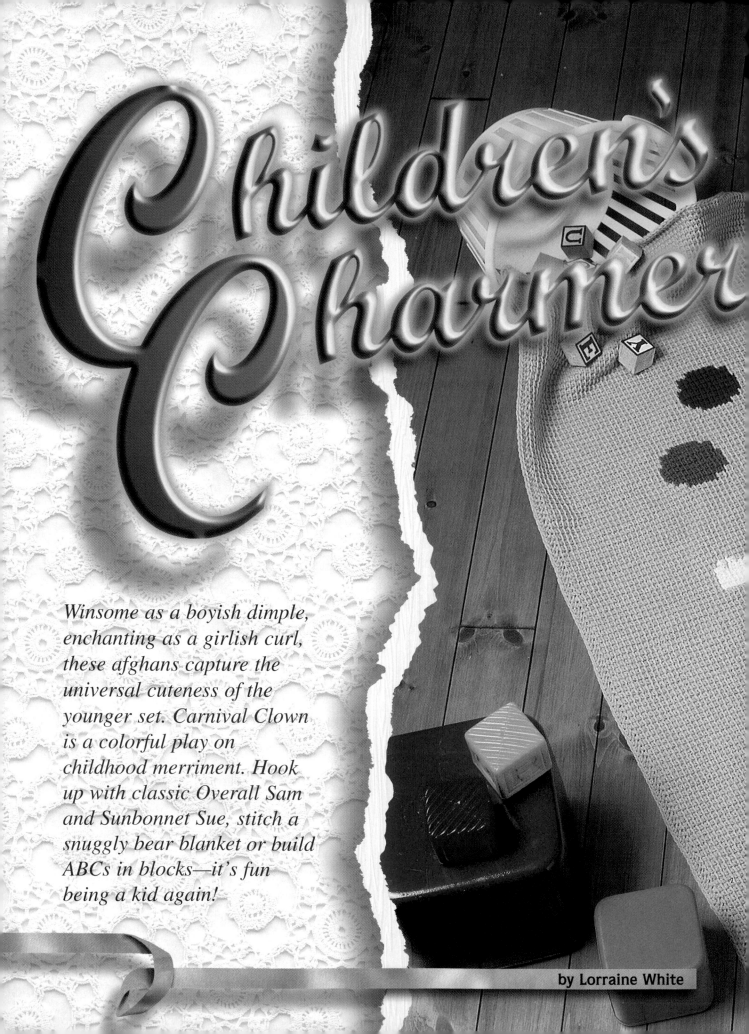

Carnival Clown

FINISHED SIZE: About 38" × 49".

MATERIALS:
- ❏ Worsted yarn:
  - 25 oz. lt. blue
  - 4 oz. purple
  - 3 oz. white
  - 2 oz. pink
  - 1 oz. each brown, red, green, lt. peach, dk. blue, black and gold
- ❏ I crochet hook
- ❏ K afghan hook or size needed to obtain gauge

GAUGE: 4 afghan sts = 1"; 3 afghan rows = 1".

NOTES:

Wind lt. blue, red and purple into 3 balls of each color. Wind pink, dk. blue, green and gold into 2 balls of each color.

One square on graph equals one afghan stitch.

To change colors on first half of afghan st, drop first color; insert hook under next vertical bar, yo with second color, pull through bar (see illustration #1).

To change colors on second half of afghan st (when working sts off hook), drop first color; with second color, pull through next 2 lps on hook (see illustration #2). Pick up dropped colors when needed.

Always drop yarn to wrong side of work. Fasten off colors when no longer needed.

1.

2.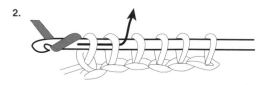

AFGHAN

Row 1: With lt. blue and afghan hook, ch 152; work first row of afghan stitch *(see Stitch Guide)*.

Rows 2–25: Work row 2 of afghan stitch *(see Stitch Guide)*.

Rows 26–115: With lt. blue, work first 21 afghan sts; changing colors according to graph *(see Notes)*, work next 110 afghan sts; with lt. blue, work last 21 afghan sts.

Rows 116–147: With lt. blue, repeat row 2.

Rnd 148: Working around outer edge in vertical bars, ends of rows and on opposite side of starting ch, with I crochet hook, sc in each bar, row and ch around with 3 sc in each corner, join with sl st in first sc. Fasten off. ❦

- = BLACK
- = BLUE
- = LIGHT BLUE
- = BROWN
- = GOLD
- = WHITE
- = GREEN
- = LIGHT PEACH
- = PINK
- = PURPLE
- = RED

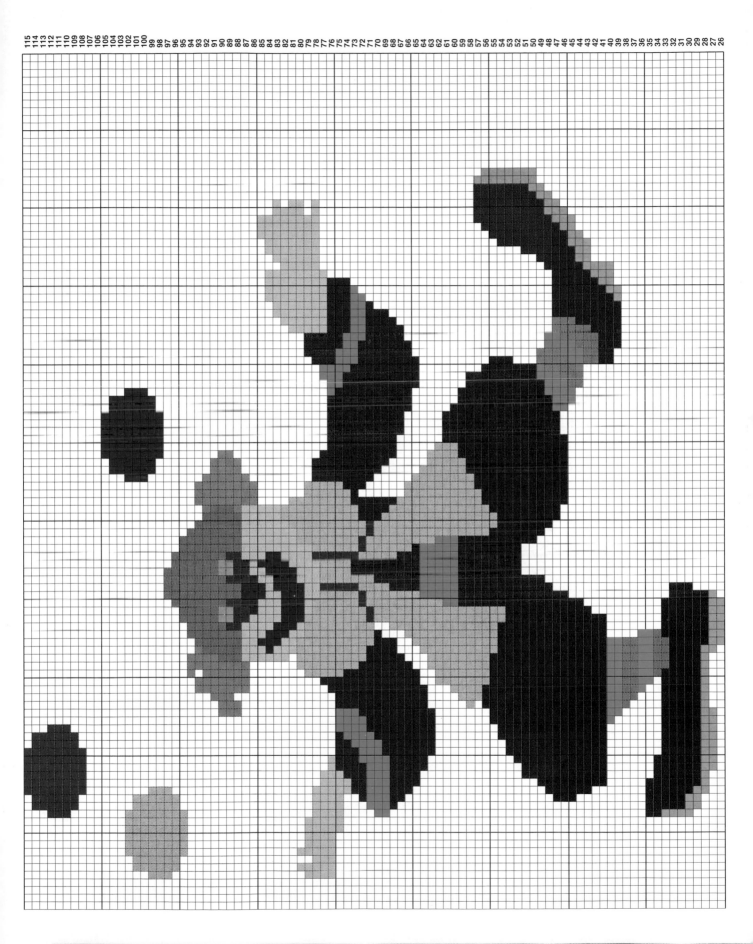

An Annie Original

Overall Sam

FINISHED SIZES: Each block is 12" square; child's Afghan is about 41" × 41"; full-size Afghan is 41" × 72".

MATERIALS:
❑ Worsted yarn:
   For Background:
   24 oz. for child's Afghan
   34 oz. for full-size Afghan
   6 oz. for Pillow
   For Each Block:
   25 yds. Overalls color
   25 yds. Shirt color
   10 yds. Hat color
   10 yds. Face, Feet color
   For Border:
   70 yds. Background color for child's Afghan
   80 yds. Background color for full-size Afghan
   70 yds. Shirt color for child's Afghan
   80 yds. Overalls color for full-size Afghan
❑ 12" square black pillow form
❑ F hook or size needed to obtain gauge

GAUGE: 4 dc = 1"; 2 dc rows = 1". Each Block measures 12" square.

NOTES:
Work all loose ends in as you go and clip unless otherwise stated.
This does not take on the shape of a Block until rnd 4 of Background.

BLOCK
Bib
With Overalls colors, ch 8, dc in fourth ch from hook and in each remaining ch across, turn. *(6 dc made)*
Strap: Ch 1, sc in dc, (ch 1, turn, sc in sc) 3 times. Leaving long tail on Strap, fasten off.
Other Strap: Join with sc in top of ch 3 at other end of Bib, (ch 1, turn, sc in sc) 3 times. Leaving long tail on Strap, fasten off. Lay Bib aside until called for in pattern.

Hat
Row 1: With Hat color, ch 7, dc in fourth ch from hook, dc in next 3 ch, turn. *(5 dc made)*
Row 2: Ch 3, dc in same st, dc in last 4 sts, turn. Fasten off.

Face
Row 1: Working in **back lps** only *(see Stitch Guide)*, join Face color with sl st in first st, ch 3, dc in last 5 sts, turn. *(6 dc made)*
Row 2: Ch 3, dc in each st across, turn.
Row 3: Ch 2, hdc in each st across, turn. Fasten off.

Shirt
Row 1: Join shirt color with sc in first st, sc in same st, sc in next 4 sts, 2 sc in last st, turn. *(8 sc made)*
Rows 2–3: Ch 3, dc in each st across, turn. Fasten off.

Overalls
Row 1: Join Overalls color with sc in first st; lay Bib as in illustration, sc in 6 sts of Bib and next 6 sts of Shirt at same time, sc in top of turning ch 3, turn. *(8 sc made)*

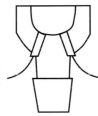

Rows 2–3: Ch 1, sc in each st across, turn.
Row 4: Ch 1, 2 sc in first st, sc in next 6 sts, 2 sc in last st, turn. *(10 sc)*
Row 5: Ch 1, sc in each st across, turn.
Row 6: Ch 1; for **First Leg,** sc in first 5 sts, turn. *(5 sc)*
Rows 7–10: Ch 1, sc in each st across, turn. At end of last row, fasten off.
For **Second Leg,** with back of doll facing you, join with sc in next st after end of row 6 and sc in next 4 sts, turn; work next 4 rows same as rows 7–10 of First Leg.

Feet
Row 1: For **First Foot,** with front of doll facing you, working in **back lps** only, join Feet color with sc in middle sc of last row on First Leg, sc in next 2 sts, turn. *(3 sc made)*

continued on page 56

continued from page 55

Rows 2–3: Ch 1, sc in each st across, turn.

Row 4: Ch 1, sc in first 2 sts, (sc, hdc, dc) in last st. Fasten off. *(5 sts)*

For **Second Foot,** with back of doll facing you, working in **front lps** only, work same as First Foot.

Sleeve (make 2)

Row 1: Join Shirt color with sc on side of Overalls *(see illustration),* work another sc on side of Overalls, turn. *(2 sc made)*

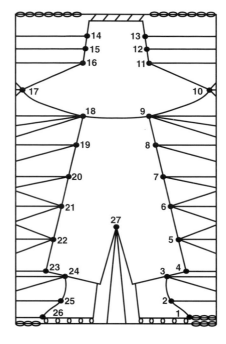

Row 2: Ch 1, sc in each st across, turn.

Row 3: Ch 1, 2 sc in first st, sc in next st, turn. *(3 sc)*

Row 4: Ch 1, sc in each st across, turn.

Row 5: Ch 1, sc in first st, 2 sc in next st, sc in last st, turn. *(4 sc)*

Rows 6–8: Ch 1, sc in each st across, turn.

Row 9: Ch 1, skip first 3 sts, sc in last st, join with sl st to top of shoulder *(at end of row 1 on Shirt).* Leaving a long tail, fasten off. Pull tail of Sleeve and tail of Bib Strap to back and tie.

Hat Brim

Row 1: With front of doll facing you, working in remaining **front lps** of row 2 of Hat, join Hat color with (sl st, ch 3, dc) in first st, dc in next st, 2 dc next 2 sts, 2 dc in last st, turn. *(10 dc made)*

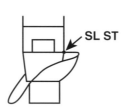

Row 2: Ch 3, dc in same st, 2 dc in each st across, turn. *(20 dc)*

Row 3: Sl st into edge between neck and Shirt, continue working in next st on last row, (dc in next st, 2 dc in next st) to end of row, dc in last st, sl st into other side of neck and Shirt edge. Fasten off.

Background

Rnd 1: See illustration for the placement of sts on this first rnd. Always try to work in a back lp when attaching background stitches to doll.

Dots are numbered to help you follow the directions on this first rnd. Starting at dot 1, work the following in each dot:

Dot 1: Join Background color with sl st and ch 3.

Dot 2: 1 tr.

Dot 3: 2 tr.

Dot 4: 1 dc.

Dot 5: 3 dc.

Dot 6: 3 tr.

Dot 7: *(Make sure arm is on top)* 2 dtr.

Dot 8: 2 dtr *(arm on top).*

Dot 9: *(Be sure not to catch hat Brim in this)* 3 ttr *(see Stitch Guide).*

Dot 10: *(Hat Brim is folded down and dot 10 is a stitch at folded edge)* 3 sc.

Dot 11: 1 ttr.

Dot 12: 1 ttr.

Dot 13: 1 ttr, ch 7, loosely sl st in 5 sts across top of Hat, ch 7.

Dot 14: 1 ttr.

Dot 15: 1 ttr.

Dot 16: 1 ttr.

Dot 17: 3 sc *(edge of Hat Brim like dot 10).*

Dot 18: 3 ttr.

Dot 19: 2 dtr.

Dot 20: 2 dtr.

Dot 21: 3 tr.

Dot 22: 3 dc.

Dot 23: 1 dc.

Dot 24: 2 tr.

Dot 25: 1 tr.

Dot 26: 1 dc, ch 3, sc in next 5 sc across bottom of Foot working in **back lps** only.

Dot 27: (Yo 6 times, insert hook in dot 27, yo and pull through, work off lps 2 at a time) 2 times.

Sc in **back lps** of 5 sts across bottom of other Foot, ch 3, sl st in top of first ch 3 *(clusters of stitches have been formed down each side of doll).*

Rnd 2: Sl st in next tr, (sl st, ch 4, 2 tr) in sp before next tr, work 3 tr between each cluster up to first ch 7 of last rnd, ch 4, work 7 sc in ch-7 lp, sc in 5 sl sts across top of Hat, 7 sc in next ch-7 lp, ch 4, 3 tr between each cluster down side to ch 3 of last rnd, ch 4, 3 sc in ch-3 sp, sc in each st across bottom *(12 sc made)*, 3 sc in next ch-3 sp, ch 3, sc in top of ch 4. *(There are 8 clusters down each side now.)*

Rnd 3: Ch 4, 2 tr in sp made by sc at end of last rnd, 3 tr between each cluster, work 3 tr in ch-4 sp, ch 5, 4 sc in same ch-4 sp, sc in next 9 sc, skip next sc, sc in next 9 sc, 4 sc in ch-4 sp, ch 5, 3 tr in same ch-4 sp, 3 tr between each cluster down side, 3 tr in ch-4 sp, ch 5, 4 sc in same ch-4 sp, sc in next 18 sc, 4 sc in ch-4 sp, ch 5, sl st in top of ch 4. Fasten off. *(9 clusters down each side)*

Rnd 4: Join Shirt color with (sl st, ch 3, 2 dc) in last ch-5 sp, 3 dc between each cluster, (3 dc, ch 2, 3 dc) in ch-5 sp, (skip 2 sc, 3 dc in next sc) 8 times, (3 dc, ch 2, 3 dc) in ch-5 sp, 3 dc between each cluster down side, (3 dc, ch 2, 3 dc) in ch-5 sp, (skip 2 sc, 3 dc in next sc) 8 times, 3 dc in ch-5 sp, ch 2, sl st in top of ch 3. Fasten off. *(10 clusters down each side)*

Rnd 5: Join Overalls color with (sl st, ch 3, 2 dc) in last ch-2 sp, work 3 dc between each cluster of last rnd and (3 dc, ch 2, 3 dc) in each ch-2 sp, ending with 3 dc in ch-2 sp, ch 2, sl st in top of ch 3. Fasten off.

Rnd 6: Join Background color with (sl st, ch 3, 2 dc) in last ch-2 sp, work 3 dc between each cluster of last rnd and (3 dc, ch 2, 3 dc) in each ch-2 sp, ending with 3 dc in ch-2 sp, ch 1, dc in top of ch 3.

Rnd 7: Ch 3, 2 dc in same st, work 3 dc between each cluster of last rnd and (3 dc, ch 2, 3 dc) in

each ch-2 sp, ending with 3 dc in ch-2 sp, ch 1, dc in top of ch 3. **If you are making an Afghan Block, fasten off here; if you are making a Pillow Block, go on.**

Rnd 8: For Pillow only, repeat rnd 7.

Rnd 9: (Ch 5, sc between next clusters) around. Do not join rnds from now on; continue working around.

Rnds 10–19: (Ch 5, sc in next ch-5 sp) around.

Rnds 20–21: (Ch 10, sc in next ch sp) around. At end of last rnd, fasten off.

Drawstring: With Background color, ch 125. Fasten off. Weave in and out of last rnd of ch-10 sps. Put Pillow over pillow form, pull Drawstring up tight and tie.

AFGHAN

You will need nine Blocks for child's size and 15 Blocks for full-size. Sew or crochet Blocks together, three wide by three long for child's size, three wide by five long for full-size.

Border

Rnd 1: Join Background color with (sl st, ch 3, 2 dc) in a corner ch-2 sp, work 3 dc between each cluster; in places where Blocks are joined, work dc in ch-2 sp, dc in seam where Blocks are joined together and dc in next ch-2 sp, work (3 dc, ch 2, 3 dc) in all corner ch-2 sps, ending with 3 dc in ch-2 sp, ch 1, dc in top of ch 3.

Rnd 2: Ch 3, 2 dc in same place, work 3 dc between each cluster of last rnd and (3 dc, ch 2, 3 dc) in each ch-2 sp, ending with 3 dc in ch-2 sp, ch 1, dc in top of ch 3 *(counts as joining ch sp).* Fasten off.

Rnd 3: Join desired Shirt color with (sl st, ch 3, 2 dc) in joining ch sp, work 3 dc between each cluster of last rnd and (3 dc, ch 2, 3 dc) in each ch-2 sp, ending with 3 dc in ch-2 sp, ch 1, dc in top of ch 3 *(counts as joining ch sp).* Fasten off.

Rnd 4: Join desired Overalls color with (sl st, ch 3, 2 dc) in joining ch sp, work 3 dc between each cluster of last rnd and (3 dc, ch 2, 3 dc) in each ch-2 sp, ending with 3 dc in ch-2 sp, ch 1, dc in top of ch 3 *(counts as joining ch sp).* Fasten off.

Rnd 5: Join desired Background color with (sl st, ch 3, 2 dc) in joining ch sp, work 3 dc between each cluster of last rnd and (3 dc, ch 2, 3 dc) in each ch-2 sp, ending with 3 dc in ch-2 sp, ch 1, dc in top of ch 3. Fasten off. ❦

An Annie Original

Sunbonnet Sue

FINISHED SIZES: Each block is 12" square; child's Afghan is about 41" × 41"; full-size Afghan is 41" × 72".

MATERIALS:
❑ Worsted yarn:
For Background:
24 oz. for child's Afghan
34 oz. for full-size Afghan
6 oz. for Pillow
For Each Block:
25 yds. Bonnet, Sleeve, Stocking color
25 yds. Dress, Shoe color
1 yd. Hand color
For Border:
70 yds. color A for child's Afghan
80 yds. color A for full-size Afghan
70 yds. color B for child's Afghan
80 yds. color B for full-size Afghan
❑ 12" square black pillow form
❑ F hook or size needed to obtain gauge

GAUGE: 4 dc = 1"; 2 dc rows = 1". Each Block measures 12" square.

NOTES:
Work all loose ends in as you go, and clip unless otherwise stated.
This does not take on the shape of a Square until rnd 4 of Background.

BLOCK
Sleeve
Row 1: With Sleeve color, ch 3, sc in second ch from hook, sc in last ch, turn. *(2 sc made)*
Row 2: Ch 1, sc in each st across, turn.
Row 3: Ch 1, 2 sc in first st, sc in last st, turn. *(3 sc)*
Row 4: Ch 1, sc in each st across, turn.
Row 5: Ch 1, sc in first st, 2 sc in next st, sc in last st, turn. *(4 sc)*
Row 6: Ch 1, 2 sc in first st, sc in next 2 sts, 2 sc in last st, turn. *(6 sc)*
Row 7: Ch 1, sc in each st across, turn.

Row 8: Ch 1, skip first st, sc in next st, (skip next st, sc in next st) 2 times, turn. *(3 sc)*
Row 9: Ch 1, skip first 2 sts, sc in last st. Fasten off.

Hand
Row 1: With Hand color, go back to beginning of Sleeve, sc in next 2 remaining lps of starting ch at bottom of sts on row 1, turn.
Row 2: Ch 1, sc in first st, sl st in next st. Fasten off. Lay Sleeve aside until called for in pattern.

Bonnet
Row 1: With Bonnet color, ch 11, dc in fourth ch from hook, dc in next 3 ch, 2 dc in next st, hdc in next st, sc in next st, sl st in next st, turn. *(10 sts made) (You do not ch any to turn here.)*
Row 2: Skip first st, sl st in next st, sc in next st, hdc in next st, dc in next st, 2 dc in next st, dc in next 3 sts, 2 dc in last st, turn. *(11 sts)*
Row 3: Ch 3, dc in same st, (dc in next 2 sts, 2 dc in next st) 2 times, hdc in next st, sc in next st, sl st in next st, sl st in beginning of row 2, sl st in very first ch of Bonnet. *(15 sts)*
Row 4: There are seven remaining lps of the starting ch across bottom of row 1, work 2 hdc in each one, turn. *(14 hdc)*
Row 5: Ch 3, dc in same st, (dc in next 2 sts, 2 dc in next st) 3 times, hdc in next st, sc in next st, skip first st, sl st in next st, turn. *(17 sts)*
Row 6: Skip first 2 sts, hdc in each st across, turn.
Row 7: Ch 3, (skip next st, dc in next st) 6 times, turn.
Row 8: (Skip next 2 sts, sc in next st) 2 times. Fasten off.

Dress
Row 1: With Dress color, starting at bottom edge of Bonnet brim *(see illustration)*, working in

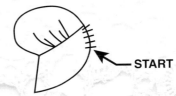

START

continued on page 60

continued from page 59

back lps only *(see Stitch Guide)*, make 5 sc in bottom edge of Bonnet trim *(you will be working in the last 4 sts of row 3 and the first hdc of row 4)*, turn. *(5 sc made)*

Row 2: Ch 3, dc in first st, dc in next st; now place top of Sleeve on other side of work *(see illustration)*, dc in next st and last st of Sleeve at same time *(this joins Sleeve to Dress)*, dc in next st, 2 dc in last st, turn. *(7 dc)*

DC TOGETHER

Row 3: Ch 3, dc in same st, dc in next 4 sts, 2 dc in next st, dc in last st, turn. *(9 dc)*

Row 4: Ch 3, dc in same st, dc in next 6 sts, 2 dc in next st, dc in last st, turn. *(11 dc)*

Row 5: Ch 3, dc in same st, dc in next 8 sts, 2 dc in next st, dc in last st, turn. *(13 dc)*

Row 6: Ch 3, dc in same st, dc in next 10 sts, 2 dc in next st, dc in last st, turn. *(15 dc)*

Row 7: Ch 2, sc in same st, sc in next st, hdc in next 3 sts, dc in next 2 sts, 2 dc in next st, dc in next 2 sts, hdc in next 3 sts, sc in next st, 2 sc in last st. Fasten off. *(18 sts)*

Stocking
Row 1: With Stocking color, working in **back lps** only, sc in middle 4 sts of last row of Dress, turn. *(4 sc made)*

Row 2: Ch 1, sc in each st across. Fasten off.

Shoe
Row 1: With Shoe color, work a sc in back lp of each st of last row, turn. *(4 sc made)*

Row 2: Ch 1, sc in first 3 sts, 2 sc in last st. Fasten off.

Tack Hand in place on Dress.

Background
Rnd 1: See illustration for the placement of stitches on this first rnd. Always try to work in a **back lp** when attaching background stitches to doll.

Dots are numbered to help you follow the directions on this first rnd. Starting at dot 1, with Background color, work the following in each dot:

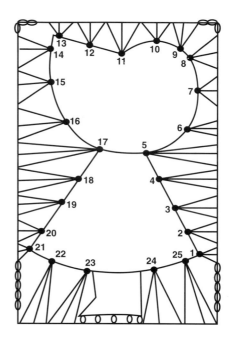

Dot 1: 3 sc.
Dot 2: 3 dc.
Dot 3: 3 tr.
Dot 4: 3 dtr
Dot 5: 3 ttr *(see Stitch Guide).*
Dot 6: 3 dc.
Dot 7: 3 hdc.
Dot 8: 3 dc, ch 3.
Dot 9: 3 hdc.
Dot 10: 3 hdc.
Dot 11: 3 dc.
Dot 12: 3 hdc.
Dot 13: 3 sc, ch 3.
Dot 14: 3 dc.
Dot 15: 3 dc.
Dot 16: 3 tr.
Dot 17: 3 ttr.
Dot 18: 3 dtr.
Dot 19: 3 tr.
Dot 20: 3 dc.
Dot 21: 3 sc, ch 6.

Dot 22: 3 ttr.

Dot 23: 3 dtr.

Sc in each of 5 sts across bottom of foot.

Dot 24: 3 dtr.

Dot 25: 3 ttr.

Ch 6, sc in first sc of dot 1.

Clusters of three have been formed down each side of doll.

Rnd 2: Ch 4, work 2 tr in same place as ch 4, 3 tr in sp between each cluster of rnd 1 up to first ch 3, 2 tr in ch-3 sp, ch 4, 3 sc in ch-3 sp, sc in next 14 sts, 3 sc in ch-3 sp, ch 4, 2 tr in ch-3 sp, 3 tr between each cluster up to ch-6 sp, 3 tr in first ch, skip 1 ch, tr in next 3 ch, ch 4, sc in next ch, sc in next 3 ttr, sc in next 3 dtr, sc in next 5 sc, sc in next 3 dtr, sc in next 3 ttr, sc in first ch, ch 4, tr in next 3 ch, sl st in top of first ch 4.

Rnd 3: Ch 4, 2 tr in same place as ch 4, 3 tr between each cluster up to ch 4, ch 5, 3 sc in ch-4 sp, sc in each sc across, 3 sc in ch-4 sp, ch 5, 3 tr between each cluster up to next ch-4 sp, ch 5, 3 sc in ch-4 sp, sc in each sc across, 4 sc in ch-4 sp, ch 5, sl st in top of first ch 4. Fasten off.

Rnd 4: Join Bonnet color with (sl st, ch 3, 2 dc) in last ch-5 sp, 3 dc between each cluster of rnd 3, in ch-5 sp work (3 dc, ch 2, 3 dc), (skip 2 sc, 3 dc in next sc) 8 times, in ch-5 sp work (3 dc, ch 2, 3 dc), work 3 dc between each cluster down side, in ch-5 work (3 dc, ch 2, 3 dc), (skip 2 sc, 3 dc in next sc) 8 times, 3 dc in ch-5 sp, ch 2, sl st in top of ch 3. Fasten off.

Rnd 5: Join Dress color with (sl st, ch 3, 2 dc) in last ch-2 sp, 3 dc between each cluster of previous rnd and (3 dc, ch 2, 3 dc) in each ch-2 sp, ending with 3 dc in ch-2 sp, ch 2, sl st in top of ch 3. Fasten off.

Rnd 6: Join Background color with (sl st, ch 3, 2 dc) in last ch-2 sp, work 3 dc between each cluster of previous rnd and (3 dc, ch 2, 3 dc) in each ch-2 sp, ending with 3 dc in ch-2 sp, ch 1, dc in top of ch 3.

Rnd 7: Ch 3, 2 dc in same place, 3 dc between each cluster of previous rnd and (3 dc, ch 2, 3 dc) in each ch-2 sp, ending with 3 dc in ch-2 sp, ch 1, dc in top of ch 3. **If you are making an Afghan Block, fasten off here; if you are making a Pillow Block, go on.**

Rnd 8: For Pillow only, ch 3, 2 dc in same place, 3 dc between each cluster of previous rnd and (3 dc, ch 2, 3 dc) in each ch-2 sp, ending with 3 dc in ch-2 sp, ch 1, dc in top of ch 3.

Rnd 9: (Ch 5, sc between next cluster) around. *(**Do not** join rnds from now on; just continue working around.)*

Rnds 10–19: (Ch 5, sc in next ch-5 sp) around.

Rnd 20–21: (Ch 10, sc in next ch sp) around. At end of last rnd, fasten off.

Drawstring: With Background color, ch 125. Fasten off. Weave in and out of last rnd of ch-10 sps. Put Pillow over pillow form, pull Drawstring up tight and tie.

AFGHAN

You will need nine Blocks for child's size and 15 Blocks for full-size. Sew or crochet Blocks together, three wide by three long for child's size, three wide by five long for full-size.

Border

Rnd 1: Join Background color with (sl st, ch 3, 2 dc) in corner ch-2 sp, work 3 dc between each cluster; in places where Blocks are joined, work dc in ch-2 sp, dc in seam where Blocks are joined together and dc in next ch-2 sp, work (3 dc, ch 2, 3 dc) in all corner ch-2 sps, ending with 3 dc in ch-2 sp, ch 1, dc in top of ch 3.

Rnd 2: Ch 3, 2 dc in same place, work 3 dc between each cluster of last rnd and (3 dc, ch 2, 3 dc) in each ch-2 sp, ending with 3 dc in ch-2 sp, ch 1, dc in top of ch 3 *(counts as joining ch sp)*. Fasten off.

Rnd 3: Join color A with (sl st, ch 3, 2 dc) in joining ch sp, work 3 dc between each cluster of last rnd and (3 dc, ch 2, 3 dc) in each ch-2 sp, ending with 3 dc in ch-2 sp, ch 1, dc in top of ch 3 *(counts as joining ch sp)*. Fasten off.

Rnd 4: Join color B with (sl st, ch 3, 2 dc) in joining ch sp, work 3 dc between each cluster of last rnd and (3 dc, ch 2, 3 dc) in each ch-2 sp, ending with 3 dc in ch-2 sp, ch 1, dc in top of ch 3 *(counts as joining ch sp)*. Fasten off.

Rnd 5: Join Background color with (sl st, ch 3, 2 dc) in joining ch sp, work 3 dc between each cluster of last rnd and (3 dc, ch 2, 3 dc) in each ch-2 sp, ending with 3 dc in ch-2 sp, ch 1, dc in top of ch 3. Fasten off. ❧

by Carlene Green

Filet Bear Blanket

FINISHED SIZE: Afghan is about 40" × 63".

MATERIALS:
- ❑ 7,600 yds. white size 10 crochet cotton
- ❑ 6 yds of ⅜" ribbon
- ❑ No. 11 steel hook or size needed to obtain gauge

GAUGE: 10 dc = 1", 4 dc rows = 1"; 7 shells = 4", 3 shells = 1".

NOTE: On graph, 1 mesh = ch 2, skip each of next 2 sts or ch. dc in next st or ch, 1 block = 3 dc. The turning chain at the beginning of each row is not shown or counted on graph.

BLANKET

Row 1: Ch 303, dc in fourth ch from hook, dc in next 58 ch, *(dc in next ch, ch 3, skip next 2 ch, sc in next ch, ch 3, skip next 2 ch) 10 times, dc in next 60 ch; repeat from *, dc in last ch, turn.

Row 2: Ch 3, work in next 59 sts according to graph, *(dc, ch 2, dc) in next dc, (dc, ch 2, dc, ch 2, dc) in each of next 9 dc, (dc, ch 2, dc) in next dc, work in next 60 sts according to graph; repeat from *, turn.

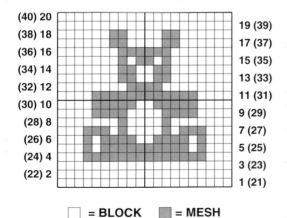

(40) 20   19 (39)
(38) 18   17 (37)
(36) 16   15 (35)
(34) 14   13 (33)
(32) 12   11 (31)
(30) 10   9 (29)
(28) 8   7 (27)
(26) 6   5 (25)
(24) 4   3 (23)
(22) 2   1 (21)

☐ = BLOCK   ▨ = MESH

Row 3: Ch 3, work in next 60 sts according to graph, *(ch 3, skip next ch-2 sp and dc, sc in next dc, ch 3, skip next ch-2 sp, dc in next st) 10 times, work in next 60 sts according to graph; repeat from *, turn.

Rows 4–20: Repeat rows 2 and 3 alternately, ending with row 2.

Row 21: Ch 6, skip next 2 sts, sc in next st, ch 3, skip next 2 sts, dc in next st, (ch 3, skip next 2 sts, sc in next st, ch 3, skip next 2 sts, dc in next st) 9 times, *(dc in next 2 ch, skip next dc, dc in next dc, dc in next 2 ch, dc in next st) 10 times, (ch 3, skip next 2 sts, sc in next st, ch 3, skip next 2 sts, dc in next st) 10 times; repeat from *, turn.

Row 22: Ch 5, dc in same st, dc in next dc, ch 2, dc in same dc as last st, (ch 2, dc in same dc as last st, dc in next dc, ch 2, dc in same dc as last st) 9 times, work in next 60 sts according to graph; repeat between ( ) 10 times, work in next 60 sts according to graph; repeat between ( ) 9 times, ch 2, dc in same dc as last st, dc in fourth ch of ch 6, ch 2, dc in same ch as last st, turn.

Row 23: Ch 6, skip next ch-2 sp and dc, sc in next dc, ch 3, skip next ch-2 sp, dc in next dc, (ch 3, skip next ch-2 sp and dc, sc in next dc, ch 3, skip next ch-2 sp, dc in next dc) 9 times, work in next 60 sts according to graph; repeat between ( ) 10 times, work in next 60 sts according to graph; repeat between ( ) 9 times, ch 3, skip next ch-2 sp and dc, sc in next dc, ch 3, dc in third ch of ch 5, turn.

Rows 24–40: Repeat rows 22 and 23 alternately, ending with row 22.

Row 41: Ch 3, *(dc in next 2 ch, skip next dc, dc in next dc, dc in next 2 ch, dc in next dc) 10 times, (ch 3, skip next 2 sts, sc in next st, ch 3, skip next 2 sts, dc in next st) 10 times; repeat from *, (dc in next 2 ch, skip next dc, dc in next dc, dc in next 2 ch, dc in next dc) 9 times, dc in next 2 ch, skip next dc, dc in next dc, dc in next 3 ch of ch 5, turn.

Rows 42–200: Repeat rows 2–41 consecutively, ending with row 40. At end of last row, **do not turn.**

Border

Rnd 1: Working around outer edge in ends of rows, sts and ch sps, ch 4, (2 tr, ch 3, 3 tr) in end of last

continued on page 67

by Jerri Akins

FINISHED SIZE: About 29" × 32½".

MATERIALS:
- ❏ Worsted yarn:
    - 14 oz. main color (MC)
    - 14 oz. contrasting color (CC)
- ❏ Tapestry needle
- ❏ J hook or size needed to obtain gauge

GAUGE: 7 sc = 2"; 4 sc rows = 1". Each Block measures 5¼" square.

NOTES:
Each diagram shows color change sts for each letter. Each square of graph = 1 sc. Each letter begins on row 4.

To change colors: Work off last 2 loops of st with second color. Carry yarn not in use along in back and crochet over it. When finished with letter color (CC) on each row, do not crochet over it, drop yarn and pick up to begin letter color on next row. When letter is completed, fasten off color and continue on with background color.

LETTER BLOCK (make 1 Block for each letter)
Row 1: With MC, ch 21, sc in second ch from hook and in each ch across, turn. *(20 sc made)*
Rows 2–3: Ch 1, sc in each st across, turn.
Rows 4–17: Ch 1, sc in each st across, changing colors according to graph being worked, turn. At end of last color change, fasten off CC.
Rows 18–20: Ch 1, sc in each st across, turn.
Rnd 21: Working around outside edges, sc in each st and in end of each row across with ch 1 in each corner, sl st in first st to join. Fasten off.

SOLID BLOCK (make 4)
Row 1: With MC, ch 21, sc in second ch from hook and in each ch across, turn.
Rows 2–20: Ch 1, sc in each st across, turn.
Rnd 21: Working around outside edges, sc in each st and in end of each row across with ch 1 in each corner, sl st in first st to join. Fasten off.

ASSEMBLY
Arrange Letter Blocks in order with one Solid Block in corner *(see photo for guide)*. Whipstitch Blocks together with CC.

BORDER
Rnd 1: Working around entire afghan, join CC with sc in any st, sc in each st around with ch 1 in each corner, join.
Rnd 2: Ch 1, hdc in each st around with ch 1 in each corner, join with sl st in top of ch 2. Fasten off. ❤

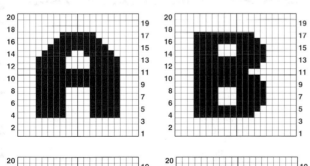

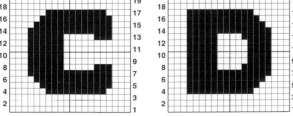

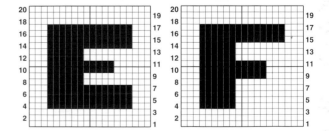

continued on page 66

continued from page 65

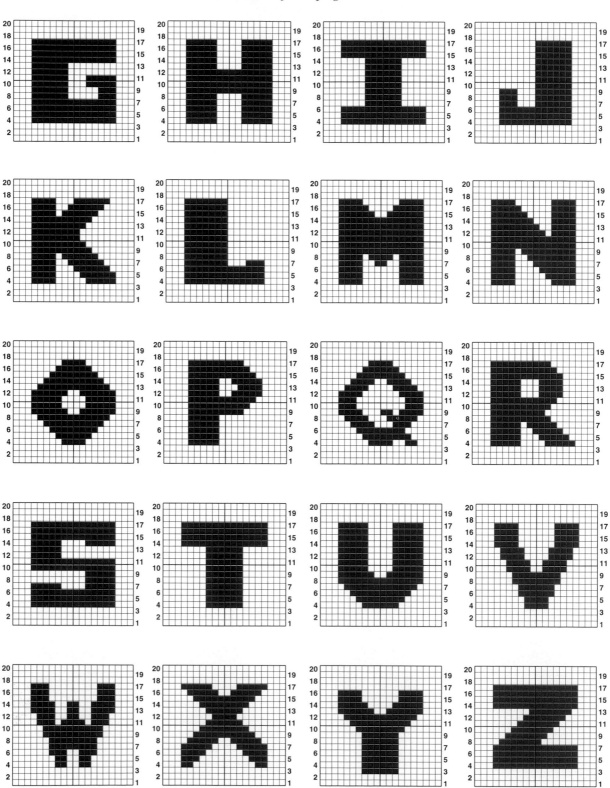

Filet Bear Blanket

continued from page 63

row, *(ch 3, skip next row, 3 tr in next row) 99 times, ch 3, (3 tr, ch 3, 3 tr, ch 3, 3 tr) in next row *; working on opposite side of starting ch, (ch 3, skip next 3 ch, tr in next 3 ch) 50 times, ch 3, (3 tr, ch 3, 3 tr, ch 3, 3 tr) in next row; repeat between first *, ch 3, 3 tr in same row as last tr group, [(ch 3, skip next 2 sts, skip next ch-2 sp, skip next st, 3 tr in next ch-2 sp) 9 times, skip next 2 sts, skip next ch-2 sp, (ch 3, tr in next 3 sts, skip next 3 sts) 10 times, ch 3, tr in next st, 2 tr in next ch-2 sp]; repeat between [ ], (ch 3, skip next 2 sts, skip next ch-2 sp, skip next st, 3 tr in next ch-2 sp) 9 times, ch 3, skip next 2 sts, 3 tr in last ch-2 sp, ch 3, join with sl st in top of ch 4. *(310 tr groups)*

Rnd 2: Sl st in next st, ch 3, (dc, ch 2, 2 dc) in same st, skip next st, sc in center ch of next ch 3, skip next st; *for **shell, (2 dc, ch 2, 2 dc) in next st;** skip next st, sc in center ch of next ch 3, skip next st; repeat from * around, join with sl st in top of ch 3. *(310 shells)*

Rnd 3: Sl st in next st, (sl st, ch 3, dc, ch 2, 2 dc, ch 2, 2 dc) in next ch sp, *shell in ch sp of next 100 shells; for **corner, (2 dc, ch 2, 2 dc, ch 2, 2 dc) in ch sp of next 2 shells;** shell in ch sp of next 51 shells*, work corner; repeat between first *, (2 dc, ch 2, 2 dc, ch 2, 2 dc) in ch sp of last shell, join. Mark two center ch sps at each corner in each rnd.

Rnd 4: Sl st in next st, (sl st, ch 3, dc, ch 2, 2 dc) in next ch sp, shell in each ch sp around, join. *(318 shells)*

Rnd 5: Sl st in next st, (sl st, ch 3, dc, ch 2, 2 dc, ch 2, 2 dc) in next ch sp, shell in ch sp of each shell around to last ch sp with corner in center two marked ch sps of each corner, (2 dc, ch 2, 2 dc, ch 2, 2 dc) in last ch sp, join.

Rnds 6–16: Repeat rnds 4 and 5 alternately.

Rnd 17: Ch 1, sc in first st, *hdc in next st, (dc, tr; for **picot, ch 4, sc in fourth ch from hook;** tr, dc) in next ch-2 sp, hdc in next st, sc in next 2 sts; repeat from * around to last shell, hdc in next st, (dc, tr, picot, tr, dc) in next ch-2 sp, hdc in next st, sc in last st, join with sl st in first sc. Fasten off.

Finishing

From ribbon, cut 2 pieces each 45" long and 2 pieces 63" long. With short pieces at top and bottom and long pieces at each side, weave ribbons through tr groups of rnd 1 on Border leaving ends at each corner. Tie ends in bows. ❦

Special Occasions

Our Hearts & Flowers
afghan romances the moment
in heart-felt sentiment shaped
by full-blown roses. Enrich
every celebration day with a
remembrance of crochet. Who
can forget tales of merry
Santa, a flag-waving Fourth,
the studious days of school
and snowfall's first craze
when retold in made-to-
treasure yarns?

by Peggy Perry

Hearts & Flowers

FINISHED SIZE: About 51" × 62".

MATERIALS:
- ❏ 45 oz. pink sport yarn
- ❏ G hook or size needed to obtain gauge

GAUGE: 9 dc = 2"; 10 dc rows = 4".

SPECIAL STITCHES:

For **beginning mesh (beg mesh),** ch 4, skip next st or ch, dc in next dc.

For **mesh,** ch 1, skip next st or ch, dc in next dc.

For **double mesh,** ch 3, skip next 3 sts or chs, dc in next dc.

For **beginning block (beg block),** ch 3, dc in next 2 sts or chs.

For **block,** dc in next 2 sts or chs.

For **beginning increase block (beg inc block),** at beginning of row only, ch 4, dc in fourth ch from hook, dc in next dc.

For **end increase block (end inc block),** for **first block** to be added, yo, insert hook in two strands at bottom of last dc made *(see illustration)*, yo, pull through strands, yo, pull through one lp on hook *(ch made)*, (yo, pull through 2 lps on hook) 2 times *(dc made)*, *yo, insert hook in last ch made, yo, pull through ch, yo, pull through one lp on hook *(ch made)*, (yo, pull through 2 lps on hook) 2 times *(dc made)*; for **each additional block** to be added, repeat between first and second * 2 times.

For **beginning decrease (beg dec),** for **first block** of row only, sl st in first 3 sts; for **next blocks** at beginning of row, sl st in next 2 sts.

For **end decrease (end dec),** leave 2 sts unworked for each unworked block on graph.

For **picot,** ch 3, sc in third ch from hook.

AFGHAN

Row 1: Ch 231; for row 1 of graph, dc in fourth ch from hook, dc in next 25 ch, (ch 1, skip next ch, dc in next 3 ch) 9 times, dc in next 12 ch, (ch 1, skip next ch, dc in next 3 ch) 9 times, dc in next 10 ch, (ch 1, skip next ch, dc in next 3 ch) 9 times, dc in next 12 ch, (ch 1, skip next ch, dc in next 3 ch) 9 times, dc in last 24 ch, turn. *(229 sts and ch made)*

NOTE: *For instructions for individual sts shown in key for graph, see Special Stitches.*

Row 2: Working according to row 2 of graph, beg block, 13 blocks, (mesh, block) 9 times, 4 blocks, (mesh, block) 10 times, 3 blocks, (mesh, block) 10 times, 4 blocks, (mesh, block) 9 times, 13 blocks, turn.

Rows 3–145: Work according to corresponding row of graph, turn. At end of last row, **do not fasten off.**

Finishing

Row 1: To complete heart shaping on straight edges of Afghan, working across row 145, ch 3, dc in next 24 dc leaving remaining sts and ch unworked, turn. *(25 dc made)*

Row 2: Sl st in first 3 sts, ch 3, dc in next 20 sts leaving last 2 sts unworked, turn. *(21 dc)*

Row 3: Sl st in first 5 sts, ch 3, dc in next 12 sts leaving last 4 sts unworked. Fasten off.

Row 4: For edging, join with sl st in last worked st of row 145, ch 2, picot *(see Special Stitches)*, ch 2, skip next 2 sts, sc in next ch sp, (ch 2, picot, ch 2, skip next 3 sts, sc in next ch sp) 8 times, sl st in next st, ch 3; for **heart shaping,** dc in next 14 sts leaving remaining sts and ch unworked, turn. *(15 dc)*

Row 5: Ch 3, dc in each st across, turn.

Row 6: Sl st in first 3 sts, ch 3, dc in next 3 sts, ch 3, sl st in next 3 sts, ch 3, dc in next 3 sts, ch 3, sl st in next st leaving 2 sts unworked. Fasten off.

Row 7: Join with sl st in last worked st of row 145, sc in next ch sp, (ch 2, picot, ch 2, skip next 3 sts, sc in next ch sp) 8 times, sl st in next st, ch 3, dc in next 12 sts leaving remaining sts and ch unworked, turn. *(13 dc)*

Row 8: Sl st in first 3 sts, ch 3, dc in next 8 sts leaving last 2 sts unworked, turn. *(9 dc)*

Row 9: Sl st in first 3 sts, ch 3, dc in next 3 sts,

ch 3, sl st in next st leaving last 2 sts unworked. Fasten off.

Row 10: Join with sl st in last worked st of row 145, sc in next ch sp, (ch 2, picot, ch 2, skip next 3 sts, sc in next ch sp) 8 times, sl st in next st, ch 3, dc in next 14 sts leaving remaining sts and ch unworked, turn. *(15 dc)*

Row 11: Ch 3, dc in each st across, turn.

Row 12: Sl st in first 3 sts, ch 3, dc in next 3 sts, ch 3, sl st in next 3 sts, ch 3, dc in next 3 sts, ch 3, sl st in next st leaving last 2 sts unworked. Fasten off.

Row 13: Join with sl st in last worked st of row 145, sc in next ch sp, (ch 2, picot, ch 2, skip next 3 sts, sc in next ch sp) 8 times, ch 2, picot, ch 2, skip next 2 sts, sl st in next st, ch 3, dc in last 24 sts, turn. *(25 dc)*

Row 14: Sl st in first 3 sts, ch 3, dc in next 20 sts leaving last 2 sts unworked, turn. *(21 dc)*

Row 15: Sl st in first 5 sts, ch 3, dc in next 12 sts leaving last 4 sts unworked. Fasten off.

Row 16: To complete shaping on other straight edge of Afghan, working in ch on opposite side of row 1, with wrong side of row 1 facing you, join with sl st in first ch, ch 3, dc in next 24 ch leaving remaining ch unworked, turn. *(25 dc)*

Rows 17–30: Working in ch on opposite side of row 1, repeat rows 2–15.

Row 31: Working in ends of rows on one side, join with sc in last worked st of row 16, ch 2, picot, ch 2, skip next 2 rows, sc in mesh on next row, (ch 2, picot, ch 2, skip next row, sc in mesh on next row) 7 times ending in row 33, **do not turn.** Fasten off.

Row 32: Skip next 7 rows, join with sc in mesh on row 41, (ch 2, picot, ch 2, skip next row, sc in mesh on next row) 14 times ending in row 69, **do not turn.** Fasten off.

Row 33: Skip next 7 rows, join with sc in mesh on row 77, (ch 2, picot, ch 2, skip next row, sc in mesh on next row) 14 times ending in row 105, **do not turn.** Fasten off.

Row 34: Skip next 7 rows, join with sc in mesh on row 113, (ch 2, picot, ch 2, skip next row, sc in mesh on next row) 7 times ending in row 127, ch 2, picot, ch 2, skip next 2 rows, sl st in last worked st of row 130, turn. Fasten off.

Rows 35–38: Working in ends of rows on other side, repeat rows 31–34. ❦

graph on pages 72 and 73

pattern on page 70

Hearts & Flowers

= BEG BLOCK
  or BLOCK
= BEG MESH
  or MESH
= DOUBLE MESH

⊠ = BEG INC BLOCK
− = BEG DEC
▢ = END INC BLOCK
● = CH 2

145 143 141 139 137 135 133 131 129 127 125 123 121 119 117 115 113 111 109 107 105 103 101 99 97 95 93 91 89 87 85 83 81

144 142 140 138 136 134 132 130 128 126 124 122 120 118 116 114 112 110 108 106 104 102 100 98 96 94 92 90 88 86 84 82 80

by Ruby Gates

Santa Claus

FINISHED SIZE: About 40" × 58".

MATERIALS:
- ❑ Worsted yarn:
  - 25 oz. black
  - 15 oz. red
  - 4 oz. each white and green
  - 2 oz. each white metallic, yellow, pink and gray
  - 1 oz. blue
- ❑ G hook or size needed to obtain gauge

GAUGE: 8 sc = 2"; 10 sc rows = 2".

AFGHAN

NOTES: Wind a separate ball of yarn for each color section.

When **changing colors** (see Stitch Guide), drop first color to wrong side of work, pick up next color; **do not** carry dropped color along back of work. Always change color in last st made.

Each square on graph equals one sc.

Row 1: With black, ch 165, sc in second ch from hook, sc in each ch across, turn. *(164 sc made)*

Rows 2–4: Ch 1, sc in each st across, turn.

Row 5: Following row 5 of graph on pages 76 and 77, ch 1, sc in first 32 sts changing to red *(see Notes),* sc in next 2 sts changing to black, sc in next 114 sts changing to red, sc in next 2 sts changing to black, sc in each st across, turn.

Rows 6–276: Ch 1, sc in each st across changing colors according to corresponding row on graph, turn.

Rnd 277: Ch 1, sc in each st and in end of each row around, join with sl st in first sc, turn. *(880 sc)*

Rnd 278: (Ch 3, 7 dc) in first st, skip next 2 sts, sc in next st, (skip next 3 sts, 6 dc in next st, skip next 3 sts, sc in next st) 32 times, skip next 3 sts, (6 dc in next st, skip next 2 sts, sc in next st, skip next 2 sts) 2 times, 8 dc in next st, skip next 2 sts, sc in next st, skip next 2 sts, 6 dc in next st, (skip next 2 sts, sc in next st, skip next 3 sts, 6 dc in next st) 22 times, skip next 2 sts, sc in next st, skip next st, 8 dc in next st, (skip next 2 sts, sc in next st, skip next 2 sts, 6 dc in next st) 2 times, (skip next 3 sts, sc in next st, skip next 3 sts, 6 dc in next st) 32 times, skip next 3 sts, sc in next st, skip next 2 sts, 8 dc in next st, skip next 2 sts, sc in next st, skip next 2 sts, 6 dc in next st, (skip next 2 sts, sc in next st, skip next 3 sts, 6 dc in next st) 22 times, skip next 2 sts, sc in next st, skip last st, join with sl st in top of ch 3. Fasten off. ❦

graph on pages 76 and 77

Santa Claus

pattern on page 75

by Mary Ann Colatuno

School Days Afghan

FINISHED SIZE: Afghan is about 52" × 62".

MATERIALS:
- ❑ Worsted yarn:
    - 20 oz. each off-white and dk. blue
    - 13 oz. burgundy
    - 7 oz. dk. green
- ❑ H hook or size needed to obtain gauge

GAUGE: 6 hdc = 2"; 5 hdc rows = 2".

NOTES:
When changing colors (see Stitch Guide), drop first color to wrong side of work, pick up next color. Always change color in last st made.

Each Square on graph equals one sc.

SQUARE *(make 12)*

Row 1: With off-white, ch 34, hdc in third ch from hook, hdc in each ch across, turn. *(33 hdc made)*

Rows 2–3: Ch 2, hdc in each st across, turn.

Row 4: Ch 2, work 12 hdc changing to burgundy in last st *(see Notes)*, work 8 hdc changing to off-white in last st, hdc in last 12 sts, turn.

Rows 5–23: Ch 2, hdc in each st across changing

- ■ = BURGUNDY
- ▩ = DK. GREEN
- ☐ = OFF-WHITE

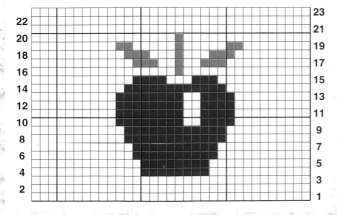

colors as colors change according to graph, turn. **Do not** carry yarn, use a separate skein of yarn.

Rnd 24: For **Edging,** working around outer edge, ch 1, sc in each st and in end of each row and on opposite side of starting ch around with 3 sc in each corner, join with sl st in first sc. Fasten off. *(116 sc)*

Rnd 25: Join dk. blue with sc in first st, sc in each st around with 3 sc in each corner st, join. *(124 sc)*

Rnds 26–27: Ch 1, sc in each st around with 3 sc in each corner st, join. At end of last rnd, fasten off. *(132 sc, 140 sc)*

ASSEMBLY

1: To connect two Squares, with apples in same direction, working in **back lps** *(see Stitch Guide)*, with right sides of two Squares together, join with sc in any corner st, sc in each st across to next corner st, sc in corner st. Fasten off. *(Ridge will be on wrong side of work.)*

2: Work three Squares across and four Squares down.

BORDER

NOTE: *Place a marker at center st of each corner worked. Remove markers and replace as needed.*

Rnd 1: Starting at top right-hand corner, join dk. blue with sc in first st after corner st, evenly space 118 sc across to next corner st, 3 sc in corner st; working across side, evenly space 119 sc across to next corner st, 3 sc in corner st; working across bottom, evenly space 119 sc across to next corner st, 3 sc in corner st; working across side, evenly space 119 sc across to last corner st, 3 sc in corner st, join with sl st in first sc. *(488 sc made)*

Rnds 2–3: Ch 1, sc in each st around with 3 sc in each corner st, join. At end of last rnd, fasten off. *(496 sc, 504 sc)*

Rnd 4: Working around Afghan, alternating 4 sc burgundy and 4 sc off-white, carry and work

continued on page 85

Afghan is by Dora Lurepa Ramirez and Pillow is by Annie Parton

Stars & Stripes

FINISHED SIZE: Afghan is about 39" × 60".

MATERIALS:
- ❑ Worsted yarn:
  - 16 oz. red
  - 15 oz. white
  - 4 oz. blue
- ❑ Tapestry needle
- ❑ K hook or size needed to obtain gauge

GAUGE: 7 dc = 2"; 4 dc rows = 3". Each Block is 3" × 3".

AFGHAN

Solid Block (make 113 red, 93 white)
Rnd 1: Ch 4, sl st in first ch to form ring, ch 3, 2 dc in ring, (ch 3, 3 dc in ring) 3 times, ch 3, join with sl st in top of ch 3. *(12 dc made)*

Rnd 2: Sl st in next 2 sts, (sl st, ch 3, 2 dc, ch 3, 3 dc) in next ch-3 sp, (3 dc, ch 3, 3 dc) in each ch-3 sp around, join. Fasten off.

Star Block (make 50)
Rnd 1: With white, ch 4, sl st in first ch to form ring, ch 3, 2 dc in ring, (ch 3, 3 dc in ring) 3 times, ch 3, join with sl st in top of ch 3. Fasten off. *(12 dc made)*

Rnd 2: Join blue with (sl st, ch 3, 2 dc, ch 3, 3 dc) in any ch-3 sp, (3 dc, ch 3, 3 dc) in each ch-3 sp around, join. Fasten off.

Black Half Block (make 8)
Row 1: With blue, ch 14, dc in fourth ch from hook, dc in next ch, ch 1, skip next 2 ch, 3 dc in next ch, ch 1, dc in last 3 ch, turn. *(9 dc made)*

Row 2: Ch 4, skip next 2 sts, 3 dc in next ch-1 sp, skip next 3 sts, 3 dc in next ch-1 sp, skip next 2 sts, dc in last st. Fasten off.

ASSEMBLY
NOTE: *All Blocks are sewn together, stitching through* **back lps** *(see Stitch Guide).*

Sew four strips with 20 red Blocks each and three strips with 11 red Blocks each. Sew three strips with 20 white Blocks each and three strips with 11 white Blocks each. Beginning with long strips at bottom, sew strips together beginning with red and alternating red and white. Sew five strips with six Star Blocks each, sew four strips with five Star Blocks each and a Half Block on each end.

Beginning with strips of six Star Blocks, sew strips together alternating six Star and five Star strips. Sew field of Stars in place at top corner of stripes.

Edging
Working around entire outer edge, with right side of Afghan facing you, join red with (sc, ch 2, 2 dc) in seam between red stripe and field of stars, (sc, ch 2, 2 dc) in center dc of each 3-dc group and in each seam around edge to field of stripes changing to blue in last st made, (sc, ch 2, 2 dc) in center dc of each 3-dc group and in each seam around, join with sl st in first sc. Fasten off.

PILLOW

FINISHED SIZE: About 12" × 16½" without Fringe.

MATERIALS:
- ❑ Worsted yarn:
  - 6 oz. blue
  - 2½ oz. each red, white and gold
- ❑ Fifty small star appliqués
- ❑ Polyester fiberfill
- ❑ Sewing needle and thread
- ❑ Tapestry needle
- ❑ F hook or size needed to obtain gauge

GAUGE: 9 sc = 2"; 9 sc rows = 2".

FRONT
Row 1: With red, ch 71, sc in second ch from hook, sc in each ch across, turn. *(70 sc made)*

Rows 2–4: Ch 1, sc in each st across, turn. At end of row 4, fasten off.

Row 5: Join white with sc in first st, sc in each st across, turn.

continued on page 85

by Teresa Garoutte

Winter Snowflakes

FINISHED SIZE: Afghan is about 52" × 65".

MATERIALS:
- ❏ Worsted yarn:
    - 36 oz. aqua
    - 21 oz. white
- ❏ Tapestry needle
- ❏ J hook or size needed to obtain gauge

GAUGE: 4 dc = 1"; 2 dc rows = 1".

NOTE:
Pattern is worked in **front lps** (see Stitch Guide) unless otherwise stated.

MOTIF (make 55)

Rnd 1: With white, ch 3, sl st in first ch to form ring, ch 1, 12 sc in ring, join with sl st in **front lp** of first sc. *(12 sc made)*

Rnd 2: (Ch 5, skip next st, sl st in next st) around. Fasten off. *(6 ch lps)*

Rnd 3: Turn work over, join aqua with sl st in any st on rnd 1, ch 2, *(dc, ch 1, dc) in next st, dc in next st; repeat from * 4 more times, (dc, ch 1, dc) in next st, join with sl st in top of ch 2. Fasten off. *(18 dc)*

Rnd 4: Turn work over, join white with sl st in any ch-1 sp of rnd 3, ch 1, *sc in ch-1 sp; for **joining ch lp, insert hook in ch lp of rnd before last and in same sp, yo, complete as sc;** sc in same sp, sc in next 3 sts; repeat from * around, join with sl st in first sc. *(36 sc)*

Rnd 5: Sl st in next st, (ch 7, skip next 5 sts, sl st in next st) 5 times, ch 7, join with sl st in first sl st. Fasten off. *(6 ch lps)*

Rnd 6: Turn work over, join aqua with sl st in first st of rnd 4, ch 4, dc in same st, *dc in next 5 sts, (dc, ch 1, dc) in next st; repeat from * 4 more times, dc in next 5 sts, join with sl st in third ch of ch 4. Fasten off. *(42 dc)*

Rnd 7: Turn work over, join white with sl st in any ch-1 sp, ch 1, (3 sc in each-1 sp, sc in next 3 sts; work joining ch lp, sc in next st, sc in next 3 sts) around, join with sl st in first sc. *(60 sc)*

Rnd 8: Sl st in next st, *ch 5, sl st in next st, (ch 5, skip next 3 sts, sl st in next st) 2 times, ch 5, sl st in next st; repeat from * 5 more times. Fasten off. *(24 ch lps)*

Rnd 9: Turn work over, join aqua with sl st in second st of rnd 7, ch 4, dc in same st, *dc in next 9 sts, (dc, ch 1, dc) in next st; repeat from * 4 more times, dc in next 9 sts, join with sl st in third ch of ch 4, sl st in next ch-1 sp, turn. *(66 dc)*

NOTE: *When joining ch-5 lps, work in **back lps** of third ch.*

Rnd 10: Ch 4, dc in ch-1 sp, [*work joining ch lp, dc in next st, dc in next 2 sts; work joining ch lp, dc in next st, dc in next 3 sts; work joining ch lp, dc in next st, dc in next 2 sts; work joining ch lp, dc in next st], (dc, ch 1, dc) in ch-1 sp; repeat from * 4 more times; repeat between [ ], join. Fasten off. *(78 dc)*

HALF MOTIF (make 4)

Row 1: With white, ch 3, sl st in first ch to form ring, ch 1, 7 sc in ring, turn. *(7 sc made)*

Row 2: Working this row in **back lps,** ch 1, sl st in first 2 sts, (ch 5, skip next st, sl st in next st) 2 times, sl st in next st. Fasten off. *(2 lps)*

Row 3: Do not turn work over, join aqua with sl st in last st of row 1, ch 2, *dc in next st, (dc, ch 1, dc) in next st; repeat from *, dc in next 2 sts. Fasten off.

Row 4: Turn work over, join white with sl st in first st, ch 1, 2 sc in first st, sc in next 2 sts, *(sc, work joining ch lp, sc)in next ch-1 sp, sc in next 3 sts; repeat from *, sc in same st as last sc, turn.

Row 5: Working this row in **back lps,** ch 7, skip next 4 sts, sl st in next st, ch 7, skip next 5 sts, sl st in next st, ch 7, skip next 4 sts, sl st in last st. Fasten off.

Row 6: Do not turn work over, join aqua with sl st in last sc of row 4, ch 2, dc in same st, dc in next 4 sts, (dc, ch 1, dc) in next st, dc in next 5 sts, (dc, ch 1, dc) in next st, dc in next 4 sts, 2 dc in next st. Fasten off. *(21 dc)*

Row 7: Turn work over, join white with sl st in first st, ch 1, 2 sc in first st, sc in next 2 sts, (work

continued on page 84

Winter Snowflakes

continued from page 83

joining ch lp, sc in next st, sc in next 3 sts, 3 sc in ch-1 sp, sc in next 3 sts) 2 times; work joining ch lp, sc in next st, sc in next 2 sts, 2 sc in next st, turn. *(29 sc)*

Row 8: Working this row in **back lps,** *(ch 5, skip next 3 sts, sl st in next st) 2 times, (ch 5, sl st in next st) 2 times; repeat from *; repeat between first ( ). Fasten off. *(10 lps)*

Row 9: Do not turn work over, join aqua with sl st in last st of row 7, ch 2, dc in same st, dc in next 8 sts, (dc, ch 1, dc) in next st, dc in next 9 sts, (dc, ch 1, dc) in next st, dc in next 8 sts, 2 dc in last st, turn. *(33 dc)*

Row 10: (Ch 2, dc) in first st, [*dc in next 2 sts; work joining ch lp, dc in next st, dc in next 3 sts; work joining ch lp, dc in next st, dc in next 2 sts]; work joining ch lp, dc in next st, (dc, ch 1, dc) in next ch-1 sp; work joining ch lp, dc in next st; repeat from *; repeat between [ ], 2 dc in next st. Fasten off. *(39 dc)*

ASSEMBLY

With wrong sides held together, join aqua with sl st in ch-1 sp of first hexagon, sl st in ch-1 sp of second hexagon, (sl st in next st of first hexagon, sl st in next st of second hexagon) across to next corner. Fasten off. Repeat, joining sides of Motifs and Half Motifs according to diagram.

To join rows of Motifs, with wrong sides together, join aqua with *sl st in ch-1 sp of hexagon on row 1, sl st in ch-1 sp of hexagon on row 2, (sl st in next st of hexagon on row 1, sl st in next st of hexagon on row 2) across to next corner, sl st in ch-1 sp of hexagon on row 1, sl st in ch-1 sp of hexagon on row 2, sl st into joining seam between 2 hexagons of row 2; repeat from * across to last seam; repeat from first * across to last corner, sl st in ch-1 sp of hexagon on row 1, sl st in ch-1 sp of hexagon on row 2. Fasten off.

Repeat, joining all Motif rows according to diagram.

BORDER

Rnd 1: Join aqua with sc in any outer ch-1 sp, 2 sc in same sp, sc in each st around, working sc in ends of sc rows and 2 sc in ends of dc rows on Half Motifs, 3 sc in each outer ch-1 sp, skipping joining seams, join with sl st in first sc. Fasten off.

Rnd 2: Join white with sc in any st, sc in each st around with 3 sc in each outer corner, skipping 2 sts at each inner corner around, join. Fasten off.

Rnd 3: Join white with sc in top right corner, (ch 2, 2 dc, ch 2, 3 dc) in same st, (skip next 2 sts, 3 dc in next st) around, working (3 dc, ch 2, 3 dc) in center st of each outer corner, skipping 4 sts at each inner corner, join with sl st in top of ch 2, turn.

Rnds 4–6: (Sl st, ch 2, 2 dc) in first ch sp between 3-dc group, *3 dc in each sp between dc groups with (3 dc, ch 2, 3 dc) in ch sp of each outer corner, skipping 4 sts at each inner corner; repeat from * around, join, turn.

Rnd 7: Ch 1, (sc in each st around with 3 sc in each ch-2 sp, skipping 2 sts at each inner corner) around, join with sl st in first sc. Fasten off.

Rnd 8: Join aqua with sl st in any st, ch 1, (sc, ch 1, sc) in same st, skip next st, *(sc, ch 1, sc) in next st, skip next st; repeat from * around, join. Fasten off. ❦

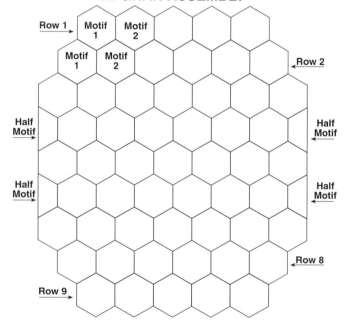

AFGHAN ASSEMBLY

Row 1 — Motif 1, Motif 2
Motif 1, Motif 2
Row 2
Half Motif
Half Motif
Half Motif
Half Motif
Row 8
Row 9

School Days Afghan

continued from page 79

over yarn as you change colors; join off-white with sc in any corner st, sc in same st changing to burgundy, sc in same st, sc in next 3 sts changing to off-white in last st, *(sc in next 4 sts changing to burgundy in last st, sc in next 4 sts changing to off-white in last st) 15 times, sc in next 2 sts, 2 sc in next st at corner changing to burgundy in last st, sc in same st, sc in next 3 sts changing to off-white in last st; repeat from * 2 more times, (sc in next 4 sts changing to burgundy in last st, sc in next 4 sts changing to off-white in last st) 15 times, sc in last 2 sts, join. *(512 sc)*

Rnds 5–7: Ch 1, work burgundy sc in burgundy sts and off-white sc in off-white sts around, join. *(Do not increase.)*

Rnd 8: Reversing colors to form checkerboard pattern as shown in photo, and continuing to change colors every 4 sts as established, ch 1, sc in each st around working 3 sc in each corner st, join. *(520 sc)*

Rnds 9–11: Ch 1, work off-white sc in off-white sts and burgundy sc in burgundy sts around, join. *(Do not increase.)* At end of last rnd, fasten off.

Rnd 12: When working 3 sc in next corner st on this rnd, keep sts in line with last corner worked on 3 rnds below; join dk. blue with sc in second st before first corner st, sc in next st, (3 sc in next st at corner, sc in each st across to next corner) around, join. *(528 sc)*

Rnd 13: Ch 1, sc in first 2 sts, (2 sc in next st, 3 sc in next corner st, 2 sc in next st, sc in each st across to st before next corner) around, join. *(544 sc)*

Rnds 14–19: Ch 1, sc in each st around with 3 sc in each corner st, join.

Rnd 20: Ch 1, reverse sc *(see Stitch Guide)* in each st around, join. Fasten off. ❦

Stars & Stripes

continued from page 81

Rows 6–24: Alternating red and white, repeat rows 2–5 consecutively.

Row 25: Join red with sc in first st, sc in next 35 sts changing to blue in last st made *(see Stitch Guide)*, sc in last 34 sts, turn.

Row 26: Ch 1, sc in first 34 sts changing to red in last st made, sc in last 36 sts, turn.

Row 27: Ch 1, sc in first 36 sts changing to blue in last st made, sc in last 34 sts, turn.

Row 28: Ch 1, sc in first 34 sts changing to red in last st made, sc in last 36 sts, turn. Fasten off.

Rows 29–52: Alternating white and red, repeat rows 25–28 consecutively. At end of row 52, fasten off. Sew stars in position on blue field.

BACK

Row 1: With blue, ch 71, sc in second ch from hook, sc in each ch across, turn. *(70 sc made)*

Rows 2–52: Ch 1, sc in each st across, turn. At end of row 52, fasten off.

Matching sts and ends of rows, sew Front and Back together, stuffing before closing.

FRINGE

For each **Fringe**, from gold, cut 5" strand. Fold strand in half, insert hook through st, pull fold through, pull ends through fold and tighten. Fringe in each st and end of each row around edge. ❦

Heirloom Treasures

Infinitely collectible is our
Antique Afghan. Exquisite in
every Old World detail, history
lives on in its ecru elegance.
Lend authentic richness to any
decor with Tree of Life filet,
Granny's homey coverlet, the
frontier sturdiness of Pioneer
Lace or a melodramatically
lush Victorian throw. Pass on
handmade wealth every family
will prize.

by Ann Parnell

Antique Afghan

FINISHED SIZE: Afghan is about 53" × 65". Pillow is about 12" square.

MATERIALS:
- ❑ 32 oz. off-white baby yarn
- ❑ 12" square pillow form
- ❑ F hook or size needed to obtain gauge

GAUGE: Rnds 1–7 = 4½" across.

SPECIAL STITCHES:

For **shell,** 5 dc in next sc.

For **dc cluster (dc cl),** ch 3, yo, insert hook in last sc made, yo, pull through 2 lps on hook, yo, insert hook in same st, yo, pull through st, yo, pull through 2 lps on hook, yo, pull through all 3 lps on hook.

For **tr cl,** yo 2 times, insert hook in st, yo, pull through st, (yo, pull through 2 lps on hook) 2 times, *yo 2 times, insert hook in same st, yo, pull through st, (yo, pull through 2 lps on hook) 2 times; repeat from *, yo pull through all 4 lps on hook.

FIRST MOTIF

Rnd 1: Ch 6, sl st in first ch to form ring, ch 3 *(counts as first dc),* 15 dc in ring, join with sl st in top of ch 3. *(16 dc made)*

Rnd 2: Ch 1, sc in first st, ch 2, sc in next st, (ch 4, sc in next st, ch 2, sc in next st) around, ch 4, join with sl st in first sc. *(8 ch-4 sps, 8 ch-2 sps)*

Rnd 3: Ch 1, (sc in next ch-2 sp; for **Petal,** 9 dc in next ch-4 sp) around, join. *(8 Petals)*

Rnd 4: Ch 2; working behind Petals into ch sps on rnd 2, (sc between second and third dc of next Petal, ch 5, sc between seventh and eighth dc of same Petal, ch 5) 7 times, sc between second and third dc of last Petal, ch 5, sc between seventh and eighth dc of same Petal; for last ch sp, ch 2, join with dc in first sc. *(16 ch sps, 16 sc)*

Rnd 5: Ch 1, sc in same ch sp, ch 5, sc in next ch sp, shell *(see Special Stitches)* in next sc, (sc in next ch sp, ch 5, sc in next ch sp, shell in next sc) around, join with sl st in first sc. *(8 shells, 8 ch sps)*

Rnd 6: (Ch 3, 2 dc) in first st—*first half of shell made,* (sc in next ch sp, shell in next sc, sc in center dc of next shell, shell in next sc) 7 times, sc in next ch sp, shell in next sc, sc in center dc of next shell, 2 dc in same sc as first ch 3—*second half of shell made,* join with sl st in top of ch 3. *(16 shells)*

Rnd 7: Ch 1, sc in first st, (shell in next sc, sc in center dc of next shell, ch 5, sc in center dc of next shell) 7 times, shell in next sc, sc in center dc of next shell, join with dc in first sc. *(8 shells, 8 ch sps)*

Rnd 8: Ch 1, sc in same ch sp, (ch 5, sc in center dc of next shell, ch 5, sc in next ch sp) 7 times, ch 5, sc in center dc of next shell, ch 2, join with dc in first sc.

Rnd 9: Ch 1, sc in same ch sp, (*shell in next sc, sc in next ch sp, ch 5, sc in next sc*, ch 5, sc in next ch sp) 7 times; repeat between first and second *, join with dc in first sc. *(8 shells, 16 ch sps)*

Rnd 10: Ch 1, sc in same ch sp, (*shell in next sc, sc in center dc of next shell, shell in next sc, sc in next ch sp, ch 5, sc in next sc*, ch 5, sc in next ch sp) 7 times; repeat between first and second *, ch 2, join with dc in first sc.

Rnd 11: Ch 1, sc in same ch sp, (*shell in next sc, sc in center dc of next shell, ch 5, sc in center dc of next shell, shell in next sc, sc in next ch sp*, ch 5, sc in next ch sp) 7 times; repeat between first and second *, ch 2, join with dc in first sc. *(16 shells, 16 ch sps)*

Rnd 12: Ch 1, sc in same ch sp, (*shell in next sc, sc in center dc of next shell, ch 5, sc in next ch sp, ch 5, sc in center dc of next shell, shell in next sc*, sc in next ch sp) 7 times; repeat between first and second *, join with sl st in first sc.

Rnd 13: (Ch 3, 2 dc) in first st—*first half of shell made,* *[sc in center dc of next shell, ch 5, sc in next ch sp, shell in next sc, sc in next ch sp, ch

5, sc in center dc of next shell, shell in next sc, sc in center dc of next shell, (ch 5, sc in next ch sp) 2 times, ch 5, sc in center dc of next shell], shell in next sc; repeat from * 2 more times; repeat between [ ], 2 dc in same st as ch 3—*second half of shell made,* join with sl st in top of ch 3.

Rnd 14: Ch 1, sc in first st, *[ch 5, sc in next st, ch 5, sc in next ch sp, shell in next sc, sc in center dc of next shell, shell in next sc, sc in next ch sp, ch 5, sc in next sc, ch 5, sc in center dc of next shell, (ch 5, sc in next ch sp) 3 times], ch 5, sc in center dc of next shell; repeat from * 2 more times; repeat between [ ], ch 2, join with dc in first sc.

Rnd 15: Ch 1, sc in same ch sp, (ch 5, sc in next ch sp) 2 times, *[shell in next sc, sc in center dc of next shell, ch 5, sc in next sc, ch 5, sc in center dc of next shell, shell in next sc, sc in next ch sp], (ch 5, sc in next ch sp) 7 times; repeat from * 2 more times; repeat between [ ], (ch 5, sc in next ch sp) 4 times, ch 2, join with dc in first sc.

Rnd 16: Ch 1, sc in same ch sp, (ch 5, sc in next ch sp) 2 times, *[ch 5, sc in next sc, ch 5, sc in center dc of next shell, shell in next sc, sc in next ch sp, ch 5, sc in next ch sp, shell in next sc, sc in center dc of next shell, ch 5, sc in next sc], (ch 5, sc in next ch sp) 7 times; repeat from * 2 more times; repeat between [ ], (ch 5, sc in next ch sp) 4 times, ch 2, join with dc in first sc.

Rnd 17: Ch 1, sc in same ch sp, (ch 5, sc in next ch sp) 4 times, *[ch 5, sc in center dc of next shell, (shell in next sc) 2 times, sc in center dc of next shell], (ch 5, sc in next ch sp) 10 times; repeat from * 2 more times; repeat between [ ], (ch 5, sc in next ch sp) 5 times, ch 2, join with dc in first sc.

Rnd 18: Ch 1, sc in same ch sp, (ch 5, sc in next ch sp) 4 times, *[ch 3, dc in next ch sp, ch 3, dc in next sc, ch 3, sc in center dc of next shell, shell in first st of next shell, sc in third dc of same shell, ch 3, dc in next sc, ch 3, dc in next ch sp, ch 3, sc in next ch sp], (ch 5, sc in next ch sp) 8 times; repeat from * 2 more times; repeat between [ ], (ch 5, sc in next ch sp) 3 times, ch 2, join with dc in first sc.

Rnd 19: Ch 1, sc in same ch sp, (ch 5, sc in next ch sp) 6 times, *[ch 5; for **Corner,** tr cl *(see Special Stitches)* in next dc, tr cl in second dc on same shell, ch 5, (tr cl, ch 7—*center corner ch sp made;* tr cl) in next dc on same shell, ch 5, tr cl in next dc on same shell, skip next dc

and next sc and next ch sp, tr cl in next dc]; (ch 5, sc in next ch sp) 12 times; repeat from * 2 more times; repeat between [ ], (ch 5, sc in next ch sp) 5 times, ch 5, join with sl st in first sc. Fasten off.

ONE-SIDE JOINED MOTIF
Rnds 1–18: Repeat rnds 1–18 of First Motif.
Rnd 19: Ch 1, sc in same ch sp, (ch 5, sc in next ch sp) 6 times, ch 5, tr cl in next dc, tr cl in second dc of next shell, ch 5, tr cl in next dc on same shell, ch 3, sc in center Corner ch sp on last motif *(see dot on joining illustration),* ch 3, tr cl in same dc as last tr cl made on this Motif, ch 2, sc in next ch sp on last Motif, ch 2, tr cl in next dc of same shell on this Motif, skip next dc and next sc and next ch sp, tr cl in next dc, (ch 2, sc in next ch sp on last Motif, ch 2, sc in next ch sp on this Motif) 12 times, ch 2, sc in next ch sp on last Motif, ch 2, tr cl in next dc on this Motif, tr cl in second dc of next shell, ch 2, sc in next ch sp on last Motif, ch 2, tr cl in next dc of same shell on this Motif, ch 3, sc in next center Corner ch sp on last Motif, ch 3, tr cl in same dc as last tr cl made on this Motif, *ch 5, tr cl in next dc on same shell, skip next dc and next sc and next ch sp, tr cl in next dc, (ch 5, sc in next ch sp) 12 times, ch 5; for **Corner,** tr cl in next dc, tr cl in second dc of next shell, ch 5, (tr cl, ch 7, tr cl) in next dc on same shell; repeat from * one more time, ch 5, tr cl in next dc on same shell, skip next dc and next sc and next ch sp, tr cl in next dc, (ch 5, sc in next ch sp) 5 times, ch 5, join with sl st in first sc. Fasten off.

TWO-SIDE JOINED MOTIF
Rnds 1–18: Repeat rnds 1–18 of First Motif.
Rnd 19: Ch 1, sc in same ch sp, (ch 5, sc in next ch sp) 6 times, ch 5, tr cl in next dc, tr cl in second dc of next shell, ch 5, tr cl in next dc on same shell, ch 3, sc in center Corner ch sp of Motif on row above *(see dot on joining illustration),* ch 3, tr cl in same dc as last tr cl made on this Motif, *ch 2, sc in next ch sp on last Motif, ch 2, tr cl in next dc of same shell on this Motif, skip next dc and next sc and next ch sp, tr cl in next dc, (ch 2, sc in next ch sp on last Motif, ch 2, sc in next ch sp on this Motif) 12 times, ch 2, sc in next ch sp on last Motif, ch 2, tr cl in next dc on this Motif, tr cl in second dc on next shell, ch 2, sc in next ch sp on last Motif, ch 2, tr cl in next dc of same shell on this Motif, ch 3, sc in next center Corner ch sp on last Motif,

continued on page 93

by Lucille LaFlamme

Tree of Life

FINISHED SIZE: About 46" × 63".

MATERIALS:
- ❏ 41 oz. off-white worsted yarn
- ❏ I hook or size needed to obtain gauge

GAUGE: 7 dc = 2"; 3 dc rows = 2".

SPECIAL STITCHES:

For **block**, dc in next 2 sts, **or,** dc in next ch sp, dc in next st, **or,** 2 dc in next double mesh.

For **beginning mesh (beg mesh),** ch 4, skip next ch, dc in next st.

For **mesh,** ch 1, skip next st or ch, dc in next st or ch.

For **double mesh,** ch 3, skip next 3 sts or ch, dc in next st or ch.

For **beginning tr cluster (beg tr cl),** ch 4, *yo 2 times, insert hook in same st or ch sp as ch 4, yo, pull through st or ch sp, (yo, pull through 2 lps on hook) 2 times; repeat from *, yo, pull through all 3 lps on hook.

For **tr cluster (tr cl),** yo 2 times, insert hook in st or sp, yo, pull through st or sp, (yo, pull through 2 lps on hook) 2 times, *yo 2 times, insert hook in same st or sp, yo, pull through st or sp, (yo, pull through 2 lps on hook) 2 times; repeat from *, yo, pull through all 4 lps on hook.

For **2-dc cluster (2-dc cl),** yo, insert hook in st or sp, yo, pull through st or sp, yo, pull through 2 lps on hook, yo, insert hook in same st or sp, yo, pull through st or sp, yo, pull through 2 lps on hook, yo, pull through all 3 lps on hook.

For **3-dc cl,** yo, insert hook in next st or sp, yo, pull through st or sp, yo, pull through 2 lps on hook, (yo, insert hook in same st or sp, yo, pull through st or sp, yo, pull through 2 lps on hook) 2 times, yo, pull through all 4 lps on hook.

AFGHAN

Row 1: Ch 124, dc in sixth ch from hook, (ch 1, skip next ch, dc in next ch) across, turn. *(60 mesh made)*

Row 2: Beg mesh, mesh across, turn. *(Front of row 2 is right side of work.)*

Rows 3–83: Work according to graph across, turn.

Row 84: Beg mesh, mesh across, **do not turn or fasten off.**

BORDER

Rnd 1: Ch 4, beg tr cl *(see Special Stitches)* in last dc made, ch 4, 2-dc cl in fourth ch from hook; working in sps at ends of rows, (3-dc cl in next sp, ch 1, 3-dc cl in next sp, ch 4, 2-dc cl in fourth ch from hook, skip next sp) 28 times; working on opposite side of starting ch, tr cl in first ch, ch 4, 2-dc cl in fourth ch from hook; repeat between ( ) 20 times, tr cl in last ch, ch 4, 2-dc cl in fourth ch from hook; repeat between ( ) 28 times, tr cl in first st, ch 4, 2-dc cl in fourth ch from hook; repeat between ( ) 20 times, join with sl st in top of first cl.

Rnd 2: Ch 4, 2-dc cl in same cl as sl st, (ch 2, 3-dc cl in same st) twice, [*ch 2, (3-dc cl, ch 2, 3-dc cl) in ch-1 sp between 3-dc cls*; repeat from * to * across to corner tr cl, ch 2, 3-dc cl in next tr cl, (ch 2, 3-dc cl in same st) twice]; repeat between [ ] 2 more times; repeat from * to * across, join with sl st in top of first cl.

Rnd 3: Ch 5 *(counts as dc and ch 2)*, in corner cl make 3 dc with ch 2 between each dc, ch 2, dc in next cl, [*ch 1, dc in ch-2 sp, (ch 1, dc in next cl) twice*; repeat from * to * across to ch-2 sp before next 3 corner cls, ch 1, dc in next ch-2 sp, ch 1, dc in next cl, ch 2, in corner cl make 3 dc with ch 2 between each dc, ch 2, dc in next cl]; repeat between [ ] 2 more times; repeat from * to * across to last ch-2 sp, ch 1, dc in last ch sp, ch 1, join with sl st in third ch of ch 5. *(86 ch-1 sps on each long side, 4 ch-2 sps at each corner, 62 ch-1 sps on each end)*

Rnd 4: Ch 5, dc in next dc, *ch 2; for **corner,** in corner dc make 3 dc with ch 2 between each dc; (ch 2, dc in next dc) twice, mesh, block, (mesh 5, block) 14 times, ch 2, dc in next dc, ch 2, corner, (ch 2, dc in next dc) twice, mesh, block*, (mesh 5, block) 10 times, ch 2, dc in next dc; repeat from * to *, (mesh 5, block) 9 times, mesh 5, dc in next ch-1 sp, join with sl st in third ch of ch 5.

continued on page 92

continued from page 91

Rnd 5: Ch 5, dc in next dc, *ch 2, dc in next dc, ch 2, corner, (ch 2, dc in next dc) 3 times, mesh 2, (block, mesh 3, block, mesh) 14 times, (ch 2, dc in next dc) twice, ch 2, corner, (ch 2, dc in next dc) 3 times, mesh 2*, (block, mesh 3, block, mesh) 10 times, ch 2, dc in next dc; repeat from * to *, (block, mesh 3, block, mesh) 9 times, block, mesh 3, block, ch 1, sl st in third ch of ch 5.

Rnd 6: Ch 5, dc in next dc, *(ch 2, dc in next dc) twice, ch 2, corner, (ch 2, dc in next dc) 4 times, mesh 3, (block, mesh, block, mesh 3) 13 times, block, mesh, block, mesh 2, (ch 2, dc in next dc) 3 times, ch 2, corner, (ch 2, dc in next dc) 4 times, mesh 3, (block, mesh, block, mesh 3) 9 times, block, mesh, block*, mesh 2, ch 2, dc in next dc; repeat from * to *, mesh, ch 1, sl st in third ch of ch 5.

Rnd 7: Ch 5, dc in next dc, *(ch 2, dc in next dc) 3 times, ch 2, corner, (ch 2, dc in next dc) 5 times, mesh 4, (block, mesh 5) 13 times, block, mesh 3, (ch 2, dc in next dc) 4 times, ch 2, corner, (ch 2, dc in next dc) 5 times, mesh 4, (block, mesh 5) 9 times, block*, mesh 3, ch 2, dc in next st; repeat from * to *, mesh 2, ch 2, sl st in third ch of ch 5.

Rnd 8: Ch 4, *[dc in next ch sp, ch 1, dc in next ch sp, ch 1, (dc in next dc, ch 1, dc in next ch sp, ch 1, dc in next ch sp, ch 1) 2 times, corner, (ch 1, dc in next ch sp) 2 times, ch 1, (dc in next dc, ch 1, dc in next ch sp, ch 1, dc in next ch sp, ch 1) 2 times, dc in next st], mesh across to next ch-2 sp; repeat from * 2 more times; repeat between [ ], mesh across, join with sl st in third ch of ch 4.

Rnd 9: For **flower edging,** (sl st, ch 3, 2-dc cl) in next ch sp, *(ch 1, 3-dc cl in next ch sp, ch 3, dc in third ch from hook, skip next dc and ch sp, sc in next dc, ch 3, dc in third ch from hook, skip next ch sp, 3-dc

■ = **BLOCK**

☐ = **MESH OR BEG MESH**

☐ = **DOUBLE MESH**

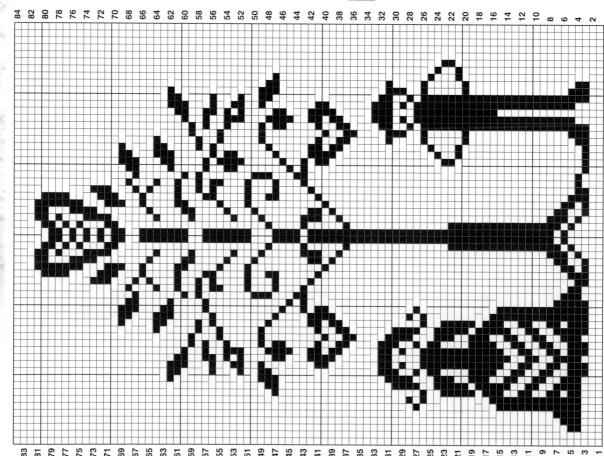

cl in next ch sp) across to corner, 3-dc cl in next ch sp; for **corner petals, (ch 3, dc in third ch from hook) twice;** skip corner dc, 3-dc cl in next sp; repeat from * 3 more times, (ch 1, 3-dc cl in next ch sp, ch 3, dc in third ch from hook, skip next dc and ch sp, sc in next dc, ch 3, dc in third ch from hook, skip next ch sp, 3-dc cl in next sp) 17 times, ch 3, 3-dc cl in next ch sp, ch 3, dc in third ch from hook, skip next dc and ch sp, sc in next dc, ch 3, dc in third ch from hook, join with sl st in top of first cl.

Rnd 10: Sl st into ch sp between cls, ch 3, make the following all in the same ch sp as sl st: dc, ch 3, sl st in same ch, ch 3, dc; ch 3, sl st in top of dc just made for picot; ch 3, sl st in same ch, ch 3, 2-dc cl; *(in ch-1 sp between next 2 cls make: ch 1, 2-dc cl, ch 3, sl st in same ch, ch 3, dc and picot, ch 3, sl st in same ch, ch 3, 2-dc cl in same ch) across to corner petals, ch 1, sl st between corner petals; repeat from * 3 more times; repeat between ( ) across, ch 1, join with sl st in top of ch 3. Fasten off. ❦

continued from page 89

ch 3, tr cl in same dc as last tr cl made on this Motif; working in ch sps of last Motif on this row; repeat from *, ch 5, tr cl in next dc on same shell, skip next dc and next sc and next ch sp, tr cl in next dc, (ch 5, sc in next ch sp) 12 times, ch 5; for **Corner,** tr cl in next dc, tr cl in second dc of next shell, ch 5, (tr, ch 7, tr cl) in next dc on same shell, ch 5, tr cl in next dc on same shell, skip next dc and next sc and next ch sp, tr cl in next dc, (ch 5, sc in next ch sp) 5 times, ch 5, join with sl st in first sc. Fasten off.

AFGHAN

Work first Motif; work One-Side Joined Motif for total of four times or to desired width of Afghan. *Work one One-Side Joined Motif onto bottom of First Motif on last row of Motifs; work Two-Side Joined Motif to width of Afghan; repeat from * for total of four more rows or to desired length.

EDGING

With right side facing you, join with sc in first ch-5 sp after any three Corner ch sps, dc cl *(see Special Stitches)* in last sc made, (sc, dc cl) in each ch sp around with (sc, dc cl, sc, dc cl) in center Corner ch sps, join with sl st in first sc. Fasten off.

PILLOW
Pillow Front
Work same as First Motif on Afghan.

Pillow Back
Rnds 1–18: Work same as rnds 1–18 of First

Motif on Afghan.

Rnd 19: Hold Pillow Front and Back wrong sides together with pillow form between; working through both thicknesses, ch 1, sc in same ch sp, (ch 2, sc in corresponding ch sp on Front, ch 2, sc in next ch sp on Back) 6 times, *[ch 2, sc in next ch sp on Front, ch 2, tr cl in next dc on Back, tr cl in second dc of next shell, ch 2, sc in next ch sp on Front, ch 2, tr cl in next dc of same shell on Back, ch 3, sc in next center Corner ch sp on Front, ch 3, tr cl in same dc as last tr cl made on Back, ch 2, sc in next ch sp on Front, ch 2, tr cl in next dc of same shell on Back, skip next dc and next sc and next ch sp, tr cl in next dc], (ch 2, sc in next ch sp on Front, ch 2, sc in next ch sp on Back) 12 times; repeat from * 2 more times; repeat between [ ], (ch 2, sc in next ch sp on Front, ch 2, sc in next ch sp on Back) 5 times, ch 2, sc in next ch sp on Front, ch 2, join with sl st in first sc. Fasten off. ❦

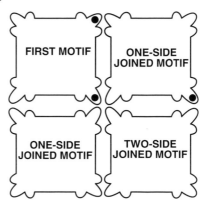

by Frieda Bell

Granny's Coverlet

FINISHED SIZE: About 65" × 94".

MATERIALS:
- ❑ Worsted yarn:
  - 68 oz. main color (MC)
  - 12 oz. contrasting color (CC)
- ❑ I hook or size needed to obtain gauge

GAUGE: 7 hdc = 1"; 2 hdc rows = 1".

SQUARE (make 36 MC, 17 CC)

Rnd 1: Ch 8, sl st in first ch to form ring, ch 2, 21 hdc in ring, join with sl st in top of ch 2. *(22 hdc made)*

Rnd 2: Ch 4, 2 tr in same st leaving last 2 lps of each st on hook, yo, pull through all lps on hook; *ch 4, skip next st; for **3 tr cluster (cl)**, **work 3 tr in next st leaving last 2 lps of each st on hook, yo, pull through all lps on hook;** repeat from * around to last st, ch 4, skip last st, join with sl st in top of ch 4. *(11 cl)*

Rnd 3: Ch 4, sc in next ch-4 sp, ch 4, (cl, ch 6, cl) in next ch-4 sp, *(ch 4, sc in next ch-4 sp) 2 times, ch 4, (cl, ch 6, cl) in next ch-4 sp; repeat from * 2 more times, ch 4, join with sl st in first ch of ch 4. *(12 ch-4 sps)*

Rnd 4: (Sl st, ch 4, 2 tr) in first ch-4 sp, 3 tr in next ch-4 sp, *(3 tr, ch 5, 3 tr) in next ch-6 sp, 3 tr in each of next 3 ch-4 sps; repeat from * 2 more times, (3 tr, ch 5, 3 tr) in next ch-6 sp, 3 tr in next ch-4 sp, join with sl st in top of ch 4. Fasten off. *(60)*

ASSEMBLY

With wrong sides together, matching sts, sl st 17 CC and 16 MC Squares together according to diagram, arranging colors shown in photograph.

INNER BORDER

Rnd 1: Working around entire outer edge of joined Squares, join MC with sc in third ch of any outer ch-5 corner *(see diagram)*, 2 sc in same ch, sc in each st and in each ch around with 3 sc in third ch of each outer ch 5 corner around, join with sl st in first sc. Fasten off.

Rnd 2: Join CC with sl st in any sc, ch 2, hdc in each st around with 3 hdc in each outer corner and hdc 2 sts tog in each inner corner, join with sl st in top of ch 2, **turn.**

Rnd 3: Working this rnd in **back lps** *(see Stitch Guide)*, ch 2, hdc in each st around with hdc 2 sts tog in outer corner and hdc 2 sts tog in inner corner, join, **turn.** Fasten off.

With MC, sl st remaining MC Squares around inner border as shown, easing to fit.

OUTER BORDER

Rnd 1: With MC, repeat rnd 1 of Inner Border. **Do not fasten off.**

Rnds 2–28: Working these rnds in **back lps**, ch 2, hdc in each st around with 3 hdc in each outer corner and hdc 2 sts tog in each inner corner, join with sl st in top of ch 2, **turn.** At end of rnd 28, fasten off. ❧

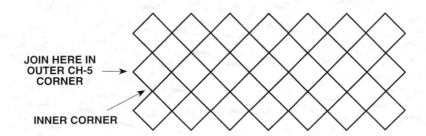

JOIN HERE IN OUTER CH-5 CORNER →

INNER CORNER →

by Joanne Whitwell

Pioneer Lace

FINISHED SIZE: About 49½" × 58½".

MATERIALS:
❏ Sport yarn:
  15 oz. off-white
  2½ oz. each lt. aqua and dk. aqua
❏ I hook or size needed to obtain gauge

GAUGE: Motif is 4½" square.

NOTES:
Alternate lt. and dk. colors at center of Motifs.
There will be 72 lt. and 71 dk. centers when
  Afghan is finished.

AFGHAN
Work First Motif; work One-Side Joined Motif for
  total of 13 Motifs or to desired length of Afghan.
*Work One-Side Joined Motif onto right-hand
  side of First Motif on last strip of Motifs; work
  Two-Side Joined Motif to length of Afghan;
  repeat from * for total of 11 strips or to desired
  width of Afghan.

FIRST MOTIF
Rnd 1: With center color, ch 5, sl st in first ch to
  form ring, ch 4, 4 tr in ring, ch 3, (5 tr in ring, ch
  3) 3 times, join with sl st in top of ch 4. Fasten
  off. *(20 tr made)*
Rnd 2: Join off-white with sl st in any ch-3 sp, ch
  7, sl st in third ch from hook, tr in same ch sp;
  (for **picot, ch 3, sl st in third ch from hook;** tr)
  in same ch-3 sp 5 times, ch 2; *for **shell, (tr,
  picot) in next ch-3 sp 6 times, tr in same ch-3
  sp;** ch 2, shell, ch 2) 2 times, join with sl st in
  fourth ch of ch 7. Fasten off.

ONE-SIDE JOINED MOTIF
NOTE: For **joined picot,** *ch 1, drop lp from hook,
insert hook in picot on first Motif, pull dropped
lp through picot, ch 2, sl st back in first ch1
from hook.*

Rnd 1: With center color, ch 5, sl st in first ch to
  form ring, ch 4, 4 tr in ring, ch 3, (5 tr in ring, ch
  3) 3 times, join with sl st in top of ch 4. Fasten
  off. *(20 tr made)*
Rnd 2: Join off-white with sl st in any ch-3 sp, ch
  7, sl st in third ch from hook, tr in same ch-3 sp,
  (picot, tr) in same ch-3 sp 3 times, work joined
  picot in second picot on any shell of last Motif
  made, tr in same ch-3 sp on this Motif, joined
  picot in first picot on last Motif, tr in same ch-3
  sp on this Motif, ch 1, sl st in ch-2 sp on last
  Motif, ch 1, tr in next ch-3 sp on this Motif,
  joined picot in sixth picot on next shell on last
  Motif, tr in same ch-3 sp on this Motif, joined
  picot in fifth picot on last Motif, tr in same ch-
  3 sp on this Motif, (picot, tr) in same ch-3 sp on
  this Motif 4 times, ch 2, (shell in next ch-3 sp,
  ch 2) 2 times, join with sl st in fourth ch of ch
  7. Fasten off.

TWO-SIDE JOINED MOTIF
Rnd 1: With center color, ch 5, sl st in first ch to
  form ring, ch 4, 4 tr in ring, ch 3, (5 tr in ring, ch
  3) 3 times, join with sl st in top of ch 4. Fasten
  off. *(20 tr made)*
Rnd 2: Join off-white with sl st in any ch-3 sp, ch
  7, sl st in third ch from hook, tr in same ch-3 sp,
  (picot, tr) in same ch sp 3 times, *joined picot
  in second picot on next corresponding Motif, tr
  in same ch-3 sp on this Motif, joined picot in
  first picot on same corresponding Motif, tr in
  same ch-3 sp on this Motif, ch 1, sl st in ch-2 sp
  on same corresponding Motif, ch 1, tr in next
  ch-3 sp on this Motif, joined picot in sixth picot
  on same corresponding Motif, tr in same ch-3
  sp on this Motif, joined picot in fifth picot on
  same corresponding Motif, tr in same ch-3 sp
  on this Motif, (picot, tr) in same ch-3 sp 2
  times; repeat from * one time, (picot, tr) in
  same ch-3 sp 2 times, ch 2, shell in last ch-3 sp,
  ch 2, join with sl st in fourth ch of ch 7. Fasten
  off. ❧

by Diane Simpson

Victorian Lace

FINISHED SIZE: Afghan is about 56" × 72" without Tassels.

MATERIALS:
- ❑ Worsted yarn:
    - 51 oz. green
    - 26 oz. rose
    - 33 oz. pink
- ❑ Tapestry needle
- ❑ H hook or size needed to obtain gauge

GAUGE: Rnd 1 = 1"; 1 Motif = 8" across.

SPECIAL STITCH:

For **puff stitch (ps)**, (yo, insert hook in st, yo, pull up lp) 3 times, yo, pull through all 7 lps on hook, ch 1.

MOTIF (make 63)

Rnd 1: With rose, ch 3, sl st in first ch to form ring, 6 ps (see Special Stitch above) in ring, ch 1, join with sl st in first ch-1 sp. (6 ps made)

NOTE: First st of each rnd is worked back into top of first ps of previous rnd.

Rnd 2: (Ps in next st, ps in next ch-2 sp) around, join. Fasten off. (12 ps)

Rnd 3: Join pink with sl st in first st, (ps in next 2 sts, ps in next ch-1 sp) around, join. (18 ps)

Rnds 4–5: (Ps in next 3 sts, ps in next ch-1 sp) around, join. (24, 32)

NOTE: To change color (see Stitch Guide), pull lp of next color through lp on hook, pull first color tight. When working with green, carry pink along back of work and crochet over it; when working with pink, drop green, pick up again when needed.

Rnd 6: (Ps in next 3 sts, changing to green, ps in next st, ps in next ch-1 sp, changing to pink) 7 times, ps in next 3 sts, changing to green, ps in next st, ps in next ch-1 sp, join. (40 ps)

Rnd 7: Ps in first st, changing to pink, (ps in next st, changing to green, ps in next 2 sts, ps in next ch-1 sp, ps in next 2 sts, changing to pink) 7 times, ps in next st, changing to green; fasten off

pink, ps in next 2 sts, ps in next ch-1 sp, ps in next st, join. (48 ps)

Rnd 8: Ps in first st, *yo, insert hook in next st and under both green strands at back, yo, pull up lp, (yo, insert hook in same st and under both strands, yo, pull up lp) 2 times, yo, pull through all lps on hook, ch 1, ps in next 3 sts, ps in next ch-1 sp, ps in next 2 sts; repeat from * 6 more times, insert hook in next st and under both strands at back, yo, pull up lp; repeat between ( ) 2 times, yo, pull through all lps on hook, ch 1, ps in next 3 sts, ps in next ch-1 sp, ps in next st, join. (56 ps)

Rnd 9: Sl st in first st, ch 2, sc in next 2 sts, *hdc in next st, (2 dc, tr, ch 1, tr, 2 dc) in next st, hdc in next st, sc in next 4 sts; repeat from * 6 more times, hdc in next st, (2 dc, tr, ch 1, tr, 2 dc) in next st, hdc in next st, sc in next st, join with sl st in top of ch 2. Fasten off. (96 sts)

Sew two points of one Motif to two points of another Motif; repeat, making 9 rows of 7 Motifs each.

FLOWERS & CHAINS

With rose, ch 5, sl st in first ch to form ring, *ch 2, (yo, insert hook in ring, yo, pull up lp, yo, pull through 2 lps on hook) 2 times, yo, pull through 3 lps on hook, ch 2, sl st in second ch from hook, ch 2, sl st in ring; repeat from * 7 more times. Fasten off. (8 petals made)

Join green with sl st in ring between any two petals, ch 8; working in circular space between 4 joined Motifs, sl st in ch-1 sp of any Motif, (*ch 8, sl st in ring between two petals, ch 8, sl st in sixth st of same Motif, ch 8, sl st in ring between next two petals*, ch 8, sl st in ch-1 sp of next Motif) 3 times; repeat between first and second *. Fasten off. Repeat in each circle between all Motifs.

TASSEL (make 64)

With rose, cut 27 strands each 16" long. Fold 25 strands in half; with another strand, tie knot in center of fold; wrap last strand around all strands 1" below fold. Tie one in each ch-1 sp around outside of Afghan. ❧

Ripple Designs

Like the stir from a stone thrown into a pond, the tasteful impression you'll make with these dramatic ripple afghans never ends. Choose Autumn Leaves' multi-layered splendor. Sample yummy Blueberry Ripple or indulge yourself with Rainbow Ripple. Fanciful Flowers is a hit, and Beef Stew, with bonus recipe, is a colorful melange that just can't miss.

by Bonnie Jenkins

Autumn Leaves

FINISHED SIZE: Afghan is about 41" × 72". Pillow is 18" × 24".

MATERIALS:
- ❑ Worsted yarn:
  - 32 oz. main color (MC)
  - 13 oz. each of 8 contrasting colors (B, C, D, E, F, G, H, I)
- ❑ Polyester fiberfill
- ❑ G hook or size needed to obtain gauge

GAUGE: 4 sc = 1"; 6 pattern rows = 2".

NOTES:

Do not turn at ends of rows.

Entire pattern is worked in **back lps** *(see Stitch Guide)* except for first and last st of each row.

Fasten off at end of every row.

AFGHAN

Row 1: With G hook and MC, ch 224, sc in second ch from hook, skip next ch, (sc in next 7 ch, 3 sc in next ch, sc in next 7 ch, skip next 2 ch) 12 times, sc in next 7 ch, 3 sc in next ch, sc in next 7 ch, skip next ch, sc in last ch. *(223 sc made)*

Rows 2–8: Join MC with sc in first st, skip next st, (sc in next 7 sts, 3 sc in next st, sc in next 7 sts, skip next 2 sts) 12 times, sc in next 7 sts, 3 sc in next st, sc in next 7 sts, skip next st, sc in last st.

NOTE: Rows 9–191 are worked changing color every three rows.

Row 9: Join B with sc in first st, skip next st, (*tr in **front lp** of next st 3 rows below, sc in next 6 sts, 3 sc in next st, sc in next 6 sts, tr in **front lp** of next st 3 rows below*, skip next 2 sts) 12 times; repeat between first and second *, skip next st, sc in last st.

Row 10: Join B with sc in first st, skip next st, (*sc in next st, tr in **front lp** of next st 3 rows below, sc in next 5 sts, 3 sc in next st, sc in next 5 sts, tr in **front lp** of next st 3 rows below, sc in next st*, skip next 2 sts) 12 times; repeat between first and second *, skip next st, sc in next st.

Row 11: Join B with sc in first st, skip next st, (*sc in next 2 sts, tr in **front lp** of next st 3 rows below, sc in next 4 sts, 3 sc in next st, sc in next 4 sts, tr in **front lp** of next st 3 rows below, sc in next 2 sts*, skip next 2 sts) 12 times; repeat between first and second *, skip next st, sc in last st.

Row 12: Join C with sc in first st, skip next st, (*sc in next 3 sts, tr in **front lp** of next st 3 rows below, sc in next 3 sts, 3 sc in next st, sc in next 3 sts, tr in **front lp** of next st 3 rows below, sc in next 3 sts*, skip next 2 sts) 12 times; repeat between first and second *, skip next st, sc in last st.

Row 13: Join C with sc in first st, skip next st, (*sc in next 4 sts, tr in **front lp** of next st 3 rows below, sc in next 2 sts, 3 sc in next st, sc in next 2 sts, tr in **front lp** of next st 3 rows below, sc in next 4 sts*, skip next 2 sts) 12 times; repeat between first and second *, skip next st, sc in last st.

Row 14: Join C with sc in first st, skip next st, (*sc in next 5 sts, tr in **front lp** of next st 3 rows below, sc in next st, 3 sc in next st, sc in next st, tr in **front lp** of next st 3 rows below, sc in next 5 sts*, skip next 2 sts) 12 times; repeat between first and second *, skip next st, sc in last st.

Row 15: Join D with sc in first st, skip next st, (*sc in next 6 sts, tr in **front lp** of next st 3 rows below, 3 sc in next st, tr in **front lp** of next st 3 rows below, sc in next 6 sts*, skip next 2 sts) 12 times; repeat between first and second *, skip next st, sc in last st.

Row 16: Join D with sc in first st, skip next st, (sc in next 7 sts, 3 tr in **front lp** of next st 3 rows below, sc in next 7 sts, skip next 2 sts) 12 times, sc in next 7 sts, 3 tr in **front lp** of next st 3 rows below, sc in next 7 sts, skip next st, sc in last st.

Row 17: With D, repeat row 9.

Rows 18–20: With MC, repeat rows 10–12.

Rows 21–23: With E, repeat rows 13–15.

Rows 24–26: With F, repeat rows 16, 9 and 10.

Rows 27–29: With MC, repeat rows 11–13.

Rows 30–32: With G, repeat rows 14–16.

Rows 33–107: Following color sequence of B, C, D, MC, E, F, MC, G, H, I, MC, beginning with row 9 and H, repeat rows 9–16 consecutively, ending with row 11 and MC.

Rows 108–191: Following color sequence of I, H, G, MC, F, E, MC, D, C, B, MC, beginning with row 12 and F, repeat rows 9–16 consecutively, ending with row 15 and B.

Rows 192–199: With MC, repeat row 2.

PILLOW

First Side

Row 1: With MC, ch 88, sc in second ch from hook, skip next ch, (sc in next 7 ch, 3 sc in next ch, sc in next 7 ch, skip next 2 ch) 4 times, sc in next 7 ch, 3 sc in next ch, sc in next 7 ch, skip next ch, sc in last ch. *(87 sc made)*

Rows 2–5: Join MC with sc in first st, skip next st, (sc in next 7 sts, 3 sc in next st, sc in next 7 sts, skip next 2 sts) 4 times, sc in next 7 sts, 3 sc in next st, sc in next 7 sts, skip next st, sc in last st.

NOTE: Rows 6–61 are worked changing color every three rows.

Row 6: Join B with sc in first st, skip next st, (*tr in **front lp** of next st 3 rows below, sc in next 6 sts, 3 sc in next st, sc in next 6 sts, tr in **front lp** of next st 3 rows below*, skip next 2 sts) 4 times; repeat between first and second *, skip next st, sc in last st.

Row 7: Join B with sc in first st, skip next st, (*sc in next st, tr in **front lp** of next st 3 rows below, sc in next 5 sts, 3 sc in next st, sc in next 5 sts, tr in **front lp** of next st 3 rows below, sc in next st*, skip next 2 sts) 4 times; repeat between first and second *, skip next st, sc in last st.

Row 8: Join B with sc in first st, skip next st, (*sc in next 2 sts, tr in **front lp** of next st 3 rows below, sc in next 4 sts, 3 sc in next st, sc in next 4 sts, tr in **front lp** of next st 3 rows below, sc in next 2 sts*, skip next 2 sts) 4 times; repeat between first and second *, skip next st, sc in last st.

Row 9: Join C with sc in first st, skip next st, (*sc in next 3 sts, tr in **front lp** of next st 3 rows below, sc in next 3 sts, 3 sc in next st, sc in next 3 sts, tr in **front lp** of next st 3 rows below, sc in next 3 sts*, skip next 2 sts) 4 times; repeat between first and second *, skip next st, sc in last st.

Row 10: Join C with sc in first st, skip next st, (*sc in next 4 sts, tr in **front lp** of next st 3 rows below, sc in next 2 sts, 3 sc in next st, sc in next 2 sts, tr in **front lp** of next st 3 rows below, sc in next 4 sts*, skip next 2 sts) 4 times; repeat between first and second *, skip next st, sc in last st.

Row 11: Join C with sc in first st, skip next st, (*sc in next 5 sts, tr in **front lp** of next st 3 rows below, sc in next st, 3 sc in next st, sc in next st, tr in **front lp** of next st 3 rows below, sc in next 5 sts*, skip next 2 sts) 4 times; repeat between first and second *, skip next st, sc in last st. Fasten off.

Row 12: Join D with sc in first st, skip next st, (*sc in next 6 sts, tr in **front lp** of next st 3 rows below, 3 sc in next st, tr in **front lp** of next st 3 rows below, sc in next 6 sts*, skip next 2 sts) 4 times; repeat between first and second *, skip next st, sc in last st.

Row 13: Join D with sc in first st, skip next st, (*sc in next 7 sts, 3 tr in **front lp** of next st 3 rows below, sc in next 7 sts*, skip next 2 sts) 4 times; repeat between first and second *, skip next st, sc in last st.

Rows 14–35: Following color sequence of B, C, D, MC, E, F, MC, G, H, I, beginning with row 6 and D, repeat rows 6–13 consecutively, ending with row 11 and I.

Rows 36–61: Following color sequence of MC, F, E, MC, D, C, B, MC, beginning with row 12 and MC, repeat rows 6–13 consecutively, ending with row 13 and MC.

Rows 62–63: With MC, repeat row 2. Fasten off.

Second Side

Row 1: Repeat row 1 of First Side.

Rows 2–63: Repeat row 2 of First Side.

Hold Pillow Sides with wrong sides together, matching ends of rows and sts; working around entire outside edge through both thicknesses, join MC with sc in any st, sc in each st around with 3 sc in each corner, stuffing before closing. Fasten off. ❧

by Phyllis Caessens

Rainbow Ripple

FINISHED SIZE: About 56" × 72".

MATERIALS:
- ❑ Worsted yarn:
  - 13 oz. dk. purple
  - 9 oz. each red, dk. orange, orange, yellow, lt. green, dk. green, lt. turquoise, dk. turquoise and lt. purple
- ❑ Tapestry needle
- ❑ J hook or size needed to obtain gauge

GAUGE: 4 post st rows = 3".

AFGHAN

Row 1: With dk. purple, ch 251, dc in fourth ch from hook, *(ch 1, skip next ch, dc in next ch) 3 times, ch 1, skip next ch, (dc, ch 2, dc) in next ch, (ch 1, skip next ch, dc in next ch) 3 times, ch 1, skip next ch; for **decrease,** yo, insert hook in next ch, yo, pull through ch, yo, pull through 2 lps on hook, yo, skip next 2 ch, insert hook in next ch, yo, pull through 2 lps on hook, yo, pull through all 3 lps on hook (decrease completed); repeat from * across. Fasten off. **Do not turn.**

Row 2: Skip beginning ch 3, join lt. purple with sl st in first st, ch 3, **tr front post (fp—see Stitch Guide)** around next st, *[ch 1, **tr bp**—see Stitch Guide—around next st, ch 1, tr fp around next st, ch 1, tr bp around next st, ch 1, (tr, ch 2, tr) in next ch-2 sp, ch 1, tr bp around next st, ch 1, tr fp around next st, ch 1, tr bp around next st, ch 1; for **decrease,** yo 2 times, insert hook around back of post of next st, yo, pull through, (yo, pull through 2 lps on hook) 2 times], yo 2 times, skip decrease, insert hook around back of post of next st, yo, pull through, (yo, pull through 2 lps on hook) 2 times, yo, pull through all 3 lps on hook (decrease completed); repeat from * 11 more times; repeat between [ ], yo 2 times, insert hook in top of next st, yo, pull through st, (yo, pull through 2 lps on hook) 2 times, yo, pull through all 3 lps on hook. Fasten off. **Do not turn.**

Row 3: Skip beginning ch 3, join dk. turquoise with sl st in first st, ch 3, tr bp around next st,

*[ch 1, tr fp around next st, ch 1, tr bp around next st, ch 1, tr fp around next st, ch 1, (tr, ch 2, tr) in next ch-2 sp, ch 1, tr fp around next st, ch 1, tr bp around next st, ch 1, tr fp around next st, ch 1; for **decrease,** yo 2 times, insert hook around front of post of next st, yo, pull through, (yo, pull through 2 lps on hook) 2 times], skip decrease, yo 2 times, insert hook around front of post of next st, yo, pull through, (yo, pull through 2 lps on hook) 2 times, yo, pull through all 3 lps on hook (decrease completed); repeat from * 11 more times; repeat between [ ], yo 2 times, insert hook in next st, yo, pull through st, (yo, pull through 2 lps on hook) 2 times, yo, pull through all 3 lps on hook. Fasten off. **Do not turn.**

Rows 4–80: Following color sequence of lt. turquoise, dk. green, lt. green, yellow, orange, dk. orange, red, dk. purple, lt. purple, dk. turquoise, repeat rows 2 and 3 alternately, ending with row 2 and red.

Row 81: Skip beginning ch 3, join dk. purple with sl st in first st, ch 3, **dc bp** around next st, *[ch 1, dc fp around next st, ch 1, dc bp around next st, ch 1, dc fp around next st, ch 1, (dc, ch 2, dc) in next ch-2 sp, ch 1, dc fp around next st, ch 1, dc bp around next st, ch 1, dc fp around next st, ch 1; for **decrease,** yo, insert hook around front of post of next st, yo, pull through, yo, pull through 2 lps on hook], yo, skip decrease, insert hook around front of post of next st, yo, pull through, yo, pull through 2 lps on hook, yo, pull through all 3 lps on hook (decrease completed); repeat from * 11 more times; repeat between [ ], yo, insert hook in next st, yo, pull through st, yo, pull through 2 lps on hook, yo, pull through all 3 lps on hook, **do not turn or fasten off.**

Rnd 82: Working in ends of rows and in sts around outer edge, ch 3, [skip first row, tr in next row; for **picot, ch 3, sl st in top of last st made;** working in front of last st made, tr in skipped row, (tr in next unworked row, picot; working in front of last st made, tr in last row) 79 times], ch 1; for **corner, (sc, picot, sc, picot, ch 1) in last row;** *(sc bp around next st, ch 1, sc fp around next st,

continued on page 107

by Carolyn Johnson

Blueberry Ripple

FINISHED SIZE: About 52" × 70".

MATERIALS:
❑ Worsted yarn:
     19 oz. dark color (A)
     15 oz. light color (B)
     15 oz. variegated (C)
❑ H hook or size needed to obtain gauge

GAUGE: 4 dc = 1"; 2 dc rows = 1".

AFGHAN

Row 1: With A, ch 261, skip first 5 ch, *sc in next 2 ch, hdc in next 2 ch, dc in next 3 ch, (2 dc, ch 1, 2 dc) in next ch, dc in next 3 ch, hdc in next 2 ch, sc in next 2 ch, skip next 2 ch; repeat from * across, dc in last ch, turn. Fasten off. *(15 patterns made)*

NOTE: *Work remainder of pattern in* **back lps** *(see Stitch Guide).*

Row 2: Join B with sl st in first st, ch 3, skip next 2 sts, *[sc in next 2 sts, hdc in next 2 sts, dc in next 3 sts, (2 tr, ch 1, 2 tr) in next ch-1 sp, dc in next 3 sts, hdc in next 2 sts, sc in next 2 sts], skip next 4 sts; repeat from * 13 more times; repeat between [ ], skip next 2 sts, dc in last st, turn. Fasten off.

Row 3: Join C with sl st in first st, ch 3, skip next 2 sts, *[sc in next 2 sts, hdc in next 2 sts, dc in next 3 sts, (2 tr, ch 1, 2 tr) in next ch-1 sp, dc in next 3 sts, hdc in next 2 sts, sc in next 2 sts], skip next 4 sts; repeat from * 13 more times; repeat between [ ], skip next 2 sts, dc in last st, turn. Fasten off.

Row 4: Join A with sl st in first st, ch 3, skip next 2 sts, *[sc in next 2 sts, hdc in next 2 sts, dc in next 3 sts, (2 tr, ch 1, 2 tr) in next ch-1 sp, dc in next 3 sts, hdc in next 2 sts, sc in next 2 sts], skip next 4 sts; repeat from * 13 more times; repeat between [ ], skip next 2 sts, dc in last st, turn. Fasten off.

Rows 5–85: Repeat rows 2–4 consecutively.

Rnd 86: With right side facing you, join A with (sc, ch 3, sc) in end of row 1 ; spacing sts evenly across side, 2 sc in end of each row; 3 sc in first st of row 85, sc in next 9 sts, (4 sc in next ch-1 sp, sc in next 7 sts, skip next 4 sts, sc in next 7 sts) 14 times, 4 sc in next ch-1 sp, sc in next 9 sts, 3 sc in next st; spacing sts evenly across side, 2 sc in end of each row, 4 sc in other end of row 1; working on opposite side of starting ch, sc in next 6 ch, skip next 3 ch, sc in next 6 ch, (3 sc in next ch-2 sp, sc in next 6 ch, skip next 3 ch, sc in next 6 ch) across, join with sl st in first sc. Fasten off. ❦

continued from page 105

picot, ch 1) 4 times, sc bp around next st, ch 1, (sc, picot, ch 1) in next ch sp*; repeat between first and second * 11 more times, (sc bp around next st, ch 1, sc fp around next st, picot, ch 1) 4 times, sc bp around next st, ch 1, corner in next row; repeat between [ ], tr in last row, picot, sc around post of same st, picot, ch 1, (sc bp around next st, ch 1, sc fp around next st, picot, ch 1) 2 times, sc bp around next st, ch 1, (sc, picot, ch 1) in next ch sp; repeat between first and second * 12 more times, (sc bp around next st, ch 1, sc fp around next st, picot, ch 1) 2 times, sc bp around next st, ch 1, corner in first ch-3 sp, join with sl st in first tr. Fasten off. ❦

by Eunice Svinicki

Fanciful Flowers

FINISHED SIZE: About 47" × 52" without Fringe.

MATERIALS:
- ❑ Cotton or worsted yarn:
  - 51 oz. off-white
  - 15 oz. lt. green
  - 3 oz. pink
- ❑ Tapestry needle
- ❑ K hook or size needed to obtain gauge

GAUGE: 4 sc = 1"; 3 sc rows = 1".

NOTE:
Work in **back lps** *(see Stitch Guide)* unless otherwise stated.

AFGHAN

Row 1: With off-white, ch 209, 2 sc in second ch from hook, sc in next 3 ch, skip next 2 ch, sc in next 4 ch, (3 sc in next ch, sc in next 4 ch, skip next 2 ch, sc in next 4 ch) 17 times, 3 sc in next ch, sc in next 4 ch, skip next 2 ch, sc in next 3 ch, 2 sc in last ch, turn. *(208 sc made)*

Rows 2–7: Ch 1, 2 sc in first st, sc in next 3 sts, skip next 2 sts, sc in next 4 sts, (3 sc in next st, sc in next 4 sts, skip next 2 sts, sc in next 4 sts) 17 times, 3 sc in next st, sc in next 4 sts, skip next 2 sts, sc in next 3 sts, 2 sc in last st, turn.

Row 8: Working this row in **both lps,** ch 7, skip next 5 sts, tr in next st, ch 1; working behind last st made, tr in third skipped st, ch 3, (skip next 4 sts, tr in next st, ch 1; working behind last st made, tr in third skipped st, ch 3, skip next 5 sts, tr in next st, ch 1; working behind last st made, tr in third skipped st, ch 3) 18 times, skip next 2 sts, tr in last st, turn. *(76 tr, 75 ch sps)*

Row 9: Working in ch-3 and ch-1 sps, ch 1, 4 sc in first ch sp, 3 sc in next 2 ch sps, (2 sc in next ch sp, 3 sc in next 3 ch sps) across, turn. *(208 sc)*

Rows 10–111: Repeat rows 2–9 consecutively, ending with row 7. At end of last row, **do not turn.** Fasten off.

Rnd 112: Working around outer edge, join green with sc in first st, sc in each st and in end of each row around with 3 sc in each corner, join with sl st in first sc. Fasten off.

FINISHING

For each design, with pink, using french knot *(see Stitch Guide)*, embroider flowers according to illustration. With green, using cross stitch *(see Stitch Guide),* embroider leaves below flowers.

Embroider 10 designs evenly spaced across every other strip between tr rows.

FRINGE

For each Fringe, cut 2 strands green each 20" long. With both strands held together, fold in half, insert hook in st, pull fold through st, pull ends through fold, tighten.

Fringe each st on each short end of Afghan. ❧

by Ann Parnell

Beef Stew Afghan

FINISHED SIZE: Afghan is about 44" × 60".

MATERIALS:
- ❏ Worsted yarn:
  - 14 oz. off-white
  - 6 oz. each red, orange, taupe, gold and green
- ❏ K hook or size needed to obtain gauge

GAUGE: 4 dc = 1½"; 2 popcorn st rows = 1½".

NOTES:
Change colors *(see Stitch Guide)* in last st at end of each row and **fasten off previous color** before turning.

AFGHAN

Row 1: With off-white, ch 140, dc in fourth ch from hook, dc in next 5 ch, *ch 1, skip next ch; for **popcorn stitch (pc), 3 dc in next ch, drop lp from hook, insert hook in top of first dc, pull dropped lp through st;** ch 2, pc in next ch, ch 1, skip next ch, dc in next 6 ch, skip next ch, dc in next 6 ch; repeat from * across, ending last repeat with skip next ch, dc in last ch, turn. *(This side is right side of work.)* (16 pc made)

Row 2: With red, ch 2, skip next dc, dc in next 5 dc, dc in ch-1 sp, *ch 1; for **reverse popcorn (rpc), 3 dc in ch-2 sp between pcs, drop lp from hook, insert hook from back to front in top of first dc, pull dropped lp through st;** ch 2, rpc in same ch-2 sp between pcs, ch 1, dc in next ch-1 sp, dc in next 5 dc, skip next dc, dc in next 5 dc, dc in next ch-1 sp; repeat from * across ending last repeat with skip next dc, dc in last dc, turn.

Row 3: With orange, ch 2, skip next dc, dc in next 5 dc, dc in ch-1 sp, *ch 1, (pc, ch 2, pc) in ch-2 sp between rpc, ch 1, dc in next ch-1 sp, dc in next 5 dc, skip next dc, dc in next 5 dc, dc in next ch-1 sp; repeat from * across ending last repeat with skip next dc, dc in ch 2, turn.

Rows 4–15: Repeat rows 2 and 3 alternately for pattern using the following color sequence for each row.

Row 4: Off-white
Row 5: Taupe
Row 6: Gold
Row 7: Off-white
Row 8: Green
Row 9: Red
Row 10: Off-white
Row 11: Orange
Row 12: Taupe
Row 13: Off-white
Row 14: Gold
Row 15: Green

Rows 16–60: (Repeat rows 2 and 3 alternately, using color sequence of rows 1–15) 3 times.

Row 61: With off-white, repeat row 3, fasten off. ❦

Baked Beef Stew

On a large piece of heavy-duty foil combine:
- ½ lb. beef, cut into small chunks
- 6 medium carrots, thinly sliced
- 3 medium potatoes, cubed
- 1 large onion, sliced
- 1 medium green pepper, sliced
- 1 cup barbecue sauce

Fold edges of foil in and seal, place in baking dish (in case of leaks) and bake at 350 degrees F. for about 75 minutes (check carrots for tenderness). Serves 2.

Just for Him

These manly colors and chunky stitch patterns are sure to appeal to masculine sensibilities. Even if he's not a cuddler, he'll appreciate the artistic detail of our Antique Autos afghan. Warm his heart with bold blocks, the look of barnyard bandannas, a motif that echoes the spokes of a wheel or Sandstone ruggedness. He'll love you for it!

by Ruth La Madrid

Antique Autos

FINISHED SIZE: About 53½" × 70½".

MATERIALS:
- ❏ Worsted yarn:
   - 45 oz. main color (MC)
   - 21 oz. contrasting color (CC)
   - 6 oz. brown
- ❏ Tapestry needle
- ❏ No. 8 afghan hook and G and F crochet hooks or sizes needed to obtain gauges

GAUGES: Afghan hook or F crochet hook, 9 sts = 2"; 9 rows = 2". **G hook,** 4 sts = 1"; (2 sc rows and 1 dc row = 1 pattern rows) 1 pattern rows = 1". Block is 13" × 14½".

NOTE:
Each square on graph equals 1 afghan stitch.

BLOCK (make 15)
Row 1: With MC and afghan hook, ch 65; work row 1 of afghan stitch *(see Stitch Guide).*

Rows 2–56: Work row 2 of afghan stitch *(see Stitch Guide).*

Row 57: Skip first vertical bar, sl st in each bar across. Fasten off.

Rnd 58: With F hook, working around outer edge, join CC with sc in any st, sc in each st, in each ch and in each row around with 3 sc in each corner, join with sl st in first sc. Fasten off.

PANEL (make 2)
NOTE: *All rows of Panel are worked in* **front lps** *(see Stitch Guide).*

Row 1: With G hook and CC, ch 21, sc in second ch from hook, sc in each ch across, turn. *(20 sc made)*

Row 2: Ch 3, dc in each st across, turn.

Row 3: Ch 1, sc in each st across, turn.

Row 4: Ch 3, dc in next 7 sts, skip next st; for **woven long dc (woven ldc), yo, insert hook from front to back around post of 10th st on row before last, yo, pull long lp through st, (yo, pull through 2 lps on hook) 2 times;** dc in next 2 sts, skip next st, woven ldc around 11th st on row before last, dc in last 8 sts, turn.

Row 5: Ch 1, sc in each st across, turn.

Row 6: Ch 3, dc in next 6 sts, (skip next st, woven ldc around post of next woven ldc on row before last, dc in next 4 sts) 2 times, dc in last 3 sts, turn.

Row 7: Ch 1, sc in each st across, turn.

Row 8: Ch 3, dc in next 5 sts, (skip next st, woven ldc around post of next woven ldc on row before last, dc in next 6 sts) 2 times, turn.

Row 9: Ch 1, sc in each st across, turn.

Row 10: Ch 3, dc in next 6 sts, (skip next st, woven ldc around post of next woven ldc on row before last, dc in next 4 sts) 2 times, dc in last 3 sts, turn.

Row 11: Ch 1, sc in each st across, turn.

Row 12: Ch 3, dc in next 7 sts, skip next st, woven ldc around post of 10th st on row before last, dc in next 2 sts, skip next st, woven ldc around 11th st on row before last, dc in last 8 sts, turn.

Row 13: Ch 1, sc in each st across, turn.

Row 14: Ch 3, dc in next 8 sts, skip next 2 sts, woven ldc around post of next 2 woven ldc, dc in last 9 sts, turn.

Rows 15–158: Repeat rows 3–14 consecutively.

Row 159: Ch 1, sc in each st across. Fasten off.

Using Cross-stitch *(see Stitch Guide),* embroider eight Blocks according to graphs.

Matching sts and corners of Blocks, working in **back lps,** sew together.

EDGING
Rnd 1: With F hook, working around outer edge in **back lps,** join CC with sc in any st, sc in each st around with 3 sc in each corner, join with sl st in first sc.

Rnd 2: Ch 2, hdc in each st around with 3 hdc in each corner, join with sl st in top of ch 2. Fasten off. ❧

= CC
= BROWN

GRAPH #1
MAKE 2

FIRST VERTICAL BAR

LAST VERTICAL BAR

GRAPH #2
MAKE 2

FIRST VERTICAL BAR

LAST VERTICAL BAR

GRAPH #3

FIRST VERTICAL BAR

LAST VERTICAL BAR

GRAPH #4

FIRST VERTICAL BAR

LAST VERTICAL BAR

GRAPH #5

FIRST VERTICAL BAR

LAST VERTICAL BAR

GRAPH #6

FIRST VERTICAL BAR

LAST VERTICAL BAR

by Anna Kemp

Sandstone Afghan

FINISHED SIZE: About 60¼" square.

MATERIALS:
- ❑ Worsted yarn:
  24 oz. each lt. beige, med. orange and rust
  2 oz. black
- ❑ G hook or size needed to obtain gauge

GAUGE: 4 sc = 1"; 4 sc rows = 1".

SPECIAL STITCH:

For **long double crochet (ldc)**, dc in **front lp** *(see Stitch Guide)* of next st on row before last.

NOTES:

For Fringe, leave 6" strand at beginning and end of each row.

Work entire pattern in **back lps** unless otherwise stated.

Join each row with sc and count as first st.

Fasten off at end of each row, **do not turn.**

AFGHAN

Row 1: With rust, ch 241. Fasten off. With rust, sc in each ch across. *(241 sc made)*

Rows 2–9. Sc in each st across.

Row 10: With black, sc in first 120 sts, ldc *(see Special Stitch)*, sc in last 120 sts.

Row 11: With lt. beige, sc in first 119 sts, ldc, sc in next st, ldc, sc in last 119 sts.

Row 12: Sc in first 118 sts, ldc, sc in next 3 sts, ldc, sc in last 118 sts.

Row 13: Sc in first 117 sts, ldc, sc in next 5 sts, ldc, sc in last 117 sts.

Row 14: Sc in first 116 sts, ldc, sc in next 7 sts, ldc, sc in last 116 sts.

Row 15: Sc in first 115 sts, ldc, sc in next 9 sts, ldc, sc in last 115 sts.

Row 16: Sc in first 114 sts, ldc, sc in next 11 sts, ldc, sc in last 114 sts.

Row 17: With med. orange, sc in first 113 sts, ldc, sc in next 13 sts, ldc, sc in last 113 sts.

Row 18: Sc in first 112 sts, ldc, sc in next 15 sts, ldc, sc in last 112 sts.

Row 19: Sc in first 111 sts, ldc, sc in next 17 sts, ldc, sc in last 111 sts.

Row 20: Sc in first 110 sts, ldc, sc in next 19 sts, ldc, sc in last 110 sts.

Row 21: Sc in first 109 sts, ldc, sc in next 21 sts, ldc, sc in last 109 sts.

Row 22: Sc in first 108 sts, ldc, sc in next 23 sts, ldc, sc in last 108 sts.

Row 23: With rust, sc in first 107 sts, ldc, sc in next 25 sts, ldc, sc in last 107 sts.

Row 24: Sc in first 106 sts, ldc, sc in next 27 sts, ldc, sc in last 106 sts.

Row 25: Sc in first 105 sts, ldc, sc in next 29 sts, ldc, sc in last 105 sts.

Row 26: Sc in first 104 sts, ldc, sc in next 31 sts, ldc, sc in last 104 sts.

Row 27: Sc in first 103 sts, ldc, sc in next 33 sts, ldc, sc in last 103 sts.

Row 28: Sc in first 102 sts, ldc, sc in next 35 sts, ldc, sc in last 102 sts.

Row 29: With lt. beige, sc in first 101 sts, ldc, sc in next 37 sts, ldc, sc in last 101 sts.

Row 30: Sc in first 100 sts, ldc, sc in next 39 sts, ldc, sc in last 100 sts.

Row 31: Sc in first 99 sts, ldc, sc in next 41 sts, ldc, sc in last 99 sts.

Row 32: Sc in first 98 sts, ldc, sc in next 43 sts, ldc, sc in last 98 sts.

Row 33: Sc in first 97 sts, ldc, sc in next 45 sts, ldc, sc in last 97 sts.

Row 34: Sc in first 96 sts, ldc, sc in next 47 sts, ldc, sc in last 96 sts.

Row 35: With med. orange, sc in first 95 sts, ldc, sc in next 49 sts, ldc, sc in last 95 sts.

Row 36: Sc in first 94 sts, ldc, sc in next 51 sts, ldc, sc in last 94 sts.

Row 37: Sc in first 93 sts, ldc, sc in next 53 sts, ldc, sc in last 93 sts.

Row 38: Sc in first 92 sts, ldc, sc in next 55 sts, ldc, sc in last 92 sts.

Row 39: Sc in first 91 sts, ldc, sc in next 57 sts, ldc, sc in last 91 sts.

Row 40: Sc in first 90 sts, ldc, sc in next 59 sts, ldc, sc in last 90 sts.

continued on page 118

Sandstone Afghan

continued from page 117

Row 41: With rust, sc in first 89 sts, ldc, sc in next 61 sts, ldc, sc in last 89 sts.

Row 42: Sc in first 88 sts, ldc, sc in next 63 sts, ldc, sc in last 88 sts.

Row 43: Sc in first 87 sts, ldc, sc in next 65 sts, ldc, sc in last 87 sts.

Row 44: Sc in first 86 sts, ldc, sc in next 67 sts, ldc, sc in last 86 sts.

Row 45: Sc in first 85 sts, ldc, sc in next 69 sts, ldc, sc in last 85 sts.

Row 46: Sc in first 84 sts, ldc, sc in next 71 sts, ldc, sc in last 84 sts.

Row 47: With black, sc in first 83 sts, (ldc, sc in next 36 sts) 2 times, ldc, sc in last 83 sts. *(241 sts)*

Row 48: With lt. beige, sc in first 82 sts, ldc, sc in next 36 sts, ldc, sc in next st, ldc, sc in next 36 sts, ldc, sc in last 82 sts.

Row 49: Sc in first 81 sts, ldc, sc in next 36 sts, ldc, sc in next 3 sts, ldc, sc in next 36 sts, ldc, sc in last 81 sts.

Row 50: Sc in first 80 sts, ldc, sc in next 36 sts, ldc, sc in next 5 sts, ldc, sc in next 36 sts, ldc, sc in last 80 sts.

Row 51: Sc in first 79 sts, ldc, sc in next 36 sts, ldc, sc in next 7 sts, ldc, sc in next 36 sts, ldc, sc in last 79 sts.

Row 52: Sc in first 78 sts, ldc, sc in next 36 sts, ldc, sc in next 9 sts, ldc, sc in next 36 sts, ldc, sc in last 78 sts.

Row 53: Sc in first 77 sts, ldc, sc in next 36 sts, ldc, sc in next 11 sts, ldc, sc in next 36 sts, ldc, sc in last 77 sts.

Row 54: With med. orange, sc in first 76 sts, ldc, sc in next 36 sts, ldc, sc in next 13 sts, ldc, sc in next 36 sts, ldc, sc in last 76 sts.

Row 55: Sc in first 75 sts, ldc, sc in next 36 sts, ldc, sc in next 15 sts, ldc, sc in next 36 sts, ldc, sc in last 75 sts.

Row 56: Sc in first 74 sts, ldc, sc in next 36 sts, ldc, sc in next 17 sts, ldc, sc in next 36 sts, ldc, sc in last 74 sts.

Row 57: Sc in first 73 sts, ldc, sc in next 36 sts, ldc, sc in next 19 sts, ldc, sc in next 36 sts, ldc, sc in last 73 sts.

Row 58: Sc in first 72 sts, ldc, sc in next 36 sts, ldc, sc in next 21 sts, ldc, sc in next 36 sts, ldc, sc in last 72 sts.

Row 59: Sc in first 71 sts, ldc, sc in next 36 sts, ldc, sc in next 23 sts, ldc, sc in next 36 sts, ldc, sc in last 71 sts.

Row 60: With rust, sc in first 70 sts, ldc, sc in next 36 sts, ldc, sc in next 25 sts, ldc, sc in next 36 sts, ldc, sc in last 70 sts.

Row 61: Sc in first 69 sts, ldc, sc in next 36 sts, ldc, sc in next 27 sts, ldc, sc in next 36 sts, ldc, sc in last 69 sts.

Row 62: Sc in first 68 sts, ldc, sc in next 36 sts, ldc, sc in next 29 sts, ldc, sc in next 36 sts, ldc, sc in last 68 sts.

Row 63: Sc in first 67 sts, ldc, sc in next 36 sts, ldc, sc in next 31 sts, ldc, sc in next 36 sts, ldc, sc in last 67 sts.

Row 64: Sc in first 66 sts, ldc, sc in next 36 sts, ldc, sc in next 33 sts, ldc, sc in next 36 sts, ldc, sc in last 66 sts.

Row 65: Sc in first 65 sts, ldc, sc in next 36 sts, ldc, sc in next 35 sts, ldc, sc in next 36 sts, ldc, sc in last 65 sts.

Row 66: With lt. beige, sc in first 64 sts, ldc, sc in next 36 sts, ldc, sc in next 37 sts, ldc, sc in next 36 sts, ldc, sc in last 64 sts.

Row 67: Sc in first 63 sts, ldc, sc in next 36 sts, ldc, sc in next 39 sts, ldc, sc in next 36 sts, ldc, sc in last 63 sts.

Row 68: Sc in first 62 sts, ldc, sc in next 36 sts, ldc, sc in next 41 sts, ldc, sc in next 36 sts, ldc, sc in last 62 sts.

Row 69: Sc in first 61 sts, ldc, sc in next 36 sts, ldc, sc in next 43 sts, ldc, sc in next 36 sts, ldc, sc in last 61 sts.

Row 70: Sc in first 60 sts, ldc, sc in next 36 sts, ldc, sc in next 45 sts, ldc, sc in next 36 sts, ldc, sc in last 60 sts.

Row 71: Sc in first 59 sts, ldc, sc in next 36 sts, ldc, sc in next 47 sts, ldc, sc in next 36 sts, ldc, sc in last 59 sts.

Row 72: With med. orange, sc in first 58 sts, ldc, sc in next 36 sts, ldc, sc in next 49 sts, ldc, sc in next 36 sts, ldc, sc in last 58 sts.

Row 73: Sc in first 57 sts, ldc, sc in next 36 sts, ldc, sc in next 51 sts, ldc, sc in next 36 sts, ldc, sc in last 57 sts.

Row 74: Sc in first 56 sts, ldc, sc in next 36 sts, ldc, sc in next 53 sts, ldc, sc in next 36 sts, ldc, sc in last 56 sts.

Row 75: Sc in first 55 sts, (ldc, sc in next 36 sts, ldc, sc in next 55 sts) across.

Row 76: Sc in first 54 sts, ldc, sc in next 36 sts, ldc, sc in next 57 sts, ldc, sc in next 36 sts, ldc, sc in last 54 sts.

Row 77: Sc in first 53 sts, ldc, sc in next 36 sts, ldc, sc in next 59 sts, ldc, sc in next 36 sts, ldc, sc in last 53 sts.

Row 78: With rust, sc in first 52 sts, ldc, sc in next 36 sts, ldc, sc in next 61 sts, ldc, sc in next 36 sts, ldc, sc in last 52 sts.

Row 79: Sc in first 51 sts, ldc, sc in next 36 sts, ldc, sc in next 63 sts, ldc, sc in next 36 sts, ldc, sc in last 51 sts.

Row 80: Sc in first 50 sts, ldc, sc in next 36 sts, ldc, sc in next 65 sts, ldc, sc in next 36 sts, ldc, sc in last 50 sts.

Row 81: Sc in first 49 sts, ldc, sc in next 36 sts, ldc, sc in next 67 sts, ldc, sc in next 36 sts, ldc, sc in last 49 sts.

Row 82: Sc in first 48 sts, ldc, sc in next 36 sts, ldc, sc in next 69 sts, ldc, sc in next 36 sts, ldc, sc in last 48 sts.

Row 83: Sc in first 47 sts, ldc, sc in next 36 sts, ldc, sc in next 71 sts, ldc, sc in next 36 sts, ldc, sc in last 47 sts.

Row 84: With black, sc in first 46 sts, (ldc, sc in next 36 sts) 4 times, ldc, sc in last 46 sts.

Row 85: With lt. beige, sc in first 45 sts, *(ldc, sc in next 36 sts) 2 times, ldc*, sc in next st; repeat between first and second *, sc in last 45 sts.

Row 86: Sc in first 44 sts, *(ldc, sc in next 36 sts) 2 times, ldc*, sc in next 3 sts; repeat between first and second *, sc in last 44 sts.

Row 87: Sc in first 43 sts, *(ldc, sc in next 36 sts) 2 times, ldc*, sc in next 5 sts; repeat between first and second *, sc in last 43 sts.

Row 88: Sc in first 42 sts, *(ldc, sc in next 36 sts) 2 times, ldc*, sc in next 7 sts; repeat between first and second *, sc in last 42 sts.

Row 89: Sc in first 41 sts, *(ldc, sc in next 36 sts) 2 times, ldc*, sc in next 9 sts; repeat between first and second *, sc in last 41 sts.

Row 90: Sc in first 40 sts, *(ldc, sc in next 36 sts) 2 times, ldc*, sc in next 11 sts; repeat between first and second *, sc in last 40 sts.

Row 91: With med. orange, sc in first 39 sts, *(ldc, sc in next 36 sts) 2 times, ldc*, sc in next 13 sts; repeat between first and second *, sc in last 39 sts.

Row 92: Sc in first 38 sts, *(ldc, sc in next 36 sts) 2 times, ldc*, sc in next 15 sts; repeat between first and second *, sc in last 38 sts.

Row 93: Sc in first 37 sts, *(ldc, sc in next 36 sts) 2 times, ldc*, sc in next 17 sts; repeat between first and second *, sc in last 37 sts.

Row 94: Sc in first 36 sts, *(ldc, sc in next 36 sts) 2 times, ldc*, sc in next 19 sts; repeat between first and second *, sc in last 36 sts.

Row 95: Sc in first 35 sts, *(ldc, sc in next 36 sts) 2 times, ldc*, sc in next 21 sts; repeat between first and second *, sc in last 35 sts.

Row 96: Sc in first 34 sts, *(ldc, sc in next 36 sts) 2 times, ldc*, sc in next 23 sts; repeat between first and second *, sc in last 34 sts.

Row 97: With rust, sc in first 33 sts, *(ldc, sc in next 36 sts) 2 times, ldc*, sc in next 25 sts; repeat between first and second *, sc in last 33 sts.

Row 98: Sc in first 32 sts, *(ldc, sc in next 36 sts) 2 times, ldc*, sc in next 27 sts; repeat between first and second *, sc in last 32 sts.

Row 99: Sc in first 31 sts, *(ldc, sc in next 36 sts) 2 times, ldc*, sc in next 29 sts; repeat between first and second *, sc in last 31 sts.

Row 100: Sc in first 30 sts, *(ldc, sc in next 36 sts) 2 times, ldc*, sc in next 31 sts; repeat between first and second *, sc in last 30 sts.

Row 101: Sc in first 29 sts, *(ldc, sc in next 36 sts) 2 times, ldc*, sc in next 33 sts; repeat between first and second *, sc in last 29 sts.

Row 102: Sc in first 28 sts, *(ldc, sc in next 36 sts) 2 times, ldc*, sc in next 35 sts; repeat between first and second *, sc in last 28 sts.

Row 103: With lt. beige, sc in first 27 sts, *(ldc, sc in next 36 sts) 2 times, ldc*, sc in next 37 sts; repeat between first and second *, sc in last 27 sts.

Row 104: Sc in first 26 sts, *(ldc, sc in next 36 sts) 2 times, ldc*, sc in next 39 sts; repeat between first and second *, sc in last 26 sts.

Row 105: Sc in first 25 sts, *(ldc, sc in next 36 sts) 2 times, ldc*, sc in next 41 sts; repeat between first and second *, sc in last 25 sts.

Row 106: Sc in first 24 sts, *(ldc, sc in next 36 sts) 2 times, ldc*, sc in next 43 sts; repeat between first and second *, sc in last 24 sts.

Row 107: Sc in first 23 sts, *(ldc, sc in next 36 sts) 2 times, ldc*, sc in next 45 sts; repeat between first and second *, sc in last 23 sts.

Row 108: Sc in first 22 sts, *(ldc, sc in next 36 sts) 2 times, ldc*, sc in next 47 sts; repeat between first and second *, sc in last 22 sts.

Row 109: With med. orange, sc in first 21 sts, *(ldc, sc in next 36 sts) 2 times, ldc*, sc in next 49 sts; repeat between first and second *, sc in last 21 sts.

Row 110: Sc in first 20 sts, *(ldc, sc in next 36 sts) 2 times, ldc*, sc in next 51 sts; repeat between

continued on page 127

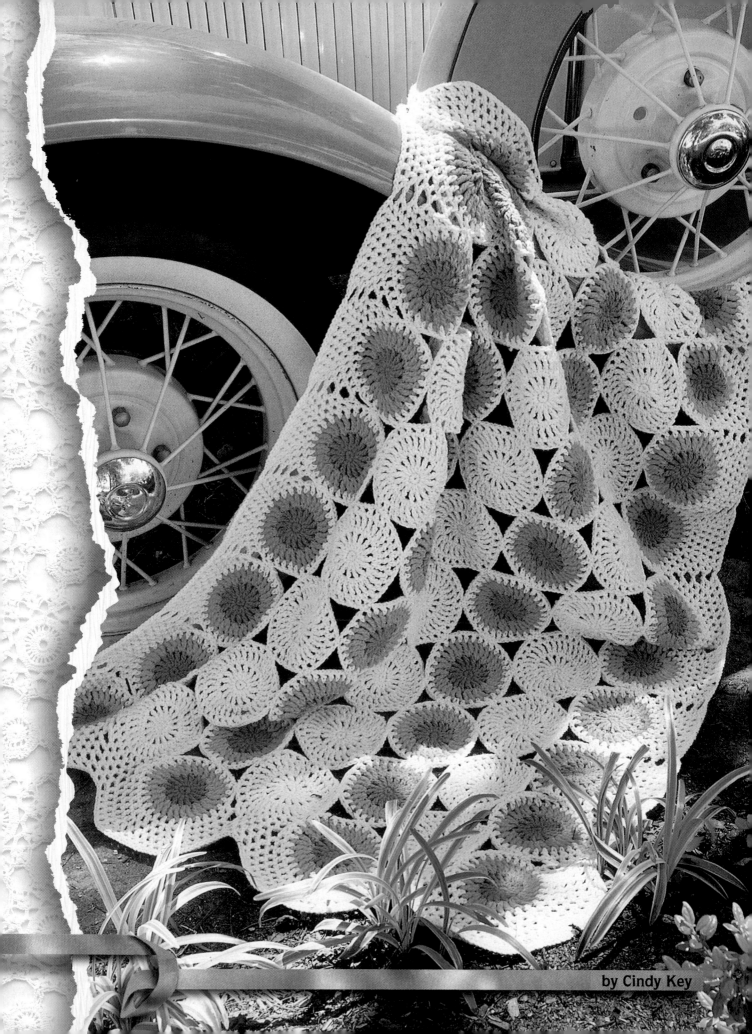

by Cindy Key

Circles & Stripes

FINISHED SIZE: About 40" × 60".

MATERIALS:
- ❏ Worsted yarn:
  - 25 oz. off-white
  - 4 oz. peach
  - 5 oz. green
- ❏ Tapestry needle
- ❏ J hook or size needed to obtain gauge

GAUGE: Each Motif — 5".

COLOR MOTIF (make 40)

Rnd 1: With peach, ch 2, 8 sc in second ch from hook, join with sl st in first sc. *(8 sc made)*

Rnd 2: Ch 4, tr in same st, (ch 1, tr, ch 1, tr) in each st around, ch 1, join with sl st in third ch of ch 4. Fasten off. *(16 tr)*

Rnd 3: Join green with (sl st, ch 4, tr) in any ch-1 sp, (ch 1, tr, ch 1, tr) in each ch-1 sp around, ch 1, join. Fasten off. *(32 tr)*

Rnd 4: Join off-white with sl st in any ch-1 sp, ch 3, (dc, ch 1) in each ch-1 sp around, join. Fasten off.

SOLID MOTIF (make 27)

Rnd 1: With off-white, ch 2, 8 sc in second ch from hook, join with sl st in first sc. *(8 sc made)*

Rnd 2: Ch 4, tr in same st, (ch 1, tr, ch 1, tr) in each st around, ch 1, join. *(16 tr)*

Rnd 3: (Sl st, ch 4, tr) in first ch-1 sp, (ch 1, tr, ch 1, tr) in each ch-1 sp around, ch 1, join. *(32 tr)*

Rnd 4: Sl st in first ch-1 sp, ch 3, (dc, ch 1) in each ch-1 sp around, join. Fasten off.

ASSEMBLY

Color Strip (make 4)

Sew first 3 sts on first Motif to 17th, 18th and 19th sts on second Motif; sew first 3 sts on second Motif to 17th, 18th and 19th sts on third Motif; repeat, joining seven more Motifs.

Solid Strips (make 3)

Work same as Color Strip.

Arrange ends of Strips as shown in illustration, sew 2 sts of Solid Motif to 2 sts of Color Motif, skip next 3 sts on Solid Motif, sew next 2 sts to 2 sts on next Color Motif, skip next 3 sts on Color Motif, sew next 2 sts to 2 sts on next Solid Motif; repeat, joining all Motifs of all Strips.

Edging

Rnd 1: As shown in illustration, join off-white with (sl st, ch 4, dc) in first ch sp, ch 1, dc in next ch sp, ch 1; for **V stitch (V st), (dc, ch 1, dc, ch 1)** in next ch sp; [[(dc in next ch sp, ch 1, V st in next ch sp) 2 times, (dc, ch 1) in next 8 ch sps, *skip next 2 ch sps at joining seam, (dc, ch 1) in next 4 ch sps, V st in next ch sp, (dc, ch 1) in next 2 ch sps, V st in next ch sp, (dc, ch 1) in next 4 ch sps; repeat from first * 7 times, skip next 2 ch sps at joining seam, (dc, ch 1) in next 8 ch sps, (V st in next ch sp, dc in next ch sp, ch 1) 4 times, (dc, ch 1) in next 8 ch sps; working across end, skip next 2 ch sps at next joining seam, (dc, ch 1) in next 8 ch sps, *skip next 2 ch sps at next joining seam, (dc, ch 1) in next 7 ch sps, V st in next ch sp, (dc, ch 1) in next 2 ch sps, V st in next ch sp, (dc, ch 1) in next 7 ch sps, skip next 2 ch sps at joining seam, (dc, ch 1) in next 8 ch sps; repeat from second * one time, skip next 2 ch sps at next joining seam, (dc, ch 1) in next 8 ch sps], V st in next ch sp, dc in next ch sp, ch 1, V st in next ch sp; repeat between [ ], join with sl st in third ch.

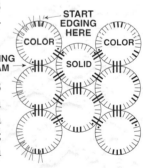

Rnd 2: (Sl st, ch 4, dc) in next ch sp, (dc, ch 1) in each ch sp and V st in each V st around skipping next 3 ch sps at joining seams, join with sl st in third ch of beginning ch 4.

Rnds 3–5: (Sl st, ch 4, dc) in next ch sp, *(dc, ch 1) in each ch sp and V st in each V st across side, skipping next 3 ch sps at joining seams; working across end, (dc, ch 1) in each ch sp and V st in each V st, skipping each ch sp at center of joining seam; repeat from * one more time, join. At end of rnd 5, fasten off. ❦

by Rise Cleary

Diamond X

FINISHED SIZE: Afghan is about 36" × 55"; Pillow is 16" square.

MATERIALS:
- ❏ Worsted yarn:
  - 27½ oz. black
  - 3 oz. each beige, red and gray
  - 2 oz. each white and off-white
- ❏ Polyester fiberfill
- ❏ Tapestry needle
- ❏ J afghan hook or size needed to obtain gauge

GAUGE: 3 sc = 1"; 3 sc rows = 1".

PILLOW

Front

Row 1: With black, ch 32, work row 1 of afghan st *(see Stitch Guide). (32 sts made)*

Rows 2–30: Work row 2 of afghan st *(see Stitch Guide).*

Row 31: Ch 1, sc in each st across. Fasten off.

Rnd 32: Working in rnds, join white with sc in first st of row 31, 2 sc in same st, sc in next 14 sts; for **long arm stitch (la), yo 9 times, insert hook in next vertical bar on row 19, yo, pull through bar, (yo, pull through 2 lps on hook) 10 times;** sc in next 16 sts, 3 sc in end of row, sc in end of next 14 rows, la in 12th vertical bar from edge on row 16, sc in end of next 15 rows; working on opposite side of starting ch, 3 sc in next ch, sc in next 14 ch, la in next vertical bar on row 12, sc in next 15 ch, 3 sc in end of row, sc in end of next 14 rows, la in 12th vertical bar from edge on row 16, sc in end of next 15 rows, join with sl st in first sc. Fasten off. *(132)*

NOTE: *Working remaining rnds in **back lps** (see Stitch Guide).*

Rnd 33: Join off-white with sc in second st on rnd 32, 2 sc in same st, (sc in next 14 sts, la in next vertical bar above la of previous rnd, sc in next st, la in next vertical bar above la of previous rnd, sc in next 15 sts) around with 3 sc in each corner, join. Fasten off. *(140)*

Rnd 34: Join beige with sc in second st of rnd 33, 2 sc in same st, (sc in next 14 sts, la in next vertical bar above la of previous rnd, sc in next 3 sts, la in next vertical bar above la of previous rnd, sc in next 15 sts) around with 3 sc in each corner, join. *(148)*

Rnd 35: Ch 1, sc in first st, 3 sc in next st, (*sc in next 14 sts, la in next vertical bar above la of previous rnd, sc in next 5 sts, la in next vertical bar above la of previous rnd*, sc in next 15 sts, 3 sc in next st) 3 times; repeat between first and second *, sc in next 14 sts, join. Fasten off. *(156)*

Rnd 36: Join gray with sc in third st on rnd 35, 2 sc in same st, (sc in next 14 sts, la in next vertical bar above la of previous rnd, sc in next 7 sts, la in next vertical bar above la of previous rnd, sc in next 15 sts) around with 3 sc in each corner, join. *(164)*

Rnd 37: Ch 1, sc in first st, 3 sc in next st, (*sc in next 14 sts, la in next vertical bar above la of previous rnd, sc in next 9 sts, la in next vertical bar above la of previous rnd *, sc in next 15 sts, 3 sc in next st) 3 times; repeat between first and second *, sc in next 14 sts, join. Fasten off. *(172)*

Rnd 38: Join red with sc in third st on rnd 37, 2 sc in same st, (sc in next 14 sts, la in next vertical bar above la of previous rnd, sc in next 11 sts, la in vertical bar above la of previous rnd, sc in next 15 sts) around with 3 sc in each corner, join. Fasten off. *(180)*

Rnd 39: Join black with sc in second st on rnd 38, 2 sc in same st, (sc in next 14 sts, la in next vertical bar above la of previous rnd, sc in next 13 sts, la in next vertical bar above la of previous rnd, sc in next 15 sts) around with 3 sc in each corner, join. *(188)*

Rnd 40: Ch 1, sc in first st, 3 sc in next st, sc in next 14 sts, la in vertical bar above la of previous rnd, sc in next 15 sts, la in next vertical bar above la of previous rnd, sc in next 14 sts, (sc in next st, 3 sc in next st, sc in next 14 sts, la in next vertical bar above la of previous rnd, sc in next 15 sts, la in next vertical bar above la of previous rnd, sc in next 14 sts) around, join. *(196)*

continued on page 126

by Sandra Smith

Bandanna Afghan

continued on page 126

FINISHED SIZE: About 56" × 71".

MATERIALS:
- ❑ Worsted yarn:
  - 36 oz. red
  - 17 oz. variegated red
  - 13 oz. white
- ❑ Tapestry needle
- ❑ I hook or size needed to obtain gauge

GAUGE: 3 dc = 1"; 2 dc rows = 1".

FLOWER MOTIF (make 4)
Triangle (make 4)
Rnd 1: With variegated red, ch 2, 9 sc in second ch from hook, join with sl st in first sc. *(9 sc made)*

Rnd 2: (Ch 3, 2 dc, ch 1, 3 dc) in first st, ch 1, skip next 2 sts, *(3 dc, ch 1, 3 dc) in next st, ch 1, skip next 2 sts; repeat from * around, join with sl st in top of ch 3. Fasten off. *(18 dc)*

Square
Rnd 1: With red, ch 2, 8 sc in second ch from hook, join with sl st in first sc. *(8 sc made)*

Rnd 2: (Ch 3, 2 dc, ch 1, 3 dc) in first st, ch 1, skip next st, *(3 dc, ch 1, 3 dc) in next st, ch 1, skip next st; repeat from * around, join with sl st in top of ch 3. Fasten off. *(24 dc)*

BLOCK ASSEMBLY
Matching sts and leaving ch-1 corners free, with white, sew **back lps** *(see Stitch Guide)* on one side of Triangle to **back lps** on one side of Square. Repeat on three other sides of Square.

NOTE: All joinings of Motifs are worked in back lps of sts and chs.

On first Motif, join white with sc in any corner ch-1 sp on Square, (sc in next 17 sts around Triangle, sc in next corner on ch-1 sp on Square) 3 times, sc in last 17 sts around Triangle, join with sl st in first sc. Fasten off. *(72 sc)*

On second Motif, join white with sc in any corner ch-1 sp on Square, sc in next 8 sts; working through both thicknesses, sc next 3 sts and 9th,

8th and 7th sts of Triangle on first Motif together *(see illustration)*, sc in next 6 sts, sc in next corner ch-1 sp on Square, sc in next 6 sts; working through both thicknesses, sc next 3 sts and 11th, 10th and 9th sts on corresponding Triangle on first Motif together *(see illustration)*, sc in next 8 sts, (sc in next corner ch-1 sp on Square, sc in next 17 sts of triangle) 2 times, join with sl st in first sc. Fasten off.

Join third Motif to first Motif the same as second Motif.

On the fourth Motif, join white with sc in corner ch-1 sp on Square, sc in next 8 sts; working through both thicknesses, sc each of next 3 sts and 9th, 8th and 7th sts on Triangle on second Motif together, sc in next 6 sts, sc in corner ch-1 of Square, sc in next 6 sts; working through both thicknesses, sc next 5 sts and 11th and 10th sts of Triangle on second Motif, 9th st of Triangle on first Motif, 8th and 7th sts on Triangle of third Motif together, sc in next 6 sts, sc in next corner ch-1 sp of Square, sc in next 6 sts; working through both thicknesses, sc each of next 3 sts and 11th, 10th and 9th sts of Triangle on third Motif together, sc in next 8 sts, sc in next corner ch-1 sp of Square, sc in next 17 sts, join with sl st in first sc. Fasten off.

BORDER
Rnd 1: Working this rnd in **back lps,** join red with sc in end st of joining seam between Flower Motifs *(see illustration)*, *sc in next 4 sts, hdc in next st, dc in next st, skip next 5 sts, dc in next st, hdc in next st, sc in next 4 sts, (2 sc, ch 1, 2 sc) in next st, sc in next 4 sts, hdc in next st, dc in next st, skip next 5 sts, dc in next st, hdc in next st, sc in next 4 sts, sc in joining seam; repeat from

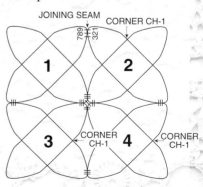

Diamond X

continued from page 125

Rnd 41: Ch 1, sc in first 2 sts, 3 sc in next st, sc in next 14 sts, la in next vertical bar above la of previous rnd, sc in next 17 sts, la in next vertical bar above la of previous rnd, sc in next 13 sts, (sc in next 2 sts, 3 sc in next st, sc in next 14 sts, la in next vertical bar above la of previous rnd, sc in next 17 sts, la in next vertical bar above la of previous rnd, sc in next 13 sts) around, join. *(204)*

Rnd 42: Ch 1, sc in first 3 sts, 3 sc in next st, sc in next 14 sts, la in next vertical bar above la of previous rnd, sc in next 19 sts, la in next vertical bar above la of previous rnd, sc in next 12 sts, (sc in next 3 sts, 3 sc in next st, sc in next 14 sts, la in next vertical bar above la of previous rnd, sc in next 19 sts, la in next vertical bar above la of previous rnd, sc in next 12 sts) around, join. *(212)*

Rnd 43: Ch 1, sc in first 4 sts, 3 sc in next st, sc in next 14 sts, la in next vertical bar above la of previous rnd, sc in next 21 sts, la in next vertical bar above la of previous rnd, sc in next 11 sts, (sc in next 4 sts, 3 sc in next st, sc in next 14 sts, la in next vertical bar above la of previous rnd, sc in next 21 sts, la in next vertical bar above la of previous rnd, sc in next 11 sts) around, join. *(220)*

Rnd 44: Working this rnd in **both lps,** ch 1, sc in each st around with 3 sc in each corner, join. Fasten off.

Back

Row 1: With black, ch 49, sc in second ch from hook, sc in each ch across, turn. *(48 sc made)*

Rows 2–54: Ch 1, sc in each st across, turn. At end of row 54, fasten off.

Assembly

With wrong sides together, easing to fit, sew Front to Back on three sides. Stuff. Sew opening closed.

AFGHAN
Square (make 6)
Work same as Pillow Front.

Assembly

Working through **back lps** and matching sts, sew Squares together.

Border

Rnd 1: Join black with sc in any st, sc in each st around with 3 sc in each corner, join with sl st in first sc.

Rnd 2: Ch 1, sc in each st around with 3 sc in each corner, join.

Rnd 3: Sl st in each st around, join with sl st in first sl st. Fasten off. ❦

Bandanna Afghan

continued from page 125

* 3 more times ending with sc in last 4 sts, join with sl st in first sc. *(120 sts made)*

Rnd 2: Ch 3, 2 dc in same st, *skip next st, 3 dc in next st, skip next 2 sts, 3 dc in next st, skip next st, 3 dc in sp between next 2 dc, skip next st, 3 dc in next st, skip next 2 sts, 3 dc in next st, skip next 3 sts, (3 dc, ch 1, 3 dc) in next ch-1 sp, skip next 3 sts, 3 dc in next st, skip next 2 sts, 3 dc in next st, skip next st, 3 dc in sp between next 2 dc, skip next st, 3 dc in next st, skip next 2 sts, 3 dc in next st, skip next st, 3 dc in next st; repeat from * around ending with skip last st, join with sl st in top of ch 3. *(156 dc)*

Rnd 3: Sl st in next 2 sts, sl st in sp between 3-dc groups, ch 3, 2 dc in same sp, 3 dc in sp between each 3-dc group around with (3 dc, ch 1, 3 dc) in each corner ch-1 sp, join.

Rnd 4: Ch 1, sc in each st around with (sc, ch 1, sc) in each corner ch-1 sp, join with sl st in first sc. Fasten off.

Rnd 5: With white, working this rnd in **back lps,** repeat rnd 4.

Rnd 6: With variegated red, working this rnd in **back lps,** repeat rnd 4.

AFGHAN ASSEMBLY
Make eleven more Blocks, sew through **back lps** with three Blocks across and four Blocks down.

EDGING

Rnd 1: Working this rnd in **back lps,** join red with (sc, ch 1, sc) in any corner ch-1 sp, sc in each st around with (sc, ch 1, sc) in each corner ch-1 sp, join with sl st in first sc. Fasten off.

Rnd 2: With white, repeat rnd 1 of Edging.

Rnd 3: With red, repeat rnd 1 of Edging. **Do not fasten off.**

Rnd 4: (Sl st, ch 3, 2 dc, ch 1, 3 dc) in next ch-1 sp, [*skip next 2 sts, 3 dc in next st; repeat from * across to last st before corner ch-1 sp, skip next st, (3 dc, ch 1, 3 dc) in next corner ch-1 sp]; repeat between [ ]; repeat from * across to last st before beginning cor-ner, skip last st, join with sl st in top of ch 3.

Rnds 5–9: Sl st in next 2 sts, (sl st, ch 3, 2 dc, ch 1, 3 dc) in next ch-1 sp, 3 dc in each sp between 3-dc groups around with (3 dc, ch 1, 3 dc) in each corner ch-1 sp, join.

Rnd 10: Ch 1, sc in each st around with (sc, ch 1, sc) in each corner ch-1 sp, join with sl st in first sc.

Rnd 11: With white, repeat rnd 1 of Edging.

Rnd 12: With red, repeat rnd 1 of Edging.

Rnd 13: Working this rnd in **back lps,** join variegated red with sl st in any st of rnd 12, ch 1, **reverse sc** *(see Stitch Guide)* in each st and each ch-1 sp around, join. Fasten off. ❦

Sandstone Afghan

continued from page 119

first and second *, sc in last 20 sts.

Row 111: Sc in first 19 sts, *(ldc, sc in next 36 sts) 2 times, ldc*, sc in next 53 sts; repeat between first and second *, sc in last 19 sts.

Row 112: Sc in first 18 sts, *(ldc, sc in next 36 sts) 2 times, ldc*, sc in next 55 sts; repeat between first and second *, sc in last 18 sts.

Row 113: Sc in first 17 sts, *(ldc, sc in next 36 sts) 2 times, ldc*, sc in next 57 sts; repeat between first and second *, sc in last 17 sts.

Row 114: Sc in first 16 sts, *(ldc, sc in next 36 sts) 2 times, ldc*, sc in next 59 sts; repeat between first and second *, sc in last 16 sts.

Row 115: With rust, sc in first 15 sts, *(ldc, sc in next 36 sts) 2 times, ldc*, sc in next 61 sts; repeat between first and second *, sc in last 15 sts.

Row 116: Sc in first 14 sts, *(ldc, sc in next 36 sts) 2 times, ldc*, sc in next 63 sts; repeat between first and second *, sc in last 14 sts.

Row 117: Sc in first 13 sts, *(ldc, sc in next 36 sts) 2 times, ldc*, sc in next 65 sts; repeat between first and second *, sc in last 13 sts.

Row 118: Sc in first 12 sts, *(ldc, sc in next 36 sts) 2 times, ldc*, sc in next 67 sts; repeat between first and second *, sc in last 12 sts.

Row 119: Sc in first 11 sts, *(ldc, sc in next 36 sts) 2 times, ldc*, sc in next 69 sts; repeat between first and second *, sc in last 11 sts.

Row 120: Sc in first 10 sts, *(ldc, sc in next 36 sts) 2 times, ldc*, sc in next 71 sts; repeat between first and second *, sc in last 10 sts.

Row 121: With black, sc in first 9 sts, *(ldc, sc in next 36 sts) 2 times, ldc*, sc in next 73 sts; repeat between first and second *, sc in last 9 sts.

NOTE: For **rows 122–241,** *starting with row 120, work back to row 2.*

Rows 122–127: With rust, repeat rows 120–115.

Rows 128–133: With med. orange, repeat rows 114–109.

Rows 134–139: With lt. beige, repeat rows 108–103.

Rows 140–145: With rust, repeat rows 102–97.

Rows 146–151: With med. orange, repeat rows 96–91.

Rows 152–157: With lt. beige, repeat rows 90–85.

Row 158: With black, repeat row 84.

Rows 159–164: With rust, repeat rows 83–78.

Rows 165–170: With med. orange, repeat rows 77–72.

Rows 171–176: With lt. beige, repeat rows 71–66.

Rows 177–182: With rust, repeat rows 65–60.

Rows 183–188: With med. orange, repeat rows 59–54.

Rows 189–194: With lt. beige, repeat rows 53–48.

Row 195: With black, repeat row 47.

Rows 196–201: With rust, repeat rows 46–41.

Rows 202–207: With med. orange, repeat rows 40–35.

Rows 208–213: With lt. beige, repeat rows 34–29.

Rows 214–219: With rust, repeat rows 28–23.

Rows 220–225: With med. orange, repeat rows 22–17.

Rows 226–231: With lt. beige, repeat rows 16–11.

Row 232: With black, repeat row 10.

Rows 233–241: With rust, repeat row 2.

Fringe

Using 6" strands at ends of rows, tie 3 strands together with black strands tied alone. ❦

Great Granny Square

Our innovative Morning Glories afghan reinvents a beloved classic by adding crisp panels of contrast. Cherished for their ease and versatility, our great grannies shape up in sunny summer brights, simulate African violets, shift into springtime with sprightly daffodils and swaddle baby with sweet delicacy. And you thought granny squares were boring!

by Michelle Maks

Morning Glories

FINISHED SIZE: About 65" × 78".

MATERIALS:
- ❑ Worsted yarn:
  - 38 oz. off-white
  - 34 oz. lt. green
  - 11½ oz. each yellow and dk. green
  - 7½ oz.each purple, dk. blue, lavender and lt. blue
- ❑ Tapestry needle
- ❑ G and H hooks or sizes needed to obtain gauge

GAUGE: H hook, 7 sc = 2"; 7 sc rows = 2". Square is 5¼" square.

NOTE:
Use H hook unless otherwise stated.

PANEL (make 4)
First Square (make 7)

Rnd 1: With yellow, ch 3, sl st in first ch to form ring, ch 4, (dc in ring, ch 1) 7 times, join with sl st in third ch of ch 4. Fasten off. *(8 dc, 8 ch sps made)*

Rnd 2: For **flower,** join lt. blue with sl st in any ch sp; for **beginning corner (beg corner), ch 3, (2 dc, ch 3, 3 dc) in same ch sp as sl st;** ch 1, skip next ch sp; *for **corner, (3 dc, ch 3, 3 dc) in next ch sp;** ch 1, skip next ch sp; repeat from * around, join with sl st in top of ch 3. Fasten off. *(Ch 3 counts as first dc.)*

Rnd 3: For **leaves,** join dk. green with sl st in any corner ch sp, beg corner, (ch 1, 3 dc in next ch-1 sp, ch 1, corner) 3 times, ch 1, 3 dc in next ch-1 sp, ch 1, join. Fasten off.

Rnd 4: Join off-white with sl st in any corner, beg corner, *(ch 1, 3 dc in next ch-1 sp) 2 times, ch 1, corner; repeat from * 3 more times, (ch 1, 3 dc in next ch-1 sp) 2 times, ch 1, join. Fasten off.

Rnd 5: For **flower trim,** working in ch sps on rnd 1, join dk. blue with sc in any ch sp on rnd 1 between lt. blue 3-dc groups in corner, ch 3, dc in next ch sp, ch 3, (sc in next ch sp between lt. blue 3-dc groups, ch 3, dc in next ch sp, ch 3) around, join with sl st in first sc. Fasten off.

Rnd 6: For **leaf trim,** working in ch sps of rnd 2 between dk. green 3-dc groups of rnd 3, join lt. green with sc on right-hand side of 3-dc group in any ch-1 sp, ch 3, sc in same ch sp on other side of 3-dc group, (*ch 3, dc in next corner ch sp on right-hand side of first 3-dc group, ch 3, sc in same ch sp between 3-dc groups, ch 3, dc in same ch sp on left-hand side of second 3-dc group, ch 3*, sc in next ch sp on right-hand side of 3-dc group, ch 3, sc in same ch sp on other side of 3-dc group) 3 times; repeat between first and second *, join. Fasten off.

Second Square (make 7)
With lavender for flower and purple for flower trim, work same as First Square.

Matching sts, working in **back lps** *(see Stitch Guide),* sew Squares together in strip alternating First and Second Squares.

Trellis
Row 1: Working on one long side of strip, join lt. green with sc in right-hand corner of First Square, evenly space 18 sc across Square, evenly space 19 sc across each Square, turn. *(266 sc made)*

Rows 2–3: Ch 1, sc in each st across, turn.

*NOTE: When **changing colors** (see Stitch Guide), drop first color, pick up when needed, carry dropped color along back of work and fasten off each color when no longer needed.*

Row 4: Ch 1, sc in first 7 sts changing to purple in last st made; for **puff st (ps), yo, insert hook in next st, yo, pull long lp through st, (yo, insert hook in same st, yo, pull long lp through st) 2 times, yo, pull through all 7 lps on hook, ch 1, changing to lt. green;** (sc in next 7 sts changing to purple in last st made, ps) across to last 2 sts, sc in last 2 sts, turn. Fasten off.

Row 5: Join dk. green with sc in first st, sc in each st across, turn. Fasten off.

Row 6: Join lt. green with sc in first st, sc in next 2 sts changing to dk. blue in last st made, ps, (sc in next 7 sts changing to dk. blue in last st made, ps) across to last 6 sts, sc in last 6 sts, turn.

Rows 7–9: Ch 1, sc in each st across, turn. At end of last row, **do not turn.** Fasten off.

Row 10: Join off-white with sc in first st, sc in each st across, turn.

Rows 11–30: Ch 1, sc in each st across, turn. At end of last row, **do not turn.** Fasten off.

Row 31: Join lt. green with sc in first st, sc in each st across, turn.

Rows 32–39: Repeat rows 2–9.

With right side facing you and Squares on left-hand side, sew long edges of Panels together.

STRIP

First Square (make 7)

Work same as Panel First Square.

Second Square (make 7)

Work same as Panel Second Square.
Sew Strip to long Trellis edge of Afghan.

EDGING

Rnd 1: Working in sts and in ends of rows around outer edge, with right side facing you, join lt. green with sc in any st; spacing sts so edge lays flat, sc around, ending in multiples of 4, join with sl st in first sc, **turn.**

Rnd 2: Ch 1, sc in each st around, join, **turn.** Fasten off.

Rnd 3: With G hook and lt. blue, join with sc in any st, ch 7, skip next st, (sc in next st, ch 7, skip next st) around, join. Fasten off.

Rnd 4: Working in skipped sts of rnd 2, with G hook and purple, join with sc in front of rnd 3 in any st; (working behind rnd 3, ch 7, sc in next st; working in front of rnd 3, ch 7, sc in next st) around; working behind rnd 3, ch 7, join with sl st in first sc. Fasten off.

FIRST FLOWER (make 28)

Rnd 1: With yellow, ch 3, sl st in first ch to form ring, ch 1, 10 sc in ring, join with sl st in first sc. Fasten off. *(10 sc made)*

Rnd 2: Join lt. blue with (sl st, ch 3, dc) in first st, 2 dc in each st around, join with sl st in top of ch 3. Fasten off. *(20 dc)*

Rnd 3: Join dk. blue with sc in first st, sc in next st; for **long sc (lsc)**, insert hook in next sc on rnd 1, yo, pull long lp through st, yo, pull through 2 lps on hook; lsc one more time, (sc in next 2 dc, lsc 2 times) around, join with sl st in first sc. Fasten off. *(10 sc, 10 lsc)*

SECOND FLOWER (make 24)

Rnd 1: With yellow, ch 3, sl st in first ch to form ring, ch 1, 10 sc in ring, join with sl st in first sc. Fasten off. *(10 sc made)*

Rnd 2: Join lavender with (sl st, ch 3, dc) in first st, 2 dc in each st around, join with sl st in top of ch 3. Fasten off. *(20 dc)*

Rnd 3: Join purple with sc in first st, sc in next st, lsc 2 times, (sc in next 2 dc, lsc 2 times) around, join with sl st in first sc. Fasten off. *(10 sc, 10 lsc)*

LEAF (make 104)

With lt. green, ch 11, sc in second ch from hook, hdc in next ch, dc in next ch, tr in next 4 ch, dc in next ch, hdc in next ch, 2 sc in last ch; continuing on opposite side of starting ch, hdc in next ch, dc in next ch, tr in next 4 ch, dc in next ch, hdc in next ch, sc in last ch, join with sl st in first sc. Fasten off.

FINISHING

Sew two Leaves to back of each Flower.

Using Cross-stitch *(see Stitch Guide)* and Lazy-Daisy Stitch *(see illustration)*, embroider each Panel according to embroidery diagram. Sew blue Flowers to Panels according to blue dots on diagram. Sew lavender Flowers to Panels according to purple dots. ❧

LAZY-DAISY STITCH

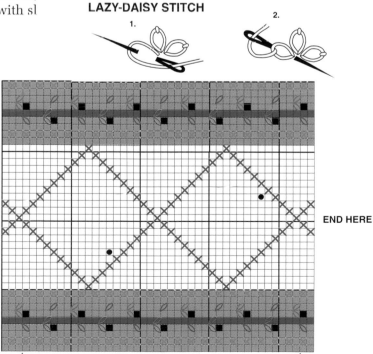

BEGIN HERE   END HERE

COLORS

- ● = BLUE FLOWER PLACEMENT
- ◉ = PURPLE FLOWER PLACEMENT
- ☒ = YELLOW CROSS-STITCHES
- ☒ = DK. GREEN CROSS-STITCHES
- ▨ = LT. BLUE LAZY-DAISY STITCHES
- ▨ = LAVENDER LAZY-DAISY STITCHES
- ▨ = DK. GREEN LAZY-DAISY STITCHES

REPEAT ACROSS

by Mary Strecker

Summer Sunglo

FINISHED SIZE: About 44" × 58½".

MATERIALS:
- ❑ Worsted yarn:
  - 16 oz. rust
  - 11 oz. each lt. gold, lt. orange, med. orange, dk. orange, red and dk. green
  - 4 oz. each dk. brown and yellow
- ❑ Tapestry needle
- ❑ G and J hooks or sizes needed to obtain gauges

GAUGES: G hook, 7 dc = 2"; 4 dc rows = 2". **J hook,** 7 dc = 2"; 3 dc rows = 2". Motif is 8" × 12".

MOTIF (make 16)
Rnd 1: With G hook and yellow, ch 4, sl st in first ch to form ring, ch 3, 2 dc in ring, ch 2, (3 dc, ch 2) 3 times in ring, join with sl st in top of ch 3, **turn.** Fasten off. *(12 dc made)*

Row 2: Working in rows, join lt. gold with (sl st, ch 3, 2 dc, ch 2, 3 dc) in any corner ch-2 sp, ch 1, 3 dc in next corner ch-2 sp leaving last 2 corner ch-2 sps unworked, turn. (9 dc)

Row 3: Ch 4, 3 dc in next ch-1 sp, ch 1, 3 dc in next corner ch-2 sp, turn.

Row 4: Ch 4, 3 dc in next ch-1 sp, ch 1, (3 dc, ch 2, 3 dc) in next ch-4 sp, ch 1, 3 dc in same corner ch-2 sp as last dc group of row 2, ch 1, (3 dc, ch 2, 3 dc) in next unworked corner ch-2 sp on rnd 1, ch 1, 3 dc in next corner ch-2 sp, turn.

Row 5: Ch 4, 3 dc in next ch-1 sp, ch 1, 3 dc in next corner ch-2 sp, turn.

Rnd 6: Working in rnds, ch 4, 3 dc in next ch-1 sp, ch 1, (3 dc, ch 2, 3 dc) in next ch-4 sp, ch 1, 3 dc in same corner ch-2 sp as last dc group of row 4, ch 1, join, **turn.** Fasten off.

Rnd 7: Join lt. orange with (sl st, ch 3, 2 dc, ch 2, 3 dc) in any corner ch-2 sp, *ch 1, (3 dc, ch 1) in each ch-1 sp across to next corner ch-2 sp, (3 dc, ch 2, 3 dc) in corner sp; repeat from * 2 more times, ch 1, (3 dc, ch 1) in each ch-1 sp across, join, **turn.** Fasten off.

Row 8: Working in rows, join med. orange with (sl st, ch 3, 2 dc, ch 2, 3 dc) in any corner ch-2 sp, ch 1, (3 dc, ch 1) in each of next 2 ch-1 sps, 3 dc in next corner ch-2 sp, **turn.**

Row 9: Ch 4, (3 dc, ch 1) in each of next 3 ch-1 sps, 3 dc in next corner ch-2 sp, **turn.**

Row 10: Ch 4, (3 dc, ch 1) in each of next 3 ch-1 sps, (3 dc, ch 2, 3 dc) in next ch-4 sp, ch 1, 3 dc in same sp as last dc group on row 8, ch 1, (3 dc, ch 1) in each unworked ch-1 sp across to next corner ch-2 sp, (3 dc, ch 2, 3 dc) in corner sp, ch 1, (3 dc, ch 1) in each of next 2 ch-1 sps, 3 dc in corner ch-2 sp, **turn.**

Row 11: Ch 4, (3 dc, ch 1) in each of next 3 ch-1 sps, 3 dc in next corner ch-2 sp, **turn.**

Rnd 12: Working in rnds, ch 4, (3 dc, ch 1) in each of next 3 ch-1 sps, (3 dc, ch 2, 3 dc) in next ch-4 sp, ch 1, 3 dc in same sp as last dc group of row 10, ch 1, (3 dc, ch 1) in each unworked ch-1 sp across, join, **turn.** Fasten off.

Rnd 13: Join dk. orange with (sl st, ch 3, 2 dc, ch 2, 3 dc) in any corner ch-2 sp, ch 1, (3 dc, ch 1) in each ch-1 sp around with (3 dc, ch 2, 3 dc) in each corner ch-2 sp, join, **turn.** Fasten off.

Rnd 14: Working in sps between sts, join red with (sl st, ch 3, dc, ch 2, 2 dc) in any corner ch-2 sp, dc in each sp around with (2 dc, ch 2, 2 dc) in each corner ch-2 sp, join, **turn.** Fasten off.

Rnd 15: Working in sps between sts, join dk. green with (sl st, ch 3, dc, ch 2, 2 dc) in any corner ch-2 sp, skip next sp; for **V st, 2 dc in next sp;** *skip next sp, (V st in next sp, skip next sp) across to next corner ch-2 sp; repeat from * 2 more times, skip next sp, (V st in next sp, skip next sp) across, join, **turn.** Fasten off.

Rnd 16: Join rust with (sl st, ch 3, dc, ch 2, 2 dc) in any corner ch-2 sp, V st in each V st around with (2 dc, ch 2, 2 dc) in each corner ch-2 sp, join. Fasten off.

Assembly
Arrange Motifs four across and four down; matching sts along edges and corner sps to corner sps, sew together with rust.

continued on page 141

by Betty Jones

African Violets

FINISHED SIZE: Afghan is about 50¾" × 64 ¾". Pillow is 15¾" square.

MATERIALS:
- ❑ Worsted yarn:
    - 60 oz. white
    - 35 oz. lt. purple
    - 11 oz. green
    - 9 oz. yellow
- ❑ ½ yd. white fabric
- ❑ Polyester fiberfill
- ❑ White sewing thread
- ❑ Sewing and tapestry needles
- ❑ I hook or size needed to obtain gauge

GAUGE: 3 dc = 1", 3 dc rows = 2". Motif is 7" square.

GRANNY SQUARE

Rnd 1: With yellow, ch 5, sl st in first ch to form ring, ch 3, 2 dc in ring, ch 2, (3 dc, ch 2) 3 times in ring, join with sl st in top of ch 3. Fasten off. *(12 dc made)*

Rnd 2: Join green with (sl st, ch 3, 2 dc, ch 2, 3 dc, ch 1) in any ch-2 sp, (3 dc, ch 2, 3 dc, ch 1) in each ch-2 sp around, join. Fasten off. *(24 dc)*

Rnd 3: Join white with (sl st, ch 3, 2 dc, ch 2, 3 dc, ch 1) in any ch-2 sp, (3 dc, ch 1) in next ch-1 sp, *(3 dc, ch 2, 3 dc, ch 1) in next ch-2 sp, (3 dc, ch 1) in next ch-1 sp; repeat from * around, join. *(36 dc)*

Rnd 4: Sl st in next 2 sts, (sl st, ch 3, 2 dc, ch 2, 3 dc, ch 1) in next ch-2 sp, (3 dc, ch 1) in each of next 2 ch-1 sps, *(3 dc, ch 2, 3 dc, ch 1) in next ch-2 sp, (3 dc, ch 1) in each of next 2 ch-1 sps; repeat from * around, join. Fasten off. *(48 dc)*

Rnd 5: Join lt. purple with (sl st, ch 3, 2 dc, ch 2, 3 dc, ch 1) in any corner ch-2 sp, (3 dc, ch 1) in each of next 3 ch-1 sps, *(3 dc, ch 2, 3 dc, ch 1) in next ch-2 sp, (3 dc, ch 1) in each of next 3 ch-1 sps; repeat from * around, join. Fasten off. *(60)*

Rnd 6: Join white with (sl st, ch 3, dc, ch 2, 2 dc) in same sp, *[for **cross-stitch (cr st), skip next st, dc in next st, dc in skipped st;** working in sts and ch sps, cr st in next 18 sts], (2 dc, ch 2, 2 dc) in next corner ch-2 sp; repeat from * 2 more times; repeat between [ ], join. Fasten off. *(40 cr sts, 16 dc)*

Flower

Rnd 1: Working through bottom lps of sts *(see illustration)* of sts on rnd 1 of Granny Squares, join lt. purple with sl st in any st, *ch 3, sl st in next 2 sts; repeat from * 4 more times, ch 3, sl st in next st, join with sl st in first sl st. *(12 sl sts made)*

Rnd 2: (Sl st, ch 1, sc, hdc, dc, 2 tr, dc, hdc, sc) in next ch-3 sp, (sc, hdc, dc, 2 tr, dc, hdc, sc) in each ch-3 sp around, join with sl st in first sc. Fasten off. *(6 petals)*

AFGHAN

For Afghan, make 63 Granny Squares.

Assembly

With wrong sides together and matching sts, working in **back lps** *(see Stitch Guide)*, sl st edges of nine Squares together to form strip. Make seven strips.

To join, sl st edges of strips together in same manner as Squares.

Border

Rnd 1: Join lt. purple with (sl st, ch 3, dc, ch 2, 2 dc) in any corner ch-2 sp, *[working in sts and ch sps, cr st in each st across to next corner ch-2 sp], (2 dc, ch 2, 2 dc) in same sp; repeat from * 2 more times; repeat between [ ], join with sl st in top of ch 3. *(412 cr sts, 16 dc)*

Rnd 2: Join white with (sl st, ch 3, dc, ch 2, 2 dc) in any corner ch-2 sp, cr st in each st across to next corner ch-2 sp, *(2 dc, ch 2, 2 dc) in next ch-2 sp, cr st in each st across to next corner ch-2 sp; repeat from * around, join. *(420 cr sts, 16 dc)*

Rnd 3: Join lt. purple with (sl st, ch 3, 8 dc) in corner ch-2 sp before either long side of Afghan, *skip next 2 sts, sc in next st, (skip next 2 sts, 7 dc in next st, skip next 2 sts, sc in next st) 39 times, skip next 3 sts, 9 dc in next corner ch-2 sp, skip next 3 sts, (sc in next st, skip next 2 sts, 7 dc

continued on page 141

by Elsie Caddey

Heirloom Baby

FINISHED SIZE: About 36" × 36".

MATERIALS:
- ❑ Sport yarn:
    - 15 oz. main color (MC)
    - 2 oz. contrasting color (CC)
- ❑ D hook or size needed to obtain gauge

GAUGE: 3 cross-stitches = 1"; 7 pattern rows = 2".

CENTER SQUARE
NOTE: *The hdc is used to place joining at center of corner.* **Do not** *count as a st.*

Rnd 1: With MC, ch 4, sl st in first ch to form ring, ch 3, 3 dc in ring, (ch 3, 4 dc in ring) 3 times, ch 1, join with hdc in top of ch 3. *(16 dc made)*

Rnd 2: Ch 3, dc around post of hdc *(see Stitch Guide)*, *dc in next 4 sts, (2 dc, ch 3, 2 dc) in next ch-3 sp; repeat from * 2 more times, dc in next 4 sts, 2 dc in next ch-1 sp, ch 1, join. *(32)*

Rnds 3–4: Ch 3, dc around post of hdc, *dc in each st across to next ch-3 sp, (2 dc, ch 3, 2 dc) in next ch-3 sp; repeat from * 2 more times; dc in each st across to ch-1 sp, 2 dc in ch-1 sp, ch 1, join. *(48) (64)*

Rnd 5: Ch 3, dc around post of hdc; for **cross-stitch (cr st), *skip next st, dc in next st, working behind dc just made, dc in skipped st;** cr st in each st across to next ch-3 sp, (2 dc, ch 3, 2 dc) in next ch-3 sp; repeat from * 2 more times, cr st in each st across to ch-1 sp, 2 dc in ch-1 sp, join.

Rnds 6–44: Repeat rnds 3 and 5 alternately. At end of rnd 44, fasten off. *(704)*

MOTIF (make 40)
Rnd 1: With CC, ch 4, sl st in first ch to form ring, ch 3, 3 dc in ring, drop lp of last dc made from hook, insert hook in top of ch 3, pick up dropped lp, pull through, ch 3; *for **popcorn st (pc),** 4 dc in ring, drop lp from hook, insert hook in first dc of group, pick up dropped lp, pull through, ch 3; repeat from * 2 more times,

join with sl st in top of ch 3. Fasten off. *(4 pc, 4 ch sps)*

Rnd 2: Join MC with (sl st, ch 3, 3 dc) in any ch-3 sp, (ch 3, 4 dc in next ch-3 sp) 3 times, ch 1, join with hdc in top of ch 3. *(16 dc)*

Rnds 3–4: Ch 3, 2 dc around post of hdc, *dc in each st across to next ch-3 sp, (3 dc, ch 3, 3 dc) in next ch-3 sp; repeat from * 2 more times, dc in each st across to ch-1 sp, 3 dc in ch-1 sp, join. At end of rnd 4, fasten off. *(40, 64)*

ASSEMBLY
NOTE: *Motif will be joined to form a frame with eleven on each end and nine on each side.*

Place two Motifs side-by-side, join MC with sl st in ch-3 sp of first Motif, ch 2, sl st in ch-3 sp of next Motif, (ch 2, skip next st on first Motif, sl st in next Motif, ch 2, skip next st on next Motif, sl st in next st) 8 times, ch 2, sl st in next ch-3 sp of first Motif, ch 2, sl st in next ch-3 sp of next Motif. Fasten off. Repeat, joining sides of all Motifs to form frame.

Place Center Square inside Motif frame, sl st in ch-3 sp at corner of Center Square, ch 2, sl st in ch-3 sp of second Motif in frame, *(ch 2, skip next st of Center Square, sl st in next st, ch 2, skip next st on Motif, sl st in next st) 8 times, ch 2, skip next st of Center Square, sl st in next st, ch 2, sl st in next ch-3 sp of Motif, ch 2, skip next st on Center Square, sl st in next st, ch 2, sl st in ch-3 sp of next Motif; repeat from * 7 more times; repeat between ( ) 8 times, ch 2, sl st in next ch-3 sp of Center Square, ch 2, sl st in next ch-3 sp of Motif, ch 2, sl st in next ch-3 of corner Motif, ch 2, sl st in ch-3 sp of Center Square, ch 2, sl st in ch-3 sp of next Motif; repeat all instructions from first * to this point around remaining sides ending with sl st in first sl st made in ch-3 sp at beginning. Fasten off.

BORDER
Rnd 1: Working around outside edge of Motif frame, join MC with sl st in ch-3 sp at corner,

continued on page 140

by Mary Strecker

Springtime Daffodils

FINISHED SIZE: About 46" × 58½".

MATERIALS:
- ❑ Worsted yarn:
  - 23 oz. dk. green
  - 12 oz. lt. green
  - 12 oz. med. green
  - 4 oz. each lt. yellow, dk. yellow and white
- ❑ Tapestry needle
- ❑ G and K hooks or sizes needed to obtain gauges

GAUGES: G hook, 7 dc = 2"; 2 dc rows = 1". **K hook,** 3 dc = 1"; 3 dc rows = 2". Motif is 5" square.

MOTIF (make 40)
Rnd 1: With G hook and dk. yellow, ch 4, sl st in first ch to form ring, (ch 2, 3 dc, sl st) 4 times in ring. Fasten off. *(4 petals made)*

Rnd 2: Join lt. yellow with sl st in back strands *(see illustration)* of second dc on any petal, ch 3, (sl st in back strands of second dc on next petal, ch 3) 3 times, join with sl st in first ch-3 sp. *(4 ch sps)*

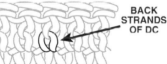

BACK STRANDS OF DC

Rnd 3: Ch 3, (2 dc, ch 1, 3 dc, ch 1) in first ch-3 sp, (3 dc, ch 1, 3 dc, ch 1) in each ch-3 sp around, join with sl st in top of ch 3. Fasten off. *(8 petals)*

Rnd 4: Join dk. green with (sl st, ch 3, 2 dc, ch 2, 3 dc) in any ch-1 sp, *ch 1, 3 dc in next ch-1 sp, ch 1; for **corner, (3 dc, ch 2, 3 dc) in next ch-1 sp;** repeat from * 2 more times, ch 1, 3 dc in next ch-1 sp, ch 1, join, **turn.** Fasten off.

Rnd 5: Join med. green with (sl st, ch 3, 2 dc, ch 2, 3 dc) in any corner ch-2 sp, *ch 1, (3 dc, ch 1) in each ch-1 sp across to next corner ch-2 sp, (3 dc, ch 2, 3 dc) in corner sp; repeat from * 2 more times, ch 1, (3 dc, ch 1) in each ch-1 sp across, join, **turn.** Fasten off.

Rnd 6: Join lt. green with (sl st, ch 3, 2 dc, ch 2, 3 dc) in any corner ch-2 sp, *ch 1, (3 dc, ch 1) in each ch-1 sp across to next corner ch-2 sp, (3 dc, ch 2, 3 dc) in corner sp; repeat from * 2 more times, ch 1, (3 dc, ch 1) in each ch-1 sp across, join, **turn.** Fasten off.

Center Motif Assembly
Arrange Motifs two across and five down; matching sts along edges and corner sps to corner sps, sew together with lt. green.

CENTER BORDER
NOTE: *At each joining seam in rnd 1, the 3-dc group is worked as follows; (dc in corner ch-2 sp of Motif, dc in seam, dc in corner ch-2 sp of next Motif, ch 1).*

Rnd 1: With K hook, join lt. green with (sl st, ch 3, 2 dc, ch 2, 3 dc) in any corner ch-2 sp, ch 1, *(3 dc, ch 1) in each ch-1 sp and at each joining seam *(see Note)* across to next corner ch-2 sp, (3 dc, ch 2, 3 dc, ch 1) in corner sp; repeat from * 2 more times, (3 dc, ch 1) in each ch-1 sp and at each joining seam across, join with sl st in top of ch 3, **turn.**

Rnds 2–4: (Sl st, ch 3, 2 dc) in first ch-1 sp, ch 1, (3 dc, ch 1) in each ch-1 sp around with (3 dc, ch 2, 3 dc, ch 1) in each corner ch-2 sp, join, **turn.** At end of last rnd, fasten off.

Rnd 5: Join dk. green with (sl st, ch 3, 2 dc, ch 2, 3 dc) in any corner ch-2 sp, ch 1, (3 dc, ch 1) in each ch-1 sp around with (3 dc, ch 2, 3 dc, ch 1) in each corner ch-2 sp, join, **turn.** Fasten off.

Rnd 6: With med. green, repeat rnd 5.

Rnd 7: Repeat rnd 5.

Rnd 8: With white, repeat rnd 5, **do not fasten off.**

Rnds 9–11: Repeat rnds 2–4.

Rnds 12–14: Repeat rnds 5–7.

Rnd 15: With lt. green, repeat rnd 5.

Outer Motif Assembly
Arrange Motifs around edge of center border *(see photograph);* matching sts along edges and corner sps to corner sps, sew together with lt. green.

continued on page 140

Springtime Daffodils

continued from page 139

OUTER BORDER

Rnd 1: Repeat rnd 1 of Center Border.

Rnds 2-4: Repeat rnds 5–7 of Center Border. At end of last rnd, **do not fasten off.**

Rnd 5: Working in sps between sts and ch sps, sl st in first sp, ch 3, dc in each sp around with (2 dc, ch 2, 2 dc) in each corner ch-2 sp, join, **turn.**

Rnd 6: Sl st in first sp, ch 2, hdc in each sp around with 3 hdc in each corner ch-2 sp, join with sl st in top of ch 2, **turn.**

Rnd 7: Sl st in first sp, ch 2, hdc in each sp around with 3 hdc in sp between second and third st of each corner, join, **do not turn.**

Rnd 8: Ch 2, **reverse sc** *(see Stitch Guide)* in each sp around, join with sl st in first ch of ch 2. Fasten off. ❦

Heirloom Baby

continued from page 137

ch 1, *(2 sc, ch 3, 2 sc) in ch-3 sp at corner, sc in next 16 sts, (sc in next ch-3 sp, 2 sc in ch-2 sp between Motifs, sc in ch-3 sp of next Motif, sc in next 16 sts) across to next corner; repeat from * 3 more times, join with sl st in first sc. Fasten off.

Rnd 2: Join CC with sl st in seventh sc of rnd 1, ch 3 *(counts as first dc)*, *(ch 1, skip next st, dc in next st) across to last st before corner, ch 1, skip next st, (dc, ch 1) 4 times in next ch-3 sp, skip next 2 sts, dc in next st; repeat from * 3 more times, skip next st, ch 1, join with sl st in third ch of ch 4. Fasten off.

Rnd 3: Join MC with sl st in last ch-1 sp of rnd 2, ch 1, [*(sc in ch-1 sp, ch 4, skip next ch-1 sp) 4 times, (dc, ch 1, dc, ch 1, dc, ch 1, dc, ch 1, dc) in next ch, ch 4, skip next ch-1 sp; repeat form * 9 more times, (sc in next ch-1 sp, ch 4, skip next ch-1 sp, ch 4) 4 times, skip next ch-1 sp, (dc in next dc, ch 1, dc in next ch-1 sp, ch 1) 3 times, dc in next dc, ch 4]; repeat between [ ] 3 more times, join with sl st in first sc.

Rnd 4: Sl st in next ch-4 sp, ch 1, [*(sc in ch-4 sp, ch 4) 3 times; for **V st,** (dc, ch 1, dc) in next st; ch 1, dc in next st, ch 1, V st in next st, ch 1, dc in next st, ch 1, V st in next st, ch 4, skip next ch-4 sp; repeat from * 9 more times, (sc in next ch-4 sp, ch 4) 3 times to next corner; (V st, ch 1) in next 6 sts, V st in next st, ch 4, skip next ch-4 sp]; repeat between [ ] 3 more times, join. Fasten off.

Rnd 5: Sl st in next ch-4 sp, ch 1, [*(sc in ch-4 sp, ch 4) 2 times, V st in next ch-1 sp, ch 1, skip next dc, (dc, ch1, dc, ch1) in each of next 4 dc, skip next dc, V st in next ch-1 sp, ch 4, skip next dc and ch-4 sp; repeat from * 9 times, (sc in next ch-4 sp, ch 4) 2 times to next corner; skip next ch-4 sp, V st in next ch-1 sp, (ch 1, dc in next ch-1 sp, ch 1, V st in next ch-1 sp) 6 times, ch 4 skip next ch-4 sp]; repeat between [ ] 3 more times, join with sl st in first sc. Fasten off.

Rnd 6: Join CC with sl st in next ch-4 sp, ch 1, [*for **picot, (sc, ch 2, sc) in ch-4 sp;** ch 4, skip next ch-4 sp, (picot in next ch-1 sp, skip next ch-1 sp) 5 times, picot in next ch-1 sp, ch 4, skip next ch-4 sp; repeat from * 9 more times, picot in next ch-4 sp, ch 4, (picot in next ch-1 sp, sc in next 3 dc) 6 times, picot in next ch-1 sp, ch 4, skip next ch-4 sp]; repeat between [ ] 3 more times, join. Fasten off. ❦

Summer Sunglo

continued from page 133

BORDER

Rnd 1: With J hook, join rust with (sl st, ch 3, dc, ch 2, 2 dc) in any corner ch-2 sp, *V st in each V st and dc in each corner ch sp of each Motif across to next corner ch-2 sp, (2 dc, ch 2, 2 dc) in corner sp; repeat from * 2 more times, V st in each V st and dc in each corner ch sp across, join with sl st in top of ch 3, **turn.** Fasten off.

NOTE: There should be 2 dc at each joining seam around edge of Afghan. These 2 dc will be counted as a V st in next rnd.

Rnd 2: Join dk. green with (sl st, ch 3, dc, ch 2, 2 dc) in any corner ch-2 sp, V st in each V st around with (2 dc, ch 2, 2 dc) in each corner ch-2 sp, join as before, **turn.** Fasten off.

Rnd 3: With yellow, repeat rnd 2.

Rnd 4: With lt. gold, repeat rnd 2.

Rnd 5: With lt. orange, repeat rnd 2.

Rnd 6: With med. orange, repeat rnd 2.

Rnd 7: With dk. orange, repeat rnd 2.

Rnd 8: With red, repeat rnd 2.

Rnd 9: Join rust with (sl st, ch 3, ch 2, 2 dc) in any corner ch-2 sp, *dc in next V st, (V st in next V st, dc in next V st) across to next corner ch-2 sp, (2 dc, ch 2, 2 dc) in corner ch-2 sp; repeat from * 2 more times, dc in next V st, (V st in next V st, dc in next V st) across, join, **turn.** Fasten off.

Rnd 10: Working in sps between sts, join dk. brown with (sl st, ch 3, dc, ch 2, 2 dc) in any corner ch-2 sp, dc in each sp around with (2 dc, ch 2, 2 dc) in each corner ch-2 sp, join, **turn.**

Rnd 11: Sl st in first sp, ch 2, hdc in each sp around with (2 hdc, ch 2, 2 hdc) in each corner ch-2 sp, join, **turn.**

Rnd 12: Sl st in first sp, ch 2, hdc in each sp around with 3 hdc in each corner ch-2 sp, join. Fasten off. ❧

African Violets

continued from page 135

in next st, skip next 2 sts) 30 times, skip next st, sc in next st, skip next 3 sts*, 9 dc in corner ch-2 sp; repeat between first and second *, join. Fasten off.

PILLOW SIDE (make 2)
For Pillow Side, make four Granny Squares.

Assembly
With wrong sides together and matching sts, working in **back lps,** sl st Granny Squares together.

Pillow Form
Using crocheted piece for pattern, from fabric, cut 2 pieces ¾" larger on all sides. Allowing ¼" for seams, sew fabric with right sides together, leaving 5" opening. Turn right side out. Stuff. Sew opening closed.

Edging
Rnd 1: Place pillow form between sides; with wrong sides together, working through both thicknesses, join lt. purple with sc in any corner ch-2 sp, 3 sc in same sp; working in sts and ch sps, (sc in each st across to next corner ch-2 sp with 2 sc in joining seam, 4 sc in corner ch-2 sp) 3 times, sc in each st across, join with sl st in first sc. *(234 sc made)*

Rnd 2: Ch 3, dc in next st, *[ch 2, dc in next 2 sts, cr st in next 52 sts], dc in next 2 sts; repeat from * 2 more times; repeat between [ ], join with sl st in top of ch 3. Fasten off. *(104 cr sts, 16 dc)*

Rnd 3: Join white with (sl st, ch 3, dc, ch 2, 2 dc) in any corner ch-2 sp, cr st in next 56 sts, *(2 dc, ch 2, 2 dc) in next corner ch-2 sp, cr st in next 56 sts; repeat from * 2 more times, join with sl st in top of ch 3. Fasten off. *(112 cr sts, 16 dc)*

Rnd 4: Join lt. purple with (sl st, ch 3, 8 dc) in any corner ch-2 sp, *[skip next 2 sts, sc in next st, (skip next 2 sts, 7 dc in next st, skip next 2 sts, sc in next st) 8 times, skip next 3 sts], 9 dc in corner ch-2 sp; repeat from * 2 more times; repeat between [ ], join. Fasten off. ❧

Favorite Stitches

Putting a twist to a foundational stitch, our Wedding Afghan marries tradition with lighthearted popcorn hearts and doves. Here are imaginative versions of all our favorites: shells for shell collectors, a Mile-a-Minute for flying fingers, pineapples for the picking and a fisherman for the Irish among us—all fit to be lovingly stitched!

by Eleanor Albano-Miles

Wedding Afghan

FINISHED SIZE: About 49" × 58".

MATERIALS:
- ❑ 58 oz. white worsted yarn
- ❑ 600 m. or 236 yds. gold metallic 8-ply thread (Kreinik Balger® 8-ply Ombre Solid Gold #2000)
- ❑ Tapestry needle
- ❑ I hook or size needed to obtain gauge

GAUGE: 3 sc = 1"; 7 sc rows = 2".

SPECIAL STITCH:

For **cluster (cl)**, yo, insert hook in next st, yo, pull through, yo, pull through 2 lps on hook, (yo, insert hook in same st, yo, pull through, yo, pull through 2 lps on hook) 2 times, yo, pull through all 4 lps on hook.

AFGHAN

Row 1: With white, ch 136, sc in second ch from hook, sc in each ch across, turn. *(135 sc made)*

Rows 2–7: Ch 1, sc in each st across, turn.

Row 8: Ch 1, sc in first 20 sts, cl in next st *(see Special Stitch—bottom of Heart made)*, sc in next 93 sts, cl in next st *(bottom of Heart made)*, sc in last 20 sts, turn. *(2 cl, 133 sc)*

Row 9: Ch 1, sc in each st across, turn.

Row 10: Ch 1, sc in first 18 sts, (cl in next st, sc in next st) 3 times, sc in next 88 sts, (cl in next st, sc in next st) 3 times, sc in last 17 sts, turn. *(6 cl, 129 sc)*

Row 11: Ch 1, sc in each st across, turn.

Row 12: Ch 1, sc in first 16 sts, (cl in next st, sc in next st) 5 times, sc in next 84 sts, (cl in next st, sc in next st) 5 times, sc in last 15 sts, turn. *(10 cl, 125 sc)*

Row 13: Ch 1, sc in each st across, turn.

Row 14: Ch 1, sc in first 14 sts, (cl in next st, sc in next st) 7 times, sc in next 80 sts, (cl in next st, sc in next st) 7 times, sc in last 13 sts, turn. *(14 cl, 121 sc)*

Row 15: Ch 1, sc in each st across, turn.

Row 16: Ch 1, sc in first 12 sts, (cl in next st, sc in next st) 9 times, sc in next 76 sts, (cl in next st, sc in next st) 9 times, sc in last 11 sts, turn. *(18 cl, 117 sc)*

Row 17: Ch 1, sc in each st across, turn.

Row 18: Ch 1, sc in first 12 sts, (cl in next st, sc in next st) 9 times, sc in next 31 sts, cl in next st *(bottom of bird's beak)*, sc in next 11 sts, cl in next st *(bottom of bird's beak)*, sc in next 32 sts, (cl in next st, sc in next st) 9 times, sc in last 11 sts, turn. *(20 cl, 115 sc)*

Row 19: Ch 1, sc in each st across, turn.

Row 20: Ch 1, sc in first 12 sts, (cl in next st, sc in next st) 4 times, sc in next 2 sts, (cl in next st, sc in next st) 4 times, sc in next 15 sts, (cl in next st, sc in next st) 5 times, sc in next 4 sts, (cl in next st, sc in next st) 2 times, sc in next 10 sts, (cl in next st, sc in next st) 2 times, sc in next 4 sts, (cl in next st, sc in next st) 5 times, sc in next 15 sts, (cl in next st, sc in next st) 4 times, sc in next 2 sts, (cl in next st, sc in next st) 4 times, sc in last 11 sts, turn. *(30 cl, 105 sc)*

Row 21: Ch 1, sc in each st across, turn.

Row 22: Ch 1, sc in first 14 sts, (cl in next st, sc in next st) 2 times *(first side on top of Heart made)*, sc in next 6 sts, (cl in next st, sc in next st) 2 times *(second side on top of Heart made)*, sc in next 15 sts, (cl in next st, sc in next st) 11 times, sc in next 6 sts, (cl in next st, sc in next st) 11 times, sc in next 15 sts, (cl in next st, sc in next st) 2 times *(first side on top of heart made)*, sc in next 6 sts, (cl in next st, sc in next st) 2 times *(second side on top of hear made)*, sc in last 13 sts, turn. *(30 cl, 105 sc)*

Row 23: Ch 1, sc in each st across, turn.

Row 24: Ch 1, sc in first 41 sts, (cl in next st, sc in next st) 12 times, sc in next 6 sts, (cl in next st, sc in next st) 12 times, sc in last 40 sts, turn. *(24 cl, 111 sc)*

Row 25: Ch 1, sc in each st across, turn.

Row 26: Ch 1, sc in first 39 sts, (cl in next st, sc in next st) 13 times, sc in next 6 sts, (cl in next st, sc in next st) 13 times, sc in last 38 sts, turn. *(26 cl, 109 sc)*

Row 27: Ch 1, sc in each st across, turn.

Row 28: Ch 1, sc in first 37 sts, (cl in next st, sc in next st) 13 times, sc in next 10 sts, (cl in next st, sc in next st) 13 times, sc in last 36 sts, turn. *(26 cl, 109 sc)*

Row 29: Ch 1, sc in each st across, turn.

Row 30: Ch 1, sc in first 31 sts, (cl in next st, sc in next st) 13 times, sc in next 22 sts, (cl in next st, sc in next st) 13 times, sc in last 30 sts, turn. *(26 cl, 109 sc)*

Row 31: Ch 1, sc in each st across, turn.

Row 32: Ch 1, sc in first 25 sts, (cl in next st, sc in next st) 15 times, sc in next 26 sts, (cl in next st, sc in next st) 15 times, sc in last 24 sts, turn. *(30 cl, 105 sc)*

Row 33: Ch 1, sc in each st across, turn.

Row 34: Ch 1, sc in first 21 sts, (cl in next st, sc in next st) 10 times, sc in next 2 sts, (cl in next st, sc in next st) 6 times, sc in next 26 sts, (cl in next st, sc in next st) 6 times, sc in next 2 sts, (cl in next st, sc in next st) 10 times, sc in last 20 sts, turn. *(32 cl, 103 sc)*

Row 35: Ch 1, sc in each st across, turn.

Row 36: Ch 1, sc in first 23 sts, (cl in next st, sc in next st) 8 times, sc in next 4 sts, (cl in next st, sc in next st) 6 times, sc in next 26 sts, (cl in next st, sc in next st) 6 times, sc in next 4 sts, (cl in next st, sc in next st) 8 times, sc in last 22 sts, turn. *(28 cl, 107 sc)*

Row 37: Ch 1, sc in each st across, turn.

Row 38: Ch 1, sc in first 23 sts, (cl in next st, sc in next st) 7 times, sc in next 4 sts, (cl in next st, sc in next st) 7 times, sc in next 26 sts, (cl in next st, sc in next st) 7 times, sc in next 4 sts, (cl in next st, sc in next st) 7 times, sc in last 22 sts, turn. *(28 cl, 107 sc)*

Row 39: Ch 1, sc in each st across, turn.

Row 40: Ch 1, sc in first 25 sts, (cl in next st, sc in next st) 6 times, sc in next 2 sts, (cl in next st, sc in next st) 7 times, sc in next 30 sts, (cl in next st, sc in next st) 7 times, sc in next 2 sts, (cl in next st, sc in next st) 6 times, sc in last 24 sts, turn. *(26 cl, 109 sc)*

Row 41: Ch 1, sc in each st across, turn.

Row 42: Ch 1, sc in first 27 sts, (cl in next st, sc in next st) 4 times, sc in next 4 sts, (cl in next st, sc in next st) 7 times, sc in next 14 sts, cl in next st *(bottom of Heart made),* sc in next 15 sts, (cl in next st, sc in next st) 7 times, sc in next 4 sts, (cl in next st, sc in next st) 4 times, sc in last 26 sts, turn. *(23 cl, 112 sc)*

Row 43: Ch 1, sc in each st across, turn.

Row 44: Ch 1, sc in first 27 sts, (cl in next st, sc in next st) 3 times, sc in next 4 sts, (cl in next st, sc in next st) 7 times, sc in next 14 sts, (cl in next st, sc in next st) 3 times, sc in next 14 sts, (cl in next st, sc in next st) 7 times, sc in next 4 sts, (cl in next st, sc in next st) 3 times, sc in last 26 sts, turn. *(23 cl, 112 sc)*

Row 45: Ch 1, sc in each st across, turn.

Row 46: Ch 1, sc in first 29 sts, (cl in next st, sc in next st) 2 times, sc in next 4 sts, (cl in next st, sc in next st) 5 times, sc in next 16 sts, (cl in next st, sc in next st) 5 times, sc in next 16 sts, (cl in next st, sc in next st) 5 times, sc in next 4 sts, (cl in next st, sc in next st) 2 times, sc in last 28 sts, turn. *(19 cl, 116 sc)*

Row 47: Ch 1, sc in each st across, turn.

Row 48: Ch 1, sc in first 35 sts, (cl in next st, sc in next st) 4 times, sc in next 18 sts, (cl in next st, sc in next st) 7 times, sc in next 18 sts, (cl in next st, sc in next st) 4 times, sc in last 34 sts, turn. *(15 cl, 120 sc)*

Row 49: Ch 1, sc in each st across, turn.

Row 50: Ch 1, sc in first 35 sts, (cl in next st, sc in next st) 2 times, sc in next 20 sts, (cl in next st, sc in next st) 9 times, sc in next 20 sts, (cl in next st, sc in next st) 2 times, sc in last 34 sts, turn. *(13 cl, 122 sc)*

Row 51: Ch 1, sc in each st across, turn.

Row 52: Ch 1, sc in first 35 sts, cl in next st *(tip of wing made on one bird),* sc in next 23 sts, (cl in next st, sc in next st) 9 times, sc in next 22 sts, cl in next st *(tip of wing made on second bird),* sc in last 35 sts, turn. *(11 cl, 124 sc)*

Row 53: Ch 1, sc in each st across, turn.

Row 54: Ch 1, sc in first 59 sts, (cl in next st, sc in next st) 4 times, sc in next 2 sts, (cl in next st, sc in next st) 4 times, sc in last 58 sts, turn. *(8 cl, 127 sc)*

Row 55: Ch 1, sc in each st across, turn.

Row 56: Ch 1, sc in first 61 sts, (cl in next st, sc in next st) 2 times *(top of one side of Heart made),* sc in next 6 sts, (cl in next st, sc in next st) 2 times *(top of second side of Heart made),* sc in last 60 sts, turn. *(4 cl, 131 sc)*

Rows 57–65: Ch 1, sc in each st across, turn.

Rows 66–114: Repeat rows 8–56.

Rows 115–127: Ch 1, sc in each st across, turn.

Rows 128–176: Repeat rows 8–56.

Rows 177–188: Ch 1, sc in each st across, turn.

EDGING

Rnd 1: Working in sts, in ends of rows and on opposite side of starting ch, ch 1, 3 sc in first st, sc in next 133 sts, 3 sc in next st; working in ends of rows, skip first row, (sc in next 2 rows, skip next row) 62 times, 3 sc in next row; working between sts on opposite side of starting ch, sc between next 133 sts, skip next st, 3 sc in next st,

continued on page 158

by Darla Fanton

Striped Shells

FINISHED SIZE: About 61" × 80".

MATERIALS:
- ❑ Worsted yarn:
  16 oz. each pale rose, lt. rose, med. rose and dk. rose
- ❑ H hook or size needed to obtain gauge

GAUGE: 7 dc = 2"; 4 dc rows = 2".

NOTE: To change colors, work off last two loops of dc with new color.

AFGHAN

Row 1: With dk. rose, ch 203, dc in fourth ch from hook, dc in each ch across, turn. *(201 dc made)*

Row 2: Ch 3, dc in next st, *ch 2, skip next 2 sts; for **shell, (2 dc, ch 2, 2 dc)** in next st; (ch 2, skip next 2 sts, dc in next st) 3 times; repeat from * across ending with ch 2, skip next 2 sts, shell, ch 2, skip next 2 sts, dc in last 2 sts, turn.

Row 3: Ch 3, dc in next st, ch 2, shell in ch-2 sp of next shell, ch 5, skip next st, (dc, ch 2, dc) in next st, *ch 5, skip next dc, shell in ch-2 sp of next shell; repeat from * across ending with ch 2, dc in last 2 sts, turn.

Row 4: Ch 3, dc in next st, ch 2, * shell in ch-2 sp of next shell, ch 4, 6 dc in next ch-2 sp, ch 4; repeat from * across ending with shell in ch-2 sp of last shell, ch 2, dc in last 2 sts, turn.

Row 5: Ch 3, dc in next st, ch 2, *shell in ch-2 sp of next shell, ch 3, dc in next st, (ch 1, dc in next st) 6 times, ch 3; repeat from * across ending with shell in ch-2 sp of last shell, ch 2, dc in last 2 sts, turn.

Row 6: Ch 3, dc in next st, *ch 2, shell in ch-2 sp of next shell, ch 2, (dc, ch 1, dc) in next 5 ch-1 sps; repeat from * across ending with shell in ch-2 sp of last shell, ch 2, dc in last 2 sts changing to med. rose *(see Note)*, turn.

Rows 7–10: Repeat rows 3–6 changing to lt. rose in last dc on last row.

Rows 11–14: Repeat rows 3–6 changing to pale rose in last dc on last row.

Rows 15–18: Repeat rows 3–6 changing to dk. rose in last dc on last row.

Rows 19–162: Repeat rows 3–18 nine times.

Rows 163–166: Repeat rows 3–6. **Do not change color at end of last row.**

Row 167: Ch 3, dc in next st, ch 2, shell in ch-2 sp of next shell, *ch 5, skip next 7 sts, (dc, ch 2, dc) in next ch-1 sp, ch 5, shell in ch-2 sp of next shell; repeat from * across ending with ch 2, dc in last 2 sts, turn.

Row 168: Ch 3, dc in next st, *(ch 3, skip next dc, dc in next st) 2 times, ch 3, dc in center ch of ch-5 sp, ch 3, dc in next ch-2 sp, ch 3, dc in center ch of ch-5 sp; repeat from * across ending with (ch 3, skip next st, dc in next st) 2 times, ch 3, dc in last 2 sts, turn.

Row 169: Ch 3, dc in each dc with 2 dc in each ch-3 sp across. Fasten off. ❦

by Debora Gardner

Strip Pillowghan

FINISHED SIZE: About 46" × 50".

MATERIALS:
- ❏ Worsted yarn:
    - 24 oz. green
    - 18 oz. variegated
- ❏ Bobby pins for markers
- ❏ Tapestry needle
- ❏ K hook or size needed to obtain gauge

GAUGE: 1 shell and 1 dc = 2"; 2 shell rows = 2".

LARGE PANEL (make 5)

Row 1: With variegated, ch 7, sl st in first ch to form ring, ch 3, (3 dc, ch 2, 4 dc) in ring, turn.

Row 2: Ch 3 *(counts as first dc)*, (3 dc, ch 2, 3 dc, ch 2, 3 dc) in ch-2 sp, dc in top of ch 3, turn.

Rows 3–46: Ch 3; for **shell, (3 dc, ch 2, 3 dc) in next ch-2 sp**; work shell in next ch-2 sp, dc in last st, turn.

Row 47: Ch 3, (3 dc in next ch-2 sp) 2 times, dc in last st, ch 4, sl st in top of beginning ch 3 on this row. Fasten off.

Rnd 48: Working around entire piece, join green with sl st in top of beginning ch 3 on row 47, ch 3; working in ends of rows, 2 dc in same sp, (3 dc in next sp) across to row 1, 6 dc in beginning ring, working on opposite ends of rows, 3 dc in each row around with 6 dc in ch-4 sp on row 47; to **join and change color, insert hook in top of first st, yo with variegated, pull through st and lp on hook;** drop green to back of work. *(294 dc)*

Rnd 49: Working in **back lps** *(see Stitch Guide)*, (sc in next st, 2 sc in next st) 2 times, sc in next 129 sts, (sc in next st, 2 sc in next st) 6 times, sc in next 129 sts, (sc in next st, 2 sc in next st) 4 times, join changing to green. Fasten off variegated. *(306 sts)*

Rnd 50: Working in **back lps,** ch 3, dc in each st around, join. Fasten off.

Mark center 20 sts on each end of Panel.

JOINING PANEL

NOTE: *Work across long straight edges of Large Panels between marked sts at ends unless otherwise stated.*

Row 1: With right sides of two Large Panels facing you, join green with sl st in marked st at end of Panel on the right, ch 5, sl st in marked st at end of Panel on the left, sl st in the next 2 sts on left Panel, turn.

Row 2: Shell in third ch of ch 5 on row 1; skip next 3 sts on next Panel, sl st in next 3 sts, turn.

Rows 3–45: Shell in ch-2 sp of shell on last row, skip next 3 sts on other Panel, sl st in next 3 sts, turn.

Row 46: Ch 2, sc in ch-2 sp of shell on last row, ch 2, skip next 3 sts on other Panel, sl st in next st. Fasten off.

Continue to join remaining Large Panels in this manner.

TRIM

Join variegated with sc in any st on outside edge of Afghan, sc in each st around, join with sl st in first sc.

PILLOW TOP

Row 1: With green, ch 46, dc in fourth ch from hook and in each ch across, turn. *(44 dc made)*

Rows 2–19: Ch 3, dc in each st across, turn. At end of last row **do not turn.**

Rnd 20: Ch 1; working around entire outer edge, sc in each st and 3 sc in end of each row around with 3 sc in each corner, join with sl st in first sc.

Rnd 21: Ch 1; working in **back lps,** sc in each st around with 3 sc in center st at each corner, join. Fasten off.

Ruffle

Rnd 1: Working in remaining **front lps** of rnd 20 on Pillow Top, join variegated with sl st in any st, ch 3, 3 dc in each st around, join with sl st in top of first ch 3.

Rnd 2: Ch 3, dc in each st around, join. Fasten off.

For **Tie,** with variegated, ch to measure 2½ yds; weave through sts and ends of rows around edges of rows 1–19, tie in bow at top.

continued on page 158

by Dorothy Moder Frantz

Violets & Pineapples

FINISHED SIZE: Fits 54" × 75" double bed.

MATERIALS:
- ❏ 60 oz. yellow pompadour baby yarn
- ❏ 4 oz. purple sport yarn
- ❏ ⅛" satin ribbon:
    88 yds. purple
    50 yds. green
- ❏ Tapestry needle
- ❏ G hook or size needed to obtain gauge

GAUGE: Rnds 1–3 of Plain Motif = 3" diameter. One popcorn shell = 1"; 5 popcorn shell rows = 3". 4 dc = 1"; 2 dc rows = 1".

PLAIN MOTIF (make 10)

Rnd 1: With G hook and yellow, ch 3, sl st in first ch to form ring, ch 1, 12 sc in ring, join with sl st in first sc. *(12 sc made)*

Rnd 2: Ch 5, (dc in next st, ch 2) around, join with sl st in third ch of beginning ch 5.

Rnd 3: Sl st in first ch sp; for **beginning popcorn (beg pc), (ch 3, 4 dc) in same sp, drop lp from hook, insert hook in top of ch 3, pull dropped lp through ch; ch 3; for popcorn (pc), 5 dc in next ch sp, drop lp from hook, insert hook in top of first dc of group, pull dropped lp through st; (ch 3, pc) in each ch sp around, ch 2, join with hdc in top of first pc.

Rnd 4: (Ch 7, sc in next ch-3 sp) 11 times, ch 3, join with tr in top of hdc.

Rnd 5: For **beginning popcorn shell (beg pc shell), ch 3, 2 dc in first ch sp, drop lp from hook, insert hook in top of ch 3, pull dropped lp through ch, ch 3, 3 dc in same sp, drop lp from hook, insert hook in first dc of group, pull dropped lp through st; ch 3, 7 dc in next ch sp, ch 3; for popcorn shell (pc shell), 3 dc in next ch sp, drop lp from hook, insert hook in first dc of group, pull dropped lp through st, ch 3, 3 dc in same sp, drop lp from hook, insert hook in first dc of group, pull dropped lp through st;** ch 3, (pc shell in next ch sp, ch 3, 7 dc in next ch sp, ch 3, pc shell in next ch sp, ch 3) around, join with sl st in top of first pc.

Rnd 6: (Sl st, beg pc shell) in ch sp of first pc shell, *[ch 3, skip next ch-3 sp, (dc in next dc, ch 1) 6 times, dc in next dc, ch 3, pc shell in ch sp of next pc shell, ch 5], pc shell in next pc shell; repeat from * 2 more times; repeat between [ ], join.

Rnd 7: (Sl st, beg pc shell) in first pc shell, *[ch 3, skip next ch-3 sp, (sc in next ch-1 sp, ch 3) 6 times, pc shell in next pc shell, ch 7], pc shell in next pc shell; repeat from * 2 more times; repeat between [ ], join.

Rnd 8: (Sl st, beg pc shell) in first pc shell, *[ch 3, skip next ch 3 sp, (sc in next ch-3 sp, ch 3) 5 times, pc shell in next pc shell, ch 5, pc shell in next ch-7 sp, ch 5], pc shell in next pc shell; repeat from * 2 more times; repeat between [ ], join.

Rnd 9: (Sl st, beg pc shell) in first pc shell, *[ch 3, skip next ch-3 sp, (sc in next ch-3 sp, ch 3) 4 times, (pc shell in next pc shell, ch 7) 2 times], pc shell in next pc shell; repeat from * 2 more times; repeat between [ ], join.

Rnd 10: (Sl st, beg pc shell) in first pc shell, *[ch 3, skip next ch-3 sp, (sc in next ch-3 sp, ch 3) 3 times, pc shell in next pc shell, ch 5, sc in next ch-7 sp, ch 5; for **double pc shell (dpc shell), 3 dc in next pc shell, drop lp from hook, insert hook in first dc of group, pull dropped lp through st, (ch 3, 3 dc in same pc shell, drop lp from hook, insert hook in first dc of group, pull dropped lp through st) 2 times;** ch 5, sc in next ch-7 sp, ch 5], pc shell in next pc shell; repeat from * 2 more times; repeat between [ ], join.

Rnd 11: (Sl st, beg pc shell) in first pc shell, *[ch 3, skip next ch-3 sp, (sc in next ch-3 sp, ch 3) 2 times, pc shell in next pc shell, ch 5, (sc in next ch-5 sp, ch 5) 2 times, pc shell in first ch sp of next dpc shell, ch 2, pc shell in next ch sp of same dpc shell, ch 5, (sc in next ch-5 sp, ch 5) 2 times], pc shell in next pc shell; repeat from * 2 more times; repeat between [ ], join.

Rnd 12: (Sl st, beg pc shell) in first pc shell, *[ch 3, skip next ch-3 sp, sc in next ch-3 sp, ch 3, pc shell in next pc shell, ch 5, (sc in next ch-5 sp,

continued on page 152

Violets & Pineapples

continued from page 151

ch 5) 2 times, skip next ch-5 sp, pc shell in next pc shell, ch 5, sc in next ch-2 sp, ch 5, pc shell in next pc shell , ch 5, skip next ch-5 sp, (sc in next ch-5 sp, ch 5) 2 times], pc shell in next pc shell; repeat from * 2 more times; repeat between [ ], join.

Rnd 13: (Sl st, beg pc shell) in first pc shell, *[ch 1, pc shell in next pc shell, ch 5, (sc in next ch-5 sp, ch 5) 3 times, pc shell in next pc shell, ch 5, sc in next ch-5 sp, ch 11, sc in next ch-5 sp, ch 5, pc shell in next pc shell, ch 5, (sc in next ch-5 sp, ch 5) 3 times], pc shell in next pc shell; repeat from * 2 more times; repeat between [ ], join. Fasten off.

FLOWER MOTIF (make 14)

Rnd 1: Hold one strand each purple ribbon and purple yarn together as one, ch 5, sl st in first ch to form ring, ch 1, (sc in ring; for **petal**, ch 4, sc in fourth ch from hook) 4 times, join with sl st in first sc. *(4 petals made)*

Rnd 2: Working this rnd in **back lps** *(see Stitch Guide),* ch 1, sc in first sc, ch 2; working behind petals, (sc in next sc between petals, ch 2) 3 times, join. *(4 ch sps)*

Rnd 3: Ch 1, sc in first st, ch 3, (sc in next sc, ch 3) 3 times, join.

Rnd 4: (Sl st, ch 1, sc, ch 1, 3 dc, ch 1, sc) in first ch sp, (sc, ch 1, 3 dc, ch 1, sc) in each ch sp around, join. Fasten off.

Rnd 5: Join green ribbon with (sl st, ch 3, 2 dc) in first st, *[ch 3, sc in center st of next 3-dc group, ch 3], skip next ch-1 sp, skip next sc, 3 dc in next sc; repeat from * 2 more times; repeat between [ ], join with sl st in top of ch 3. Fasten off.

Rnd 6: Join yellow with (sl st, beg pc) in first ch-3 sp, *ch 3, pc in next sc, (ch 3, pc) in next 2 ch sps; repeat from * 2 more times, ch 3, pc in next sc, ch 3, pc in next ch sp, ch 2, join with hdc in top of first pc.

Rnds 7–16: Repeat rnds 4–13 of Plain Motif.

For **center of flower,** cut 3 strands yellow each 6" long. With all strands held together, insert hook in one lp of any st at center of rnd 1, pull ends through lp; with both ends on front, tie in double knot. Trim ends ¼" from knot.

ASSEMBLY

With yellow, working in ch sps only, matching 2 blocks together, weaving yarn through ch and sts as you work, [starting at ch 11 of each square, tack together at center ch, *tack ch-5 sps together at edge of pc shell, tack ch-3 sps between pc shells together, tack ch-5 sps together at edge of pc shell, tack center ch on each of next 3 ch-5 sps together*, (tack ch-3 sps of next pc shell together) 2 times; repeat between first and second *, tack ch-3 sp of next pc shell together, tack ch-5 sp together at edge of pc shell, tack center ch of ch 11 together]; repeat between [ ] according to assembly diagram.

PILLOW COVER SECTION

Sew four Flower Motifs together to form one row.

Top Trim

Row 1: With right side facing you, join yellow with (sl st, ch 3, 2 dc) in ch-11 sp at one end of one long edge on Pillow Cover Section; skipping ch sp of each pc shell, (ch 2, 3 dc) in each ch sp and in sp between 2 pc shells at top of each pineapple across with last 3 dc in opposite ch-11 sp, turn.

Row 2: Ch 5, 3 dc in first ch sp, (ch 2, 3 dc) in each ch sp across, ch 2, dc in last st, turn.

Row 3: Ch 3, 2 dc in first ch sp, (ch 2, 3 dc) in each ch sp across, turn.

Rows 4–13: Repeat rows 2 and 3 alternately. At end of last row, fasten off.

Bottom Trim

Rows 1–10: Working on opposite side of Pillow Cover Section, repeat rows 1–10 of Top Trim. At end of last row, fasten off.

Matching 3 sts to each ch sp, sew sts of row 10 to top edge of Bedspread.

RIGHT SIDE TRIM

Row 1: With right side facing you, working in ch sps on Motifs and in ch-5 sps at ends of rows on Pillow Cover Section, join yellow with (sl st, ch 3, 2 dc) in ch-11 sp on Motif at bottom right corner; skipping ch sp of each pc shell, (ch 2, 3 dc) in each ch sp and in sp between pc shells at top of each pineapple across, turn. *(89 dc groups made)*

Row 2: Ch 5, 3 dc in first ch sp, (ch 2, 3 dc) in each ch sp across, ch 2, dc in last st, turn.

Row 3: Ch 3, 2 dc in first ch sp, (ch 2, 3 dc) in each ch sp across, **do not turn.** Fasten off.

Row 4: Join purple with sl st in top of ch 3, ch 5, dc in next st, ch 2, skip next st, dc in next ch sp, ch 2, (skip next st, dc in next st, ch 2, dc in next ch sp, ch 2) across to last 3 sts, skip next st, dc in next st, ch 2, dc in last st, turn. Fasten off. *(179 dc)*

Row 5: Join yellow with (sl st, ch 3, 2 dc) in first ch sp, (ch 1, 3 dc) in each ch sp across, turn.

Row 6: Ch 4, 3 dc in each ch sp across, ch 1, dc in last st, turn.

Row 7: Ch 6, (skip next ch sp, tr in next st, ch 2, skip next st, tr in next st, ch 2) across to ch 4, tr in third ch of ch 4, turn. *(356 tr)*

Rows 8–12: Ch 6, tr in first ch sp; for **V st, (tr, ch 2, tr)** in next ch sp; V st in each ch sp across, turn. *(355 V sts)*

Row 13: Ch 8, skip first V st, tr in sp between next 2 V sts, (ch 5, skip next V st, tr in sp between next 2 V sts) across to last 3 V sts, ch 5, skip next V st, tr in ch sp of next V st, ch 5, tr in fourth ch of ch 6, turn.

Rows 14–15: Ch 8, (tr in next tr, ch 5) across, tr in fourth ch of ch 8, turn.

Row 16: Ch 8, *(tr in next tr, ch 5) 3 times, sc in next tr; repeat from * across to last tr and ch sp, ch 5, tr in last tr, ch 5, tr in fourth ch of ch 8, **do not turn.** Fasten off.

Row 17: Join purple with sl st in fourth ch of ch 8, ch 8, *(tr in next tr, ch 5) 3 times, sc in next sc; repeat from * across to last 2 tr, ch 5, tr in next tr, ch 5, tr in last tr, **do not turn.** Fasten off.

Row 18: Join yellow with sl st in fourth ch of ch 8, ch 3, sc in first ch sp, ch 3, sc in next st, (ch 3, sc in next ch sp, ch 3, sc in next st) across. Fasten off.

LEFT SIDE TRIM

Row 1: Joining in ch sp at end of row 12 on Pillow Cover Section Top Trim, repeat row 1 of Right Side Trim.

Rows 2–18: Repeat rows 2–18 of Right Side Trim.

END TRIM

Row 1: With right side facing you, working in ch sps on Motifs, join yellow with (sl st, ch 3, 2 dc) in ch-11 sp at bottom right corner; skipping ch sp of each pc shell, (ch 2, 3 dc) in each ch sp and in each sp between pc shells at top of each pineapple across, turn. *(52 dc groups made)*

Rows 2–15: Repeat rows 2–15 of Right Side Trim, ending with 105 tr in last row.

Row 16: Ch 8, tr in next tr, ch 5, sc in next tr, *(ch 5, tr in next tr) 3 times, ch 5, sc in next tr; repeat from * across to last ch sp, ch 5, tr in fourth ch of ch 8, **do not turn.** Fasten off.

Row 17: Join purple with sl st in fourth ch of ch 8, ch 8, tr in next tr, ch 5, sc in next sc, *(ch 5, tr in next tr) 3 times, ch 5, sc in next sc; repeat from * across to last tr, ch 5, tr in last tr, **do not turn.** Fasten off.

Row 18: Join yellow with sl st in fourth ch of ch 8, ch 3, sc in first ch sp, ch 3, sc in next st, (ch 3, sc in next ch sp, ch 3, sc in next st) across. Fasten off. ❦

Flower	Plain	Plain	Flower
Plain	Flower	Flower	Plain
Flower	Plain	Plain	Flower
Plain	Flower	Flower	Plain
Flower	Plain	Plain	Flower

by Ann Parnell

Fisherman Afghan

FINISHED SIZE: Afghan is about 40" × 54".

MATERIALS:
- ❏ 27 oz. off-white sport yarn
- ❏ K hook or size needed to obtain gauge

GAUGE: 2 dc and 2 shells = 2"; 3 sc rows, one 3-dc shell row and one dc row = 2".

SPECIAL STITCHES:

For **3-dc shell,** 3 dc in next ch sp.

For **5-dc shell,** 5 dc in next ch sp.

For **back cross st (bcr),** skip next 2 sts, dc in next 2 sts; working behind last 2 sts made, dc in last 2 skipped sts.

For **front cross st (fcr),** skip next 2 sts, dc in next 2 sts; working in front of last 2 sts made, dc in last 2 skipped sts.

For **sc in space (sc in sp),** work sc between 2 dc **or** between one dc and one 3-dc shell **or** 5-dc shell.

AFGHAN

Row 1: Ch 155, sc in second ch from hook, sc in next ch, *(ch 1, skip next ch, sc in next ch) 11 times, sc in next ch, dc in next ch, sc in next 16 ch, dc in next ch, sc in next 2 ch; repeat from * 2 more times, (ch 1, skip next ch, sc in next ch) 11 times, sc in last ch, turn. *(Front of row 1 is right side of work—110 sts, 44 ch sps made)*

Row 2: (Ch 2, dc) in first st, *(skip next st, dc in next ch sp, skip next st, **3-dc shell**—see Special Stitches—in next ch sp) 5 times, skip next st, dc in next ch sp, skip next st, 2 dc in next st, **dc back post (bp**—see Stitch Guide) around next st, (**bcr**—see Special Stitches—across next 4 sts, **fcr**—see Special Stitches—across next 4 sts) 2 times, dc bp around next st, 2 dc in next st; repeat from * 2 more times, (skip next st, dc in next ch sp, skip next st, 3-dc shell in next ch sp) 5 times, skip next st, dc in next ch sp, skip next st, 2 dc in last st, turn. *(Ch 2 counts as first dc—40 dc, 20 3-dc shells, 6 bcr sts, 6 fcr sts, 6 dc bp)*

Row 3: Ch 1, sc in first st, sc in sp *(see Special Stitches),* *(ch 1, sc in sp) 11 times, skip next st, sc in next st, dc fp around next post st, sc in next 16 sts, dc fp around next post st, sc in next st, sc in sp; repeat from * 2 more times, (ch 1, sc in sp) 11 times, skip next st, sc in last st, turn.

Row 4: Ch 2, 3-dc shell in first ch sp, *(dc in next ch sp, 3-dc shell in next ch sp) 5 times, skip next st, dc in next st, dc bp around next post st, (fcr st, bcr st) 2 times, dc bp around next post st, dc in next st, 3-dc shell in next ch sp; repeat from * 2 more times, (dc in next ch sp, 3-dc shell in next ch sp) 5 times, skip next st, dc in last st, turn.

Row 5: Ch 1, sc in first st, sc in sp, *(ch 1, sc in sp) 11 times, sc in next st, dc fp around next post st, sc in next 16 sts, dc fp around next post st, sc in next st, sc in sp; repeat from * 2 more times, (ch 1, sc in sp) 11 times, sc in last st, turn.

Row 6: (Ch 2, dc) in first st, dc in first ch sp, *(3-dc shell in next ch sp, dc in next ch sp) 2 times, 5-dc shell *(see Special Stitches)* in next ch sp, (dc in next ch sp, 3-dc shell in next ch sp) 2 times, dc in next ch sp, skip next st, 2 dc in next st, dc bp around next post st, (bcr st, fcr st) 2 times, dc bp around next st, 2 dc in next st, dc in next ch sp; repeat from * 2 more times, (3-dc shell in next ch sp, dc in next ch sp) 2 times, 5-dc shell in next ch sp, (dc in next ch sp, 3-dc shell in next ch sp) 2 times, dc in last ch sp, skip next st, 2 dc in last st, turn. *(Push 5-dc shells to front of work throughout.)*

Row 7: Ch 1, sc in first st, sc in sp, *(ch 1, sc in sp) 11 times, skip next st, sc in next st, dc fp around next post st, sc in next 16 sts, dc fp around next post st, sc in next st, sc in sp; repeat from * 2 more times, (ch 1, sc in sp) 11 times, skip next st, sc in last st, turn.

Row 8: Ch 2, 3-dc shell in first ch sp, dc in next ch sp, 3-dc shell in next ch sp, dc in next ch sp, *(5-dc shell in next ch sp, dc in next ch sp) 2 times, 3-dc shell in next ch sp, dc in next ch sp, 3-dc shell in next ch sp, skip next st, dc in next st, dc bp around next post st, (fcr st, bcr st) 2 times, dc bp around next post st, dc in next st, skip next st, (3-dc shell in next ch sp, dc in next ch sp) 2

continued on page 156

times; repeat from * 2 more times, (5-dc shell in next ch sp, dc in next ch sp) 2 times, 3-dc shell in next ch sp, dc in next ch sp, 3-dc shell in last ch sp, skip next st, dc in last st, turn.

Row 9: Ch 1, sc in first st, sc in sp, *(ch 1, sc in sp) 11 times, sc in next st, dc fp around next post st, sc in next 16 sts, dc fp around next post st, sc in next st, sc in sp; repeat from * 2 more times, (ch 1, sc in sp) 11 times, sc in last st, turn.

Row 10: (Ch 2, dc) in first st, dc in first ch sp, *(3-dc shell in next ch sp, dc in next ch sp, 5-dc shell in next ch sp, dc in next ch sp) 2 times, 3-dc shell in next ch sp, dc in next ch sp, skip next st, 2 dc in next st, dc bp around next post st, (bcr st, fcr st) 2 times, dc bp around next post st, 2 dc in next st, dc in next ch sp; repeat from * 2 more times, (3-dc shell in next ch sp, dc in next ch sp, 5-dc shell in next ch sp, dc in next ch sp) 2 times, 3-dc shell in next ch sp, dc in last ch sp, skip next st, 2 dc in last, turn.

Row 11: Ch 1, sc in first st, sc in sp, *(ch 1, sc in sp) 11 times, skip next st, sc in next st, dc fp around next post st, sc in next 16 sts, dc fp around next post st, sc in next st, sc in sp; repeat from * 2 more times, (ch 1, sc in sp) 11 times, skip next st, sc in last st, turn.

Row 12: Ch 2, 3-dc shell in first ch sp, *dc in next ch sp, 5-dc shell in next ch sp, (dc in next ch sp, 3-dc shell in next ch sp) 2 times, dc in next ch sp, 5-dc shell in next ch sp, dc in next ch sp, 3-dc shell in next ch sp, skip next st, dc in next st, dc bp around next post st, (bcr st, fcr st) 2 times, dc bp around next post st, dc in next st, 3-dc shell in next ch sp; repeat from * 2 more times, dc in next ch sp, 5-dc shell in next ch sp, (dc in next ch sp, 3-dc shell in next ch sp) 2 times, dc in next ch sp, 5-dc shell in next ch sp, dc in next ch sp, 3-dc shell in last ch sp, skip next st, dc in last st, turn.

Row 13: Ch 1, sc in first st, sc in sp, *(ch 1, sc in sp) 11 times, sc in next st, dc fp around next post st, sc in next 16 sts, dc fp around next post st, sc in next st, sc in sp; repeat from * 2 more times, (ch 1, sc in sp) 11 times, sc in last st, turn.

Row 14: (Ch 2, dc) in first st, dc in first ch sp, *(5-dc shell in next ch sp, dc in next ch sp, 3-dc shell in next ch sp, dc in next ch sp) 2 times, 5-dc shell in next ch sp, dc in next ch sp, skip next st, 2 dc in next st, dc bp around next post st, (bcr st, fcr st) 2 times, dc bp around next post st, 2 dc in next st, dc in next ch sp; repeat from * 2 more times, (5-dc shell in next ch sp, dc in next ch sp, 3-dc shell in next ch sp, dc in next ch sp) 2 times, 5-dc shell in next ch sp, dc in last ch sp, skip next st, 2 dc in last st, turn.

Row 15: Ch 1, sc in first st, sc in sp, *(ch 1, sc in sp) 11 times, skip next st, sc in next st, dc fp around next post st, sc in next 16 sts, dc fp around next post st, sc in next st, sc in sp; repeat from * 2 more times, (ch 1, sc in sp) 11 times, skip next st, sc in last st, turn.

Row 16: Ch 2, 3-dc shell in first ch sp, *dc in next ch sp, 5-dc shell in next ch sp, (dc in next ch sp, 3-dc shell in next ch sp) 2 times, dc in next ch sp, 5-dc shell in next ch sp, dc in next ch sp, 3-dc shell in next ch sp, skip next st, dc in next st, dc bp around next post st, (bcr st, fcr st) 2 times, dc bp around next post st, dc in next st, 3-dc shell in next ch sp; repeat from * 2 more times, dc in next ch sp, 5-dc shell in next ch sp, (dc in next ch sp, 3-dc shell in next ch sp) 2 times, dc in next ch sp, 5-dc shell in next ch sp, dc in next ch sp, 3-dc shell in last ch sp, skip next st, dc in last st, turn.

Row 17: Ch 1, sc in first st, sc in sp, *(ch 1, sc in sp) 11 times, sc in next st, dc fp around next post st, sc in next 16 sts, dc fp around next post st, sc in next st, sc in sp; repeat from * 2 more times, (ch 1, sc in sp) 11 times, sc in last st, turn.

Row 18: (Ch 2, dc) in first st, dc in first ch sp, *(3-dc shell in next ch sp, dc in next ch sp, 5-dc shell in next ch sp, dc in next ch sp) 2 times, 3-dc shell in next ch sp, dc in next ch sp, skip next st, 2 dc in next st, dc bp around next post st, (bcr st, fcr st) 2 times, dc bp around next post st, 2 dc in next st, dc in next ch sp; repeat from * 2 more times, (3-dc shell in next ch sp, dc in next ch sp, 5-dc shell in next ch sp, dc in next ch sp) 2 times, 3-dc shell in next ch sp, dc in last ch sp, skip next st, 2 dc in last st, turn.

Row 19: Ch 1, sc in first st, sc in sp, *(ch 1, sc in sp) 11 times, skip next st, sc in next st, dc fp around next post st, sc in next 16 sts, dc fp around next post st, sc in next st, sc in sp; repeat from * 2 more times, (ch 1, sc in sp) 11 times, skip next st, sc in last st, turn.

Row 20: Ch 2, 3-dc shell in first ch sp, dc in next ch sp, 3-dc shell in next ch sp, dc in next ch sp, *(5-dc shell in next ch sp, dc in next ch sp) 2 times, 3-dc shell in next ch sp, dc in next ch sp, 3-dc shell in next ch sp, skip next st, dc in next st, dc bp around next post st, (fcr st, bcr st) 2 times, dc bp around next post st, dc in next st, (3-dc shell in next ch sp, dc in next ch sp) 2 times; repeat from * 2 more times, (5-dc shell in next ch sp, dc in next ch sp) 2 times, 3-dc shell in next ch sp, dc in next ch sp, 3-dc shell in last ch sp, skip next st, dc in last st, turn.

Row 21: Ch 1, sc in first st, sc in sp, *(ch 1, sc in sp) 11 times, sc in next st, dc fp around next post st, sc in next 16 sts, dc fp around next post st, sc in next st, sc in sp; repeat from * 2 more times, (ch 1, sc in sp) 11 times, sc in last st, turn.

Row 22: (Ch 2, dc) in first st, dc in first ch sp, *(3-dc shell in next ch sp, dc in next ch sp) 2 times, 5-dc shell in next ch sp, (dc in next ch sp, 3-dc shell in next ch sp) 2 times, dc in next ch sp, skip next st, 2 dc in next st, dc bp around next post st, (bcr st, fcr st) 2 times, dc bp around next st, 2 dc in next st, dc in next ch sp; repeat from * 2 more times, (3-dc shell in next ch sp, dc in next ch sp) 2 times, 5-dc shell in next ch sp, (dc in next ch sp, 3-dc shell in next ch sp) 2 times, dc in last ch sp, skip next st, 2 dc in last st, turn.

Row 23: Ch 1, sc in first st, sc in sp, *(ch 1, sc in sp) 11 times, skip next next st, sc in next st, dc fp around next post st, sc in next 16 sts, dc fp around next post st, sc in next st, sc in sp; repeat from * 2 more times, (ch 1, sc in sp) 11 times, skip next st, sc in last st, turn.

Row 24: Ch 2, 3-dc shell in first ch sp, *(dc in next ch sp, 3-dc shell in next ch sp) 5 times, skip next st, dc in next st, dc bp around next post st, (fcr st, bcr st) 2 times, dc bp around next post st, dc in next st, 3-dc shell in next ch sp; repeat from * 2 more times, (dc in next ch sp, 3-dc shell in next ch sp; repeat from * 2 more times, (dc in next ch sp, 3-dc shell in next ch sp) 5 times, skip next st, dc in last st, turn.

Row 25: Ch 1, sc in first st, sc in sp, *(ch 1, sc in sp) 11 times, sc in next st, dc fp around next post st, sc in next 16 sts, dc fp around next post st, sc in next st, sc in sp; repeat from * 2 more times, (ch 1, sc in sp) 11 times, sc in last st, turn.

Rows 26–147: Repeat rows 2–25 consecutively, ending with row 3. At end of last row, **do not turn or fasten off.**

Rnd 148: For **Edging**, working around outer edges, ch 1, sc in end of next 146 rows; working on opposite side of row 1, 3 sc in first ch, *2 sc in each of next 11 ch sps, sc in next 2 ch sps, (sc next 2 sps together, sc in next sp) 5 times, sc next 2 sps together, sc in next 2 ch sps; repeat from * 2 more times, 2 sc in each of next 11 ch sps, 3 sc in last ch, sc in end of next 146 rows, 3 sc in end of last row, 2 sc in each ch sp across to last ch sp, 3 sc in last ch sp, join with sl st in first sc.

Rnd 149: Sl st in each st around, join with sl st in first sl st. Fasten off. ❦

Wedding Afghan

continued from page 145

(sc in next 2 rows, skip next row) 62 times, join with sl st in first sc, **turn.** *(526 sc made)*

Rnd 2: Ch 1, sc in first st, ch 3, skip next st, (sc in next st, ch 3, skip next st) around, join, **turn.**

Rnds 3–5: (Sl st, ch 1, sc) in first ch sp, ch 3, (sc in next ch sp, ch 3) around, join, **turn.**

Rnd 6: (Sl st, ch 1, sc) in first ch sp, ch 4, (sc in next ch sp, ch 4) around, join. Fasten off.

FINISHING

Double Ring (make 3)

Rnd 1: For **First Ring,** with two strands of metallic thread held together, ch 32, sl st in first ch to form ring, ch 1, 32 sc in ring, join with sl st in first sc. Fasten off. *(32 sc made)*

Rnd 2: For **Second Ring,** with two strands of metallic thread held together, ch 32, run one end of ch through First Ring, sl st in first ch to form ring, ch 1, 32 sc in ring, join. Fasten off.

Attach one Double Ring over rows 10–18 with edge of Rings touching between 10th and 11th cl at birds' beaks on row 18, sewing through **back lps** *(see Stitch Guide).*

Attach second Double Ring over rows 69–76 with edge of Rings touching between 10th and 11th cl at birds' beaks on row 76, sewing through **back lps.**

Attach third Double Ring over rows 130–138 with edge of Ring touching between 10th and 11th cl at birds' beaks on row 138, sewing through **back lps.**

Heart Trim

Rnd 1: With two strands metallic thread held together, working between sts around one Heart, join with sc at bottom of Heart, sc between each 2 sts around Heart to first sc, join.

Rnd 2: Ch 1, sc in first st, ch 3, (sc in next st, ch 3) around, join. Fasten off.

Repeat Heart Trim around each Heart. ❧

Strip Pillowghan

continued from page 149

FINISHING

1: With right side of Afghan facing you, fold Afghan with wrong side out according to illustrations 1–3.

2: With tapestry needle and green yarn, folding Ruffle to the inside, sew rnd 21 on right side of Pocket to **one layer** of folded Afghan according to dotted lines on illustration 3, sewing only three sides and leaving the fourth side open at center of Afghan.

3: Turn Pocket right side out over the folded Afghan and flatten. The bulk of the Afghan stuffs the Pocket to form a pillow. ❧

1: Fold in thirds.
LONG STRAIGHT EDGE

2: Fold ends to center.

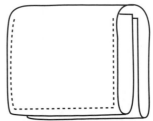

3: Fold ends to inside.

Stitch Guide

Chain—ch:
Yo, pull through lp on hook.

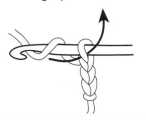

Single crochet—sc:
Insert hook in st, yo, pull through st, yo, pull through both lps on hook.

Half double crochet—hdc:
Yo, insert hook in st, yo, pull through st, yo, pull through all 3 lps on hook.

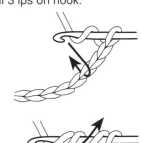

Slip stitch–sl st:
Insert hook in st, yo, pull through st and lp on hook.

Treble crochet—tr:
Yo 2 times, insert hook in st, yo, pull through st, (yo, pull through 2 lps) 3 times.

Double crochet—dc:
Yo, insert hook in st, yo, pull through st, (yo, pull through 2 lps) 2 times.

Double treble crochet—dtr:
Yo 3 times, insert hook in st, yo, pull through st, (yo, pull through 2 lps on hook) 4 times.

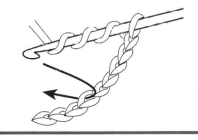

Triple treble crochet—ttr:
Yo 4 times, insert hook in st, yo, pull through st, (yo, pull through 2 lps on hook) 5 times.

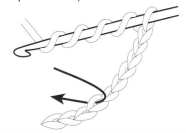

continued on page 160

For row 1 of afghan stitch:

Work starting ch for width of piece, insert hook in 2nd ch from hook, yo, pull through, (insert hook in next ch, yo, pull through) repeat across leaving all lps on hook; to *work lps off hook,* working from left to right, yo, pull through first lp on hook, (yo, pull through next 2 lps on hook—see illustration 1) repeat across. The lp left on hook is the first lp for the next row.

1.

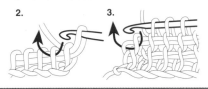

For row 2 of afghan stitch:

Skip first vertical bar, (insert hook under next vertical bar—see illustration 2; yo, pull through bar) repeat across to last vertical bar, insert hook under last vertical bar and the bar directly behind it—see illustration 3; yo, pull through both bars; work lps off hook same as for row 1. Repeat row 2 for number of rows needed.

2.   3.

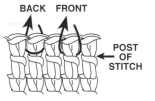

Front post stitch—fp; Back post stitch—bp:

When working post st, insert hook from right to left around post of st on previous row specified.

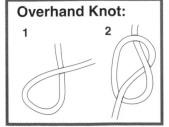

Reverse sc: Working from left to right, insert hook in next st to the right, complete as sc.

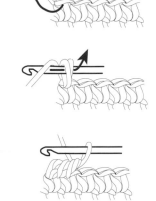

Color change: Drop first color; with second color, pull through last 2 lps of st.

Front loop—front lp; Back loop—back lp:

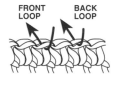

Embroidery Stitches

Overhand Knot:

1   2

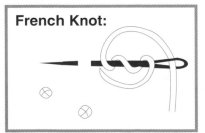

French Knot:

Cross Stitch:

2 4
3 1

Cross Stitch on Afghan Stitch: